LLEWELLYN'S

COMPLETE BOOK OF PREDICTIVE

ASTROLOGY

Lamar Studios

ABOUT THE AUTHOR

Kris Brandt Riske, M.A., is executive director and a professional member of the American Federation of Astrologers, the oldest U.S. astrological organization, founded in 1938. She is also a member of the NCGR (National Council for Geocosmic Research) and served on its board of directors.

Kris has been a speaker at various astrological conferences and has written for several astrological publications. She currently writes for *Llewellyn's Sun Sign Book*, *Llewellyn's Moon Sign Book*, and American Media. Kris is also the author of *Mapping Your Future* and *Mapping Your Money* and co-author of *Mapping Your Travels & Relocation*. She is particularly interested in astrometeorology (astrological weather forecasting) and is the author of *Astrometeorology: Planetary Power in Weather Forecasting* and the annual weather forecast published in *Llewellyn's Moon Sign Book*.

Kris is an avid stock car (NASCAR) fan, although she'd rather be driving than watching. She also enjoys gardening, needlework, and computer gaming. An Illinois native, Kris has a master's degree in journalism and is a Chinese language student.

TO WRITE TO THE AUTHOR

If you wish to contact the author or would like more information about this book, please write to the author in care of Llewellyn Worldwide and we will forward your request. Both the author and publisher appreciate hearing from you and learning of your enjoyment of this book and how it has helped you. Llewellyn Worldwide cannot guarantee that every letter written to the author can be answered, but all will be forwarded. Please write to:

Kris Brandt Riske, M.A.
% Llewellyn Worldwide
2143 Wooddale Drive
Woodbury, MN 55125-2989

Please enclose a self-addressed stamped envelope for reply,
or $1.00 to cover costs. If outside U.S.A., enclose
international postal reply coupon.

Many of Llewellyn's authors have websites with additional information and resources. For more information, please visit our website at www.llewellyn.com.

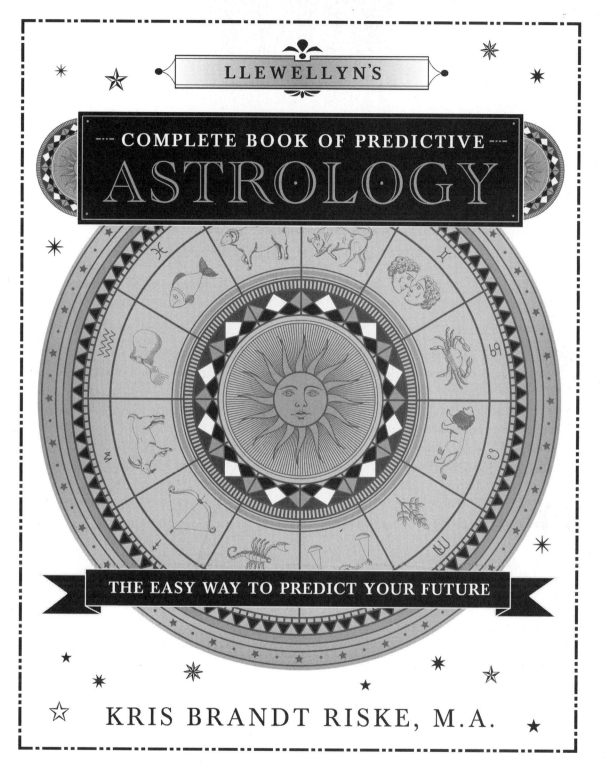

LLEWELLYN'S

--- COMPLETE BOOK OF PREDICTIVE ---
ASTROLOGY

THE EASY WAY TO PREDICT YOUR FUTURE

KRIS BRANDT RISKE, M.A.

Llewellyn Publications

Woodbury, Minnesota

FIRST EDITION
First Printing, 2011

Book design and format by Donna Burch
Cover zodiac image © iStockphoto.com/omergenc
Cover design by Kevin R. Brown
Editing by Sharon Leah

Llewellyn is a registered trademark of Llewellyn Worldwide Ltd.

The Chart wheels were produced by the Solar Fire Gold ver. 7 program, licensed for use by Astrolabe
    at www.astrolabe.com

Astro America's Daily Ephemeris, 2000–2020 at Midnight is reprinted with the kind permission of David R. Roell at Astrology
    Classics (www.astroamerica.com).

Library of Congress Cataloging-in-Publication Data (Pending)
ISBN: 978-0-7387-2755-4

Llewellyn Publications
A Division of Llewellyn Worldwide Ltd.
2143 Wooddale Drive
Woodbury, MN 55125-2989
www.llewellyn.com

Printed in the United States of America

OTHER BOOKS AND ARTICLES BY KRIS BRANDT RISKE, M.A.

Mapping Your Travels & Relocation (co-author)
(Llewellyn Publications, 2005)

Mapping Your Money
(Llewellyn Publications, 2005)

Mapping Your Future
(Llewellyn Publications, 2004)

Astrometeorology: Planetary Power in Weather Forecasting
(American Federation of Astrologers, 1997)

Llewellyn's Moon Sign Book (contributor)
(Llewellyn Publications, 2002–2013)

Llewellyn's Sun Sign Book (contributor)
(Llewellyn Publications, 2007–2013)

Llewellyn's Starview Almanac (contributor)
(Llewellyn Publications, 2005–2006)

Civilization Under Attack (contributor)
(Llewellyn Publications, 2001)

Llewellyn's Complete Book of Astrology
(Llewellyn Publications, 2007)

DEDICATION

To Mother and Dad

ACKNOWLEDGMENTS

Many thanks to my editor Sharon Leah for her exceptional skills, guidance, and insights in shaping this book into its final edition. An author is only as good as her editor.

Once again, Donna Burch has worked her magic in shaping the text into a user-friendly format, and Kevin Brown has done the same with the cover.

I also extend my appreciation to the people whose charts and life stories are included in this book, and to Dave Roell of Astrology Center of America for granting permission to use a page from the ephemeris published by him.

CONTENTS

LIST OF CHARTS

INTRODUCTION

S ome people are content with the present, while others live in the past. Then there are those people, like me, who live in the future.

Maybe it's because of my Aquarius Sun, or some other influence I've yet to identify, but I've always wanted to know about the future and what would happen and when. This was my main motivation to learn astrology. I didn't fully comprehend at the time how useful astrology could be in predicting the future; I just knew the subject was worth pursuing, and this has proved to be true time and again.

After all, life really is about the future. The past is history, albeit of great benefit to us as a learning experience. The present is a nanosecond at best. The future is what we have to look forward to, the days and months and years during which we can take advantage of life and our innate talents. The future is all about the choices we have yet to make. Life is also about timing. When you know the timing and what the future might bring, you are better prepared to take advantage of life's opportunities and to minimize life's challenges. You are reading this book because you're one of the wise souls who knows, or at least senses, that your future can be far more promising with this knowledge.

If you heed the messages of the astrological chart, you can better live your life to its fullest. You will know when your realistic hopes and wishes can come true. When a soul mate will enter your life. When you will achieve your career goals. When saving is better than spending. When to take it easy to avoid an accident. When your children need extra attention. When you will begin or complete your educational goals. When to plan the trip of a lifetime. When … the list is endless!

There is nothing mysterious or magical about predictive astrology, as you will learn. In essence, planet A contacts planet B and results in C, the action or event. Interpreting A+B=C involves the symbolic meanings of the zodiacal signs, the planets, and the astrological houses. As is true in all areas of life, however, some decisions are not quite so simplistic. This is where we humans are faced with choices. Like life, astrology is not fateful, but our choices certainly can be, with one action triggering the next and the next and so on. Making the right choices—choosing our actions—is a life task that benefits from having as much quality information as possible. When you can see into the future, you make much better choices for yourself and your life.

You arrived in the world with as much potential as any other human being. Why not make the most of it?

And making the most of it begins with your birth chart. In fact, this is the most important part of predictive astrology. If, for example, you wish you could be a software engineer but your birth chart indicates you're a people-person, you would be unhappy in such a solitary job. However, you might do very well in software sales. The same would be true of someone who is drawn to the creative arts. A career as an artist is unrealistic if the birth chart doesn't show high potential in this area. Instead, a career in architecture or interior design might provide an income and the freedom to paint during leisure-time hours.

I am often asked if astrology can be of assistance in winning millions in the lottery. Possibly. The reason is that the odds of winning are just as astronomical as the number of birth charts with the potential to win. More common is a birth chart that indicates the potential to win $100.

So, *potential* is the keyword here. If your birth chart has the potential for any of the thousands of events, situations, relationships, and opportunities possible in life, sooner or later you are likely to experience them to a greater or lesser degree. And by knowing your birth chart, you can use predictive astrology techniques to know when to maximize the positives in your birth chart. Likewise, you can predict when caution is advisable to minimize the negatives. For example, suppose your birth chart indicates you tend to be too trusting of people. Astrology can alert you to the years when you'll be especially vulnerable, which enables you to take extra precautions to prevent negative outcomes.

This book is about predictive astrology, which is what draws many people to this ancient subject. But do yourself a favor before delving too deeply into the future, as irresistible as it might be. Get a copy of my book on birth chart astrology—*Llewellyn's Complete Book of Astrology*—and use it to learn the basics of astrology as you gain an understanding of your birth chart. You will quickly see that when you use these two books together, your knowledge of astrology will grow exponentially and you'll be far better prepared to accurately forecast your future.

PREDICTIVE TECHNIQUES

Like all else in astrology, the predictive art is both simple and complex. Some charts are very straightforward, with the probable outcome plainly evident even to the novice. Others are incredibly complex, so much so that they can stump even the most seasoned astrologer.

Each chart is something of a puzzle that requires the astrologer to follow a trail of clues, unraveling them to find a solution. The clues are, in essence, a set of rules that, when observed, can help you pinpoint anything from a job offer to an inheritance to a romantic opportunity. Success is all in knowing the rules and applying them to the chart in question.

THE ROOTS OF PREDICTION

Astrology came into existence about 3,000 years ago when people first began to observe a correlation between the planetary positions and life on Earth. Then, and for hundreds of years following, the birth chart and the predictive chart were one and the same. There were no separate predictive tools.

The birth chart was used to predict the person's overall life. As deterministic as this sounds today, people had few choices at that time. A person born into a family of serfs, for example, had little hope of becoming an educated clergyman. In other situations, the ancient astrologers would observe the planetary positions and predict the outcome of, for example, a war. All the charts were, in essence, horary charts. Horary astrology is the branch of astrology used to answer a specific question. Ancient chart reading was the equivalent of asking what a person's life would be like:

whether a child would become king, if a certain individual would become a thief, or if there would be drought and famine.

The first use of predictive astrology can be traced to Ptolemy, an astronomer and astrological writer who lived in the second century. Much of his work, including the well-known *Tetrabiblos*, is a compilation of the Greek astrological knowledge in existence at the time. His predictive method involved advancing every planet one degree for every year of the individual's life.

It wasn't until the sixteenth century that predictive methods took a step forward. By then, people were using trigonometry, and astrologer Valentine Naibod began using what today we call the solar arc method, where every planet is advanced 0°59'08" per year. This is the Sun's annual motion, and the method is called Naibod's Measure.

A technique called primary directions was used for centuries, but this involved complicated computations and so it eventually fell out of favor. Solar and lunar returns have also been used for centuries.

Seventeenth century astrologer Placidus de Titus created two techniques that are widely used today: the Placidus system of house division and secondary progressions.

PREDICTIVE TECHNIQUES

Astrologers use a variety of techniques when working on a predictive forecast. Each is valid, although not every astrologer uses every technique. The choice of technique depends upon a number of factors, including what astrologers learned as students, what their mentors used, and what they believe from experience work best. The most popular are outlined below and will be fully explained in succeeding chapters.

Progressions

Also called directions (mainly in older books), progressions use a day-for-a-year formula. For example, if your birthday is June 1, the planets in your progressed chart at age twenty-four would be their zodiacal location on June 24, or your twenty-fourth year of life. You will need an ephemeris, which lists the planetary positions by degree and sign for each day of the year to find the position of progressed planets. Count June 1 as first year of life, June 2 as second year, and so on. (Ephemeris books are compiled in volumes from one year to 151 years. A more complete explanation about how to use an ephemeris can be found in Chapter 2.) Progressions indicate major trends that are in effect as long as a year.

Solar Arcs

Solar arcs are similar to progressions and also indicate major trends. The difference is that they are calculated based on the motion of the Sun. In this system, every planet moves at the same rate of speed, making it easy to calculate solar arcs based on your age alone. For example, at age forty-four, every planet in your birth chart will have moved forward approximately forty-four degrees by solar arc, thus maintaining the same distance relationship to every other planet in your birth chart.

Transits

This is where the planets are on any given day. If you're interested in knowing what events might transpire on November 5 of a given year, you would consult an ephemeris for the planetary positions on that date. The outer planet transits indicate major trends, and the inner planet transits function as triggers to initiate action indicated by progressions, solar arcs, and outer planet transits.

Lunations and Eclipses

There are two lunations each month: the New Moon and the Full Moon. Four or more of these each year are also solar (New Moon) or lunar (Full Moon) eclipses. In addition to indicating an area of emphasis for that month (or six months to a year in the case of an eclipse), lunations also can function as triggers for progressed planets, solar arcs, and outer planet transits.

Solar, Lunar, and Planetary Returns

Two of these predictive tools, the solar and lunar returns, indicate the trends for a year (solar) or a month (lunar). A solar return is a chart calculated for the exact moment the Sun returns to its place in your birth chart, and thus occurs on your birthday (or possibly the day before or after, depending upon your birth time). A lunar return uses the same principle, but on a monthly basis, when the Moon returns to where it was when you were born. Planetary return charts are also calculated for the time a natal planet, such as Mercury or Venus, returns to where it was at your birth. Mercury returns occur annually, and Venus returns occur annually or biannually, depending on the retrograde motion of transiting Venus. Usually, but not always, these returns are near your birth date.

The timing of other planetary return charts varies according to the speed, measured in years, at which the planet transits the entire zodiac.

Diurnal

Diurnal charts are used for daily forecasting. Using the current transiting planets in combination with your birth time and place, the diurnal chart offers insight into the general tone of the day, what your focus will be, and whether it will be easygoing or hectic, for example.

Horary

Mastering this branch of astrology can take a lifetime of study, and is well beyond the scope of this book. However, some of these charts are relatively easy to read and can be an asset as an adjunct to other techniques, primarily when you need a yes or no answer. Beyond that, this "ask a question, get an answer" technique requires the use of extensive rules and an in-depth study of the chart, which is calculated for the moment the question is asked.

Mundane

This branch of astrology is used to forecast trends and events for cities, states, provinces, and countries, as well as the weather. Lunation, eclipse, and solar ingress charts are the most commonly used, and transits and progressions to the charts of cities, states, provinces, and countries can also be revealing. Reading these charts takes practice and it's necessary to become familiar with the meaning of the houses, planets, and signs from a mundane perspective. Financial astrology, which is used for investing, also falls in this category.

PREDICTIVE ASTROLOGY: WHAT IT IS, AND ISN'T

Is it really possible to predict when you'll earn a promotion or meet the man or woman of your dreams? Yes and no.

Unlike the weather, people have free will. Think of all the choices you've made in your life. Did you choose option A or option B, or choose to do nothing at all? Unfortunately, the world is filled with people who made unwise choices at one point or another, choices that changed their lives. It's also filled with people who made wise choices and changed their lives.

The point is this: never depend upon astrology to make decisions for you (or for others, no matter how much they plead). Instead, consider predictive astrology to be another tool in your life tool box. When used in combination with your own reasoning power and your knowledge of a given situation, predictive astrology can often give you the edge. As a wise person once said, "It's all in the timing."

Astrology can indicate when the timing is right, for example, to aim for a promotion, send out your resume, socialize with friends in hopes of meeting a romantic interest, save rather than spend, return to school, relocate, or purchase property. Without this knowledge, you could miss out on a fantastic career opportunity. Or you could buy a home or sign a lease when there are strong astrological indicators that a second relocation might be on the horizon. By being aware of periods when money might be tight, you can plan ahead to increase savings.

Even the best trends will produce absolutely nothing if you don't act on them. The job offer won't be forthcoming if you don't submit your resume, the spectacular sale won't save you money if you don't shop, and you won't earn a college degree until you first apply for admission. The goal is to find the right time to act.

Predictive astrology can also give you the edge in daily activities. Say you have an important meeting or presentation on a given day. By looking at the planetary positions for that day, you can determine whether people will be generally impatient, open-minded, emotional, hot-headed, or agreeable. With this knowledge, you'll be better prepared to handle the day's events.

SUN-SIGN ASTROLOGY

Friends, relatives, and acquaintances will be quick to ask you to tell them their future when they discover you're learning predictive astrology. Their requests will be followed by: "My birthday is…"

This is, of course, the downside of Sun-sign astrology (the daily horoscopes found on the Internet and in newspapers and magazines that most people define as astrology because they have no other knowledge of the subject). Sun-sign forecasts are valid up to a point, but they're based only on the sign the Sun was in at birth. That's only one planet out of ten! Not to mention the all-important angles of the chart (Ascendant, Midheaven, Descendant, and IC). Unfortunately, much of the general public isn't aware of the difference, so be prepared to explain the reason why you can't forecast someone's future off the top of your head.

In order to fully understand (and to explain to others) the difference between a Sun-sign chart and a timed chart, it's helpful to know how both are derived. A timed chart has a sign on the Ascendant, which is the cusp of the first house; a succeeding sign on the cusp of the second house; and so on around the chart. A Sun-sign chart, which is untimed, has no Ascendant. Instead, the Sun sign functions as the first house cusp. To illustrate this, your timed chart might have transiting Saturn in the tenth house, pointing to a strongly emphasized career period. But your Sun-sign chart might show transiting Saturn in the fifth house of recreation and children, completely missing the strong career trend in your life. Your individualized house emphasis, an important part of interpretation, is completely missing in your Sun-sign forecast.

However, in-depth Sun-sign forecasts that target particular birth dates can be very insightful. This is because these forecasts focus on the effects of outer planet transits to a particular birth date (month and day). These transits are nearly as powerful in both timed and untimed charts. After all, the Sun represents you, the person, in the birth chart, no matter in what house and sign your Sun is located. Just ask anyone who has lived through a year or two with transiting Uranus or Pluto contacting his or her Sun! Because of the many other factors taken into consideration in in-depth forecasts versus short daily forecasts, they can also (often with a good deal of accuracy) forecast other trends based only on the Sun sign. However, absolutely nothing can take the place of an accurately timed chart.

PREDICTING WITH THE BIRTH CHART

It is not only impossible but unwise to try and derive an accurate forecast without first studying the birth chart. This point cannot be over-emphasized. Doing so can be equated to driving to a new destination without first getting directions. Every turn and road traveled is based on those directions, the map that guides you.

The birth chart is often called a map, meaning a map of life. It is your starting point, the skills, talents, challenges, strengths, and weaknesses with which you are equipped at birth. No matter how hard you wish or how much effort you put into something, if the potential isn't there at birth, it's unlikely to happen. This is why some people are engineers, others are financial wizards, and still others are astrologers. So before attempting to predict your future, please read the companion book to this volume, *Llewellyn's Complete Book of Astrology*.

As your birth chart—your map of life—unfolds in tune with the ever-moving planets, so too does your potential unfold through many experiences, much experimentation, learning, and increasing self-knowledge. How does this apply to predictive astrology?

Suppose a birth chart indicates fear of commitment and every predictive tool indicates that a once-in-a-lifetime period for the start of a lasting relationship is approaching. If the person has not yet dealt with that fear of commitment, the positive predictive indications are unlikely to overcome that trait. On the other hand, these positive predictive influences could motivate the individual to seek counseling to overcome the pattern.

Or suppose a birth chart indicates there is a tendency for an individual to be not only a risk-taker but also accident-prone. A day with a strong Mars transit would not be a good choice for sky diving or race car driving!

It's thus vital to begin with the birth chart, from which you can gain a full understanding of the individual it represents. Only at that point can you forecast how someone might respond to current planetary influences.

Your chart is the best learning tool you have because you know yourself best. By looking for upcoming predictive influences and then noting what effect they have, you will begin to learn how your chart—and you—respond in various events and situations. Be prepared to be surprised. Charts do not always respond in predictable ways, just as people do not. Or so it will seem at first. The astrology is accurate if correctly interpreted, but it's tough to maintain an objective perspective when looking at your own chart. In the process, and in addition to learning how your chart responds to various predictive factors, you will learn much more about yourself. That can definitely help you become the best you can be.

PROGRESSIONS AND SOLAR ARCS

Secondary progressions and solar arc directions are the two most commonly used methods to "advance" the birth chart to the current year in an individual's life. They indicate current trends, the themes of the year, and areas of life that will be emphasized. Both are valid predictive tools, but most astrologers use secondary progressions. I prefer secondary progressions because there are generally more aspects to consider and I've found them to be more insightful and to work better than solar arcs. But solar arcs can add valuable information and confirmation to what the progressions show, so give both a try.

Secondary progressions, commonly referred to as progressions (also called directions), are a relatively new addition to the astrologer's tool box. First proposed in the seventeenth century by astrologer Placidus de Titus, it was late in the nineteenth century, after astrologer Alan Leo revived the technique, that secondary progressions gained popularity. Prior to this, astrologers had used primary directions, which are difficult to calculate without knowledge of spherical astronomy and trigonometry. Secondary progressions, on the other hand, are relatively easy to calculate because they are based on the positions of the planets in an ephemeris, a book that lists the sign, degrees, and minutes of each planet on a daily basis. (This was, of course, before the advent of the computer in the days when astrologers calculated all charts by hand.)

Progressions use the day-for-a-year method of planetary movement. They are based on the actual—not the average—daily movement of the planets, with each day corresponding to a year in the individual's life. For example, to determine the progressed influences in effect when you were age ten, count forward ten days in an ephemeris, beginning with the date of your birth (month,

PROGRESSED AND SOLAR ARC PLACEMENT FOR AUGUST 1, 2008, BIRTH DATE

	Birth Placement	Progressed Placement	Solar Arc Placement
Sun	09 Leo 36	19 Leo 11	19 Leo 36
Venus	24 Leo 15	06 Virgo 32	04 Libra 15
Mars	18 Virgo 44	24 Virgo 59	28 Virgo 44

day, year). The planets at age ten for a July 20 birth would be those listed for July 29 of the same year, an October 8 birth date would be October 17, and so on.

Solar arc directions are the simplest of all to calculate. Based on the motion of the Sun (approximately one degree per day, or exactly 0°59'08"), the planets are progressed forward one degree for every year of life. Thus, for a birth date of February 5, you would add ten degrees to every planet's birth position in order to find its placement at age fifteen. This predictive tool was devised by Ptolemy and refined by Valentine Niabod.

The following example illustrates the difference in movement between the two systems for someone born August 1, 2008, at age eleven:

Note how the Sun in both methods is approximately the same, while planetary placements for Venus and Mars are quite different. This raises the question as to how both methods can work. They do, as we will see in several examples later in this chapter.

A basic understanding of planetary motion is essential in order to fully understand how the planets appear in a progressed chart. Although each planet has an average annual motion, the only two that maintain this constant are the Sun and Moon. They are always direct in motion and never turn retrograde, as do the other planets. The Sun moves approximately one degree for every year of life, and the progressed Moon returns to its natal place about every twenty-eight years, that number being the approximate number of days it takes the Moon to move through the twelve signs each month.

When planets turn retrograde they appear to move backward in the heavens. The ephemeris will show the degrees and minutes of the planet to be decreasing instead of increasing. Planets appear to slow their speed as they approach retrograde and direct stations (the points at which they appear to stop before changing direction, either backward or forward).

Pluto can remain at the same degree for ten to fifteen days, which equates to ten to fifteen years by progression. Progressed Saturn can do the same for five years, progressed Mars for two or three years, and progressed Mercury for a year.

Venus moves more than one degree a day (one year by progression) at its fastest, gradually slowing to a one to two day (one to two years by progression) stationary period as it prepares to reverse direction. Depending upon the birth date, Venus usually progresses through one to three signs in a lifetime, while progressed Mercury, due to its overall faster motion, usually travels through two, three, or four signs.

Progressed Jupiter sometimes changes signs in progression, but the outer planets—Saturn, Uranus, Neptune, and Pluto—must be in the last (or first, if retrograde) degrees of a sign to change signs, because their movement is so slow. The outer planets sometimes progress no more than a degree or two.

Planetary motion is expressed in degrees, minutes, and seconds of a sign.

One sign = 30 degrees (30°)

One degree = 60 minutes (60')

One minute = 60 seconds (60")

The average annual movement of progressed planets is:

Sun—1 degree (1°)

Moon—12 degrees (12°)

Mercury—1 degree, 23 minutes (1° 23')

Venus—1 degree, 12 minutes (1° 12')

Mars—31 minutes (0° 31')

Jupiter—5 minutes (0° 5')

Saturn—2 minutes (0° 2')

Uranus—42 seconds (0° 0'42")

Neptune—24 seconds (0° 0'24')

Pluto—1 second (0° 0'01")

The Sun, Moon, Mercury, Venus, Mars, and sometimes Jupiter can move fast enough in a lifetime to perfect (make exact) a natal aspect. That is, the first of two planets in a natal aspect could progress forward (or backward if retrograde) until it reaches the same degree as the second planet. For example, a birth chart trine of Mars at 8 Aquarius to Uranus at 14 Gemini (an orb of six degrees, with Mars applying to Uranus) would, if Mars were moving at its average speed, become exact approximately twelve years after birth.

The progressed outer planets (Saturn, Uranus, Neptune, Pluto) move so slowly that they rarely form aspects not present at birth. If a natal aspect involving an outer planet is nearly exact, the planet could progress forward and close the gap, thereby eliminating the orb. But this in itself is unlikely to manifest as an event unless triggered by a faster moving planet. If this happens, it usually presents a once in a lifetime opportunity to fully realize the natal potential.

THE CHART UNFOLDS

With this understanding of planetary movement, it's easier to grasp the concept that progressions and solar arcs represent the birth chart potential unfolding throughout an individual's life. This concept is at the core of predictive astrology because it underlines the fact that each person arrives in the world with a set of talents, personality traits, and skills that can be developed. The potential is there, but it is up to each individual to develop it, while emphasizing strengths and minimizing (or resolving) weaknesses.

The progressed chart (versus solar arc) is particularly important in this respect. The inner planets are what differentiate the individual from the collective represented by the outer planets. Because the outer planets move so slowly, everyone born within months, and sometimes several years, has these planets within a few degrees. Not so, however, with any of the inner planets, such as Mercury, which moves through the entire zodiac (all twelve signs) every year. As these inner planets advance in the progressed chart, they perfect birth chart aspects, contact other planets in the birth chart (forming new aspects not in the birth chart), and change house and sign position.

As an example, consider an individual born with Saturn in the ninth house of higher education. That placement alone indicates a probable delay in post-secondary education. The approximate time frame for this education can be determined by progressing the chart and finding the year when progressed Mercury (planet of learning), will aspect natal Saturn. For someone born July 14, 2008, with Mercury at 06 Cancer and Saturn at 05 Virgo, this could be at age thirty, when Mercury will have progressed through the rest of Cancer, all of Leo, and advanced to 05 Virgo, where it will conjunct natal Saturn. Note that in this example, solar arc Mercury would be at 06 Leo, forming a semi-sextile to natal Saturn.

Although the above example is something of an over-simplification, especially because predictive astrology involves far more than one planetary indicator, it nevertheless illustrates how the universe offers the opportunity to fulfill one's natal potential. This is also a good example of how astrologers forecast the future.

You can quickly spot potentially significant years simply by scanning the ephemeris in the weeks after your birth. Look for the years (represented by days) when progressed planets will aspect your natal planets. With this advance knowledge, you can determine which year, for example, might be a career high point, and then use several predictive techniques to refine the forecast and zero in on the timing. This can be invaluable in long-range planning and goal setting. Just as important will be a close study of

the chart in the years leading up to the designated year so you can incorporate those planetary indications into your plans.

SIGN AND HOUSE CHANGES

Although natal characteristics always dominate, their energy is modified when a progressed or solar arc planet enters another sign. The effect is that of adding or opening up another layer of resources that you can explore and tap into. For example, family and security are major areas of interest if you have Mars in Cancer. This will be true throughout your lifetime, but if Mars progresses into Leo, personal needs will become a higher priority than in previous years.

These energy shifts are most easily felt with the faster moving progressed Moon, which progresses through a sign in about two and a half years. But you'll also experience the subtle shift in emphasis when the other inner planets change signs.

A similar effect occurs when planets change houses. If your natal Venus is in the seventh house, relationships will be prominent throughout your life. However, when progressed Venus enters the eighth house, you could form a business/financial partnership or otherwise learn to meld your resources with those of others. Or if you have a twelfth house Sun, your self-confidence will rise when the Sun enters your first house.

RETROGRADE AND STATIONARY PROGRESSED PLANETS

The easiest way to spot the years when progressed planets station to turn retrograde or direct is, again, to look at an ephemeris. Look forward in the ephemeris for two to three months, beginning with the day of your birth and make a note of the age at which a planet turns retrograde (R) or direct (D). A year in which a progressed planet reverses direction signals a major turning point. The immediate effect is usually apparent when Venus, Mercury, or Mars changes direction; but it is more subtle with the outer planets, and you may not realize the full impact until several years later. (An ephemeris is also the easiest way to discover whether you were born on a day when a planet reversed its direction.)

Again using the higher education example, a delay could occur at the beginning of a course of study if there is a natal retrograde Mercury-Saturn opposition from the ninth to third houses. The year that progressed Mercury turns direct could bring a sudden urge to enroll in college. Fulfilling that goal will then have a major effect in your career when progressed Mercury, which will continue to advance, eventually forms a conjunction with the Midheaven.

Venus or a seventh house planet changing direction brings relationships into focus, often resulting in marriage or divorce. A tenth house planet can indicate a shift in career direction, and a second or eighth house planet can influence finances. House rulerships also provide clues to the potential outcome. Mercury turning direct in a chart with Virgo rising can act as a confidence builder.

Retrograde progressed planets manifest in yet another way that might or might not release the promised potential of the natal chart. This occurs when a faster moving retrograde planet (usually Mercury, Venus, Mars, or Jupiter) precedes by degree a planet it aspects.

For example, one possible outcome of a natal Jupiter-Pluto trine is a sizable inheritance. But suppose that, at birth, Pluto is at 16 degrees, and Venus is retrograde at 14 degrees. The natal promise of an inheritance would most likely occur during the year(s) that progressed Venus is exactly trine natal Pluto. That could be one year or sixty or more, depending on how long it takes Venus to retrograde into its station, resume forward movement and move past its natal position to form the exact aspect with Pluto. For people born during the stationary or early retrograde period, it may never reach exactitude.

Retrograde and stationary planets have no bearing in solar arc directions because all planets move forward at the same speed when this method is used.

ASCENDANT AND MIDHEAVEN

The progressed or solar arc Ascendant and Midheaven (two of the angles) are highly significant in predictive astrology. Their opposing points, the Descendant and IC (the other two angles), are of course simultaneously aspected. The method used to progress the Ascendant and Midheaven is a matter of personal preference. I have found that angles progressed by Naibod in longitude are the most accurate, but it's wise to experiment with various methods before choosing one. In a solar arc chart, the angles are also advanced according to the motion of the Sun, or about a degree a year.

As in the natal chart, the progressed or solar arc Ascendant is a personality factor, and the Midheaven governs career, status, and achievements. Although these angles, like the progressed and solar arc planets, are key components in predictive astrology, their strength is less significant than the natal angles, just as it is for progressed planets versus natal planets. Nevertheless, there are instances when progressed or solar arc angles are just as strong, such as when the progressed or solar arc Ascendant-Descendant aspects Venus or Mars, often an indication of a serious relationship or marriage.

A progressed or solar arc planet aspecting the natal Ascendant or Midheaven signals a major event ninety-nine percent of the time. The event usually focuses on self (Ascendant), partners (Descendant), career (Midheaven) and/or home and family (IC), and the years when these events occur are generally memorable and sometimes momentous and life-changing.

ASPECTS AND ORBS

Progressed planets form aspects with natal and progressed planets and angles. Solar arc planets, because they advance at the same rate of motion, can only form aspects to natal planets. All of these planetary contacts are important indicators in predictive astrology.

The Ptolemaic, or major, aspects are easy to spot, but they seldom tell the full story. Although more difficult to see at a glance, the semisquare (45°) and sesquisquare (135°) are similar to the square and often signal events. If you don't want to do the math, purchase an aspectarian to help you find the 45° and 135° aspects. Or use astrological software to run a "hit list" of progressed aspects for two or three years so you can spot upcoming trends.

Generally, progressed and solar arc aspects to planets and angles, react like this:

- Conjunction (0°)—intensity, action, joins the forces of two planets
- Trine (120°)—rarely an action aspect, it provides luck and harmony
- Sextile (60°)—creates opportunities, but requires action to realize gain
- Opposition (180°)—usually involves relationships, people at odds, separation
- Square (90°)—action, conflict, matters requiring attention
- Semisquare (45°) and sesquisquare (135°)—action, conflict, need for resolution

Usually, you will see a combination of easy and difficult aspects; the latter are necessary to generate action. The difficult aspects often act as incentives for action rather than manifesting as negative events. Practice and experience are invaluable here, and it's vital to take the birth chart into consideration. A difficult natal aspect aspected by a progressed or solar arc planet will often result in a less than favorable outcome, and the reverse is true when an easy natal alignment is aspected. It's equally important to look at the overall picture—all the planets and aspects involved. When, for example, positive indicators outweigh negative ones, the situation could ultimately have the desired, or close to desired, outcome after overcoming some hurdles.

Effective orbs vary according to the progressed planet, and based on their speed of movement:

Sun—1°

Moon—1½°

Mercury—1°

Venus—1°

Mars—30'

Jupiter—15'

Outer planets—5'

The above are guidelines. Be flexible, and look for both separating and approaching aspects that could indicate prior events related to the current one, or those that might indicate the ultimate outcome.

Because all solar arc planets move at the same rate, the natal aspects never change, even when a planet enters a new sign. Therefore, look only for aspects between solar arc planets and natal ones. The relationship of the solar arc planets to each other is the same as in the natal chart. The orb of influence is one degree for all solar arc planets and angles.

STEP-BY-STEP ANALYSIS

With practice and experience, you'll reach the point where you can fairly quickly spot the pertinent progressed and solar arc indicators and sum up the current trends active in someone's life. In fact, you'll know almost instantly why someone wants your astrological input.

Be careful! It's easy even for experienced astrologers to overlook an important factor because not all of them are quite so apparent. Therefore, you should get into the habit of first studying the birth chart before moving on to the progressions and solar arcs in order to learn about the individual's personality, motivations, skills, talents, and attitudes.

Once your study of the birth chart is complete, make a list of all the progressed and solar arc aspects, noting the house(s) each planet rules, the planet's house position, and the birth chart planet(s) it activates, along with comments or keywords to aid your interpretation. Note progressed to progressed, progressed to natal, and solar arc to natal planets.

Going through this exercise might seem like a lot of work, especially at first. Trust me. It will help you to organize your thoughts and develop a cohesive forecast. A main theme will quickly begin to emerge and you'll see that it is repeated over and over in the aspects (see Three Aspect Rule on page 33). Although it doesn't often happen, there are times when you'll see little activity in the progressions and solar arcs. Don't be concerned. Outer planet transits, which act much like progressions and solar arcs, add another level to the predictive analysis (see Chapter 5).

Each of the examples that follow use this method of analysis, focusing on the aspects pertinent to the event that occurred at the time.

PAMELA ANDERSON

Actress Pamela Anderson was discovered at a Canadian Football League game she attended with friends in the summer of 1989. A video camera focused on her and flashed her image on the stadium screen, and when the crowd cheered she was invited onto the field. At the time she was wearing a Labatt's beer t-shirt, and that company subsequently hired her as a model. That was just the beginning of a career as a model and actress that took off in a flash.

She was featured as a cover girl in the October 1989 issue of *Playboy,* and returned as Playmate of the Month in February 1990. In between, she moved from Vancouver to Los Angeles to

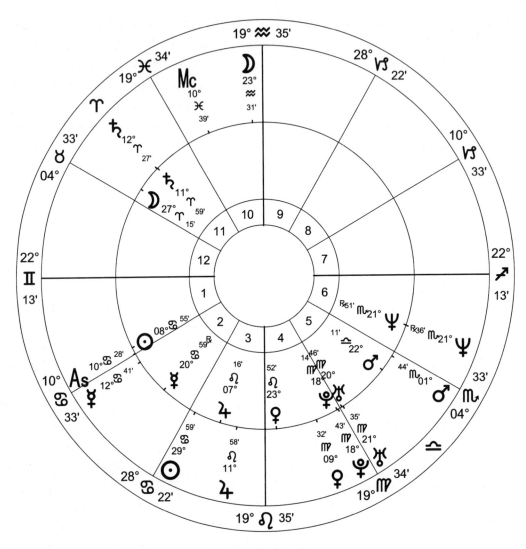

Chart 1: Pamela Anderson
Inner wheel: Birth Chart / July 1, 1967 / 4:08 am PDT /Ladysmith, Canada / Placidus House
Outer wheel: Secondary Progressed / Aug. 1, 1989 / 8:48:31 am PDT / Ladysmith, Canada / Placidus House

pursue an acting career. After a series of small roles, she landed a role on the popular series *Baywatch*, where she was a regular character from 1992 to 1997. She has appeared in many movies.

Pamela's chart (Chart 1) is an excellent example of how the progressed chart can indicate both initial and ongoing career success. This progressed chart is cast for August 1, 1989, to indicate the trends that were active at the time; the exact date of the football game is unavailable.

First, notice the progressed Moon, which had a few months previously entered the tenth house of career and status. It makes a number of important aspects, including an opposition to natal Venus (popularity), a separating trine to natal Mars, a separating square to the natal Ascendant, and a sesquisquare to natal Sun. The progressed Moon was thus the key factor that set up the potential for career success and fame, especially because it activated the decidedly sexy natal Venus-Mars sextile that aspects the natal Midheaven by opposition (Venus) and trine (Mars).

The progressed angles are also active, with the progressed Midheaven (career) in an approaching semisquare to natal Moon (the public), and the progressed Ascendant (self) approaching a square to natal Saturn (career planet). Note that these are approaching aspects, which indicates that she was just beginning a new career phase.

Luck was definitely with Pamela, putting her in the right place at the right time, with progressed Jupiter in an exact trine to natal Saturn, the old ruler of Aquarius and thus co-ruler of her tenth house. This aspect fully illustrates the concept of the chart unfolding, because Jupiter was at 7 Leo when she was born, just under five degrees from a trine with natal Saturn.

When Jupiter progressed to the exact aspect, her career took off, bringing with it all the natal potential for major success and income (Saturn rules the eighth house). This progressed aspect is one that an astrologer could have identified at any time in the previous years, and then alerted her to the potential for an opportunity of a lifetime at age twenty-two. Progressed Jupiter continued to move forward, eventually forming a trine to progressed Saturn in early 1992, when she landed the role on *Baywatch*.

There were other approaching aspects that indicated her discovery would be more than a momentary flash of stardom. The progressed Sun, which was just about to enter Leo (acting, glitz, and glamour), would square progressed Mars in 1991. In turn, progressed Mars was moving into a semisquare with the natal and progressed Uranus-Pluto conjunction. This aspect was active from 1992 to 1997, when she was a *Baywatch* star.

The solar arc chart (Chart 2) was also active, with solar arc Mercury (Ascendant ruler) trine tenth-house co-ruler Saturn. (The solar arc Sun made the same aspects as the progressed Sun.)

Most evident in the solar arc chart are the approaching aspects that would be active during her time on *Baywatch*. The solar arc Moon, which was square the natal Midheaven in 1989, bringing her to public attention, would advance to a square to natal Venus in 1994. Between 1992 and 1995, solar arc Venus was conjunct the Pluto-Uranus conjunction, and in 1995, solar arc Mars was square the natal Midheaven. Although she stayed with the show until 1997, she probably began to feel it was time to move on when these aspects were at their strongest in 1995.

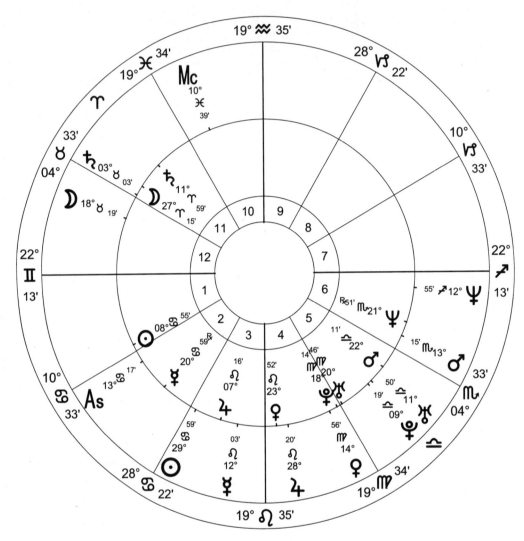

Chart 2: Pamela Anderson
Inner wheel: Birth Chart / July 1, 1967 / 4:08 am PDT /Ladysmith, Canada / Placidus House
Outer wheel: Directed Solar Arc / Aug. 1, 1989 / 3:04:57 pm PDT / Ladysmith, Canada / Placidus House

PROGRESSED AND SOLAR ARC INFLUENCES IN PAMELA ANDERSON'S CHART			
Progressed Planet	**Aspect or House**	**Planet or Angle**	**Comments**
Moon	Tenth House		Moon (public) in tenth (career, fame) rules Cancer, ruler of the second (income) and third (communication)
Moon	Opposition	Natal Venus	Moon (public) in tenth (career, fame) opposition Venus (popularity); Venus co-rules the fifth (recreation, drama/theatre, sex appeal), where Libra is intercepted; Moon activates the natal Venus-Mars-Midheaven configuration, indicating potential for fame as an actor and sex symbol
Moon	Trine	Natal Mars	Moon (public) in tenth (career, fame) trine (easy connection) Mars, ruler of the sixth (work, job) and eleventh house (friends and goals)
Moon	Sextile	Natal Ascendant	Moon in tenth (public attention) trine (opportunity) Ascendant (self)
Moon	Sesquisquare	Natal Sun	Moon in tenth (public attention) focused on self (Sun) indicates a new awareness of "self"; Sun rules the fourth (home, family), indicating possible relocation, along with the above-mentioned Moon opposition natal Venus in the fourth
Midheaven	Semisquare	Natal Moon	Midheaven in tenth (career, fame) semisquare (action) natal Moon in eleventh (friends); she came to the attention of many while attending an event with friends
Prog. Ascendant	Square	Natal Saturn	Ascendant (self) in second (income) square (action, challenge) Saturn, ruler of eighth (money), and co-ruler of the tenth (career) in the eleventh (friends)

Venus	Sextile	Natal Sun	Venus (popularity) sextile (opportunity) natal Sun (self) square Saturn, co-ruler of tenth (career, fame); Saturn rules the eighth (money); natal Sun is also semisquare natal Venus, so progressed Venus-natal Sun aspect also activates natal Venus-Mars-Midheaven configuration
Prog. Jupiter	Trine	Natal Saturn	Prog. Jupiter (luck, abundance) ruler of seventh (relationships) and eleventh (friends) perfects natal Jupiter-Saturn (realistic optimism) trine and activates natal Saturn aspects (ambition)
Sun	Enters	Leo	Sun (self) in Leo (popularity, acting)

Solar Arc Planet	Aspect or House	Planet	Comments
Mercury	Trine	Natal Saturn	Mercury, ruler of first (self) and fifth (recreation, acting, and sex appeal) trine (easy connection) natal Saturn, ruler of eighth (money) and co-ruler of tenth (career) in the eleventh (friends); also activates natal Saturn aspects
Moon	Square	Natal Mid-heaven	Moon (public) and ruler of second (income) square (action) Midheaven (career, fame)

Summary: A recreational event (fifth house) with friends (eleventh house) has the potential to bring you luck (Jupiter) that will put you in the public spotlight (Moon, Venus) and advance your career aims and popularity (tenth house).

MARTHA STEWART

Entrepreneur Martha Stewart built a small, home-based catering business into a global empire: Martha Stewart Living Omnimedia, Inc. She was indicted June 4, 2003, on charges of securities fraud, conspiracy, and obstruction of justice, among others. She was found guilty of four counts on March 5, 2004, after a jury trial in New York. Sentenced to five months in prison, five months house arrest, and two years supervised probation, she entered prison October 8, 2004, and was released March 4, 2005.

The ninth house rules the legal system and publishing, and the twelfth house rules prisons. Martha's chart (Chart 3) has three planets in the natal ninth house, indicative of her publishing

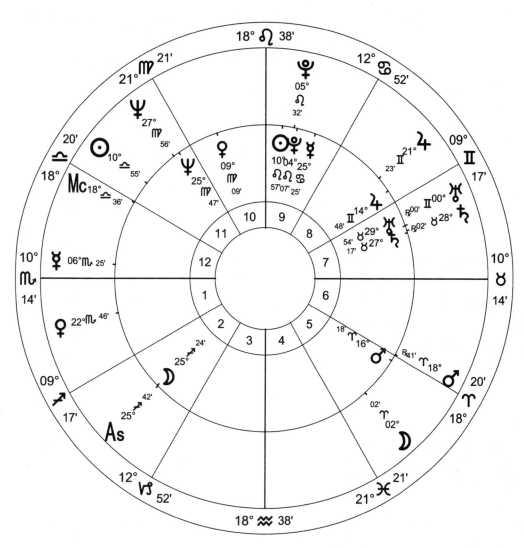

Chart 3: Martha Stewart
Inner wheel: Birth Chart / Aug. 3, 1941 / 1:33 pm EDT / Jersey City, NJ / Placidus House
Outer wheel: Secondary Progressed / June 4, 2003 / 8:48:31 am EDT / Jersey City, NJ / Placidus House

empire and the potential for legal problems. The planets and planetary rulers associated with these houses are: Venus (twelfth house ruler), Moon (ninth house ruler), and Sun, Pluto, and Mercury in the ninth house. We would thus expect to see active progressions involving some (or all) of these planets during the period of Martha's legal difficulties, and specifically, a connection between the ninth and twelfth houses.

Note that Martha's chart has natal Venus, ruler of the twelfth house, semisquare natal Mercury in the ninth. This hard aspect indicates that she was born with the potential for legal difficulties and a prison sentence. It is reinforced by the Moon, ruler of the ninth house, square Neptune, natural ruler of the twelfth house, an aspect that was active during Martha's ordeal. The natal Moon is also inconjunct natal Mercury in the ninth house.

At the time of the indictment, progressed Mercury was separating from a square to natal and progressed Pluto. This aspect was exact in June 2002, when rumors first surfaced that she was being investigated by the United States Justice Department. Progressed Mercury was also sesquisquare progressed Jupiter (universal ruler of the ninth house) in the eighth house of other people's money. From the beginning of this event, progressed Mercury was approaching a sextile to natal Venus, an aspect that was exact at the completion of her two-year probation period.

The timing of the rumors and the indictment are also reflected in the progressed Ascendant, which had been exactly conjunct natal Moon in 2002, and which was exactly square progressed Neptune at the time of her release from prison. Also at the time of her release, progressed Venus in Scorpio was trine natal Mercury (remember the natal Mercury-Venus semisquare that indicates the potential for time in prison).

There were aspects involving the progressed Moon as well. It was applying to a trine to natal and progressed Pluto when she was indicted, semisquare natal Saturn when she was sentenced, and square natal Mercury when she was released from prison, again activating the natal Mercury-Venus semisquare. The progressed Moon was also approaching a trine to natal Moon when she was released.

If Martha's natal chart had more difficult aspects involving the ninth and twelfth houses, her sentence would probably have been much longer. She also has put these planets to effective use in her media career, and benefitted from the income-attracting Jupiter in the eighth house. The Jupiter placement, which is one of the best for attracting money, may have contributed to her belief that her actions were business as usual and that she had done nothing wrong.

There are several important aspects in the solar arc chart (Chart 4), where all solar arc planets sextile their natal positions and thus activate the natal aspects.

Solar arc Mercury was conjunct natal Neptune and square natal Moon at the time of the indictment, setting off the natal configuration with the potential for legal trouble and a prison sentence. Venus by solar arc was close to the natal Ascendant, which it crossed, moving out of the twelfth house and into the first, about the time she was released. Upon her release from prison, solar arc Venus was square natal Sun, ruler of the tenth house, indicating her motivation to get back to business, which she did.

But the most interesting aspect in the June 4, 2003, chart is solar arc Jupiter approaching

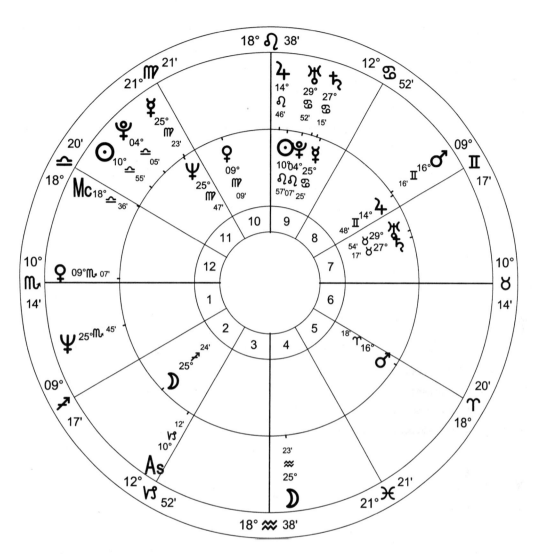

Chart 4: Martha Stewart
Inner wheel: Birth Chart / Aug. 3 1941 / 1:33 pm EDT / Jersey City, NJ / Placidus House
Outer wheel: Directed Solar Arc / June 4, 2003 / 8:48:31 am EDT / Jersey City, NJ / Placidus House

a conjunction with the natal Midheaven. This in itself indicates that Martha would again be at the top of her career just four years later, in 2007, and indeed she was.

PROGRESSED AND SOLAR ARC INFLUENCES IN MARTHA STEWART'S CHART			
Progressed Planet	**Aspect or House**	**Planet**	**Comments**
Mercury	Twelfth house		Twelfth (institutions, secrets, and hidden activities)
Mercury	Sesquisquare	Prog. Jupiter	Jupiter in the eighth (other people's money, investments); Mercury rules the eighth, and Jupiter rules the second (personal money) and co-rules the fifth (speculation)
Ascendant	Square	Prog. Neptune	Prog. Ascendant activates natal Moon-Neptune square (action); Moon in second (money) rules ninth (legal matters), and Neptune in eleventh (high aspirations with regard to friends) rules fifth (speculation)
Venus	Trine	Mercury	Activates natal Mercury-Venus (charm, beneficial communication) semisquare (challenge)
Solar Arc Planet	**Aspect or House**	**Planet**	**Comments**
Mercury	Conjunction	Neptune	Activates natal Moon-Neptune (fantasy, intuition) square (action)

Note: The aspects listed above were in effect at the time Martha was indicted. If you were preparing a thorough analysis of her chart, you would also want to list the obvious approaching aspects. If Martha were your client, she would want your assessment of possible penalties, including incarceration.

Summary: Martha will be involved in a legal matter (ninth house) concerning finances—probably speculation or investments (second, fifth, and eighth houses)—that could result in a significant fine and/or other penalties, including probation and/or incarceration. Note that the only positive aspect activates a difficult natal aspect, which is also generally true of the progressions and solar arcs a year before and for the following two to three years.

MARILYN MONROE

Marilyn Monroe, the iconic sex symbol, had a difficult childhood. Her mother likely was affected by a bipolar disorder that resulted in her institutionalization at various times and Marilyn's placement in foster homes and an orphanage. Reportedly, she married Jim Dougherty, the first of three husbands, on June 19, 1942, at age sixteen in order to avoid returning to an orphanage. They had been married only a short time when Dougherty was shipped out to the Pacific during World War II, and Marilyn went to work in an airplane factory. That's where the photograph that jump-started her modeling and film career was taken. Marilyn and Jim divorced in August 1946.

A number of the classic marriage/serious relationship indicators were active in Marilyn's chart when she married (Chart 5). There is almost always a significant aspect involving the natal and/or progressed Ascendant-Descendant (self-partner), Venus (love), Mars (passion and sex), planets in and ruling the seventh house of partnership, and often the natal and/or progressed Midheaven-IC.

The progressed Sun was sextile/trine the progressed Ascendant-Descendant, and progressed Mercury (ruler of her Sun sign, Gemini) was semisquare/sesquisquare the same angles. When she married, she changed her living situation, as reflected in the progressed Midheaven opposition natal Saturn (co-ruler of the seventh house) in the fourth house of home. The progressed Midheaven was also square natal and progressed Neptune, which indicates her "escape" from the orphanage into what she probably perceived as an ideal solution and situation. At the time of the marriage, the progressed Moon was separating from a trine to Venus, an aspect that was exact a month earlier when initial wedding plans were probably made.

Of all the aspects, there were three that were the most telling that she would marry in this year of her life: progressed Sun trine and progressed Ascendant opposition natal Jupiter in the seventh house, and progressed Venus semisquare progressed Mars. Based on these aspects alone, an astrologer could have forecast at the time of her birth that she would have a marriage opportunity in 1942.

In her solar arc chart (Chart 6), the most significant aspects were solar arc Pluto trine natal Uranus, ruler of her seventh house, solar arc Sun trine natal Jupiter in the seventh house, solar arc Mercury sextile natal Neptune. The latter two aspects were present in the progressed chart, with the Pluto-Uranus trine indicating this "arranged" marriage (Pluto in the secretive twelfth house). Pluto, along with the solar arc Midheaven opposition natal Saturn, reinforces the new living situation. But the solar arc Ascendant inconjunct natal Uranus suggests she wasn't completely comfortable with the marriage idea.

The 1946 divorce occurred with the progressed and solar arc Sun square Uranus, ruler of the seventh house.

Two other events in Marilyn's life were strongly reflected in her chart. She said she had been raped at age eleven, a period when she was in foster care and an orphanage. At that time, the progressed Ascendant was conjunct natal/progressed Neptune, ruler of the eighth house,

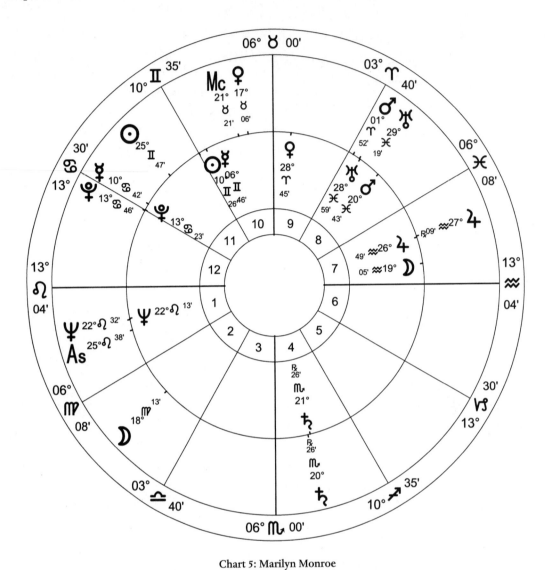

Chart 5: Marilyn Monroe
Inner wheel: Birth Chart / June 1, 1926 / 9:30 am / Los Angeles, California
Outer wheel: Secondary Progressed / June 19, 1942 / 8:48:31 am / Los Angeles, California
Placidus House

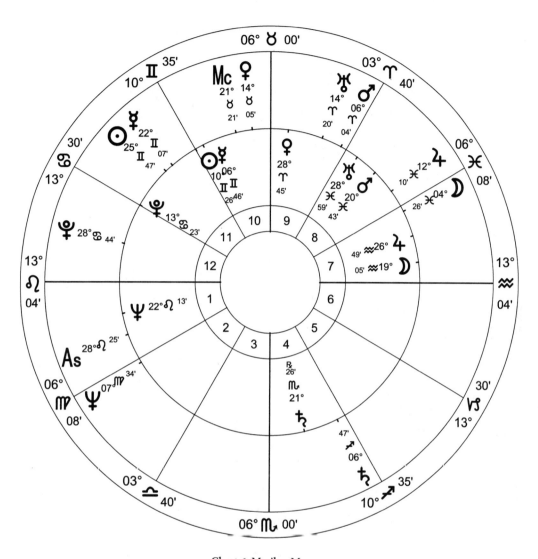

Chart 6: Marilyn Monroe
Inner wheel: Birth Chart / June 1, 1926 / 9:30 am / Los Angeles, California
Outer wheel: Directed Solar Arc / June 19, 1942 / 8:48:31 am / Los Angeles, California
Placidus House

and progressed Mars in the eighth house was conjunct natal/progressed Uranus, ruler of the seventh house.

Many rumors and allegations continue to surround Marilyn and her alleged relationships with Jack and Bobby Kennedy. Marilyn reportedly told several friends in early 1962 that she and Bobby would marry. She was decidedly in love with someone that year, as indicated by one of the classic serious relationship/marriage indicators: progressed Venus conjunction natal Sun. This aspect is one of the most common when people marry.

PROGRESSED AND SOLAR ARC INFLUENCES IN MARILYN MONROE'S CHART			
Progressed Planet	**Aspect or House**	**Planet**	**Comments**
Sun	Trine	Prog. Descendant	Sun (self) rules Ascendant (self) trine (easy connection) with partner (Descendant)
Mercury	Sesquisquare	Prog. Descendant	Mercury (ruler of Sun sign, Gemini) sesquisquare (action to connect with partner (Descendant)
Midheaven	Opposition	Saturn	Midheaven (recognition)/IC (home, family); Saturn in fourth (home, family) co-rules Descendant (partner)
Midheaven	Square	Neptune	IC (home, family) square (action, incentive) to escape via romance (Neptune)
Venus	Semisquare	Prog. Mars	Venus (love, romance, partner) semisquare (action) Mars (sex)
Sun	Trine	Jupiter	Sun (self) trine (easy connection) with partner (Jupiter in the seventh house)
Ascendant	Opposition	Jupiter	Ascendant (self) opposition (contact with partner (Jupiter in the seventh house)
Solar Arc Planet/Angle	**Aspect or House**	**Planet**	**Comments**
Midheaven	Opposition	Natal Saturn	IC (home, family) conjunction (merges) Saturn in the fourth (home family); provided incentive to remove herself from a difficult home life
Mars	Sesquisquare	Solar Arc Midheaven	Mars, co-ruler of fourth (home, family) sesquisquare (action) IC (home, family); also provided incentive to remove herself from difficult home life

Mercury	Trine	Natal Neptune	Mercury, ruler of Sun sign (self) trine (opportunity) Neptune (fantasy, escape)
Sun	Trine	Natal Jupiter	Sun (self) trine (easy connection) natal Jupiter in the seventh house (partner)
Pluto	Trine	Natal Uranus	Pluto (ruler of fourth/home and family) trine (ease) natal Uranus (co-rules seventh/partner); change in living situation because of a partner
Ascendant	Inconjunct	Natal Uranus	Ascendant (self) inconjunct (unease) natal Uranus (co-rules seventh/partner)

Summary: Marilyn may choose to marry, but not necessarily for the best reasons. The relationship may be based more on fantasy and the lure of escape from a difficult situation into one that probably will not live up to expectations. She should consider whether she's in love or in love with love.

VAL

Relocation has been a central theme in Val's life, the first move occurring when she was only a few months old. This is to be expected with a natal Jupiter-IC conjunction, a Uranus-Pluto conjunction in the fourth house of home and family, and Mercury (first and fourth house ruler) sextile the Jupiter-IC conjunction. These planetary placements make it easier for an astrologer to identify time periods when yet another move might take place.

When looking at a chart for relocation, it's also important to consider the progressed Midheaven-IC and the second house. A second-house influence is often active because this represents the individual's possessions. At times, the Ascendant-Descendant are also aspected, reflecting a personal change. Moving is usually stressful and would be indicated by a hard aspect to the aforementioned configurations

Val moved to a new state in early September 2002 (Charts 7 and 8). This example is also a good illustration of how the solar arc chart can add more information to the interpretation.

Progressed Mercury (fourth house ruler) was separating from a sextile to progressed Jupiter (seventh house ruler) in the fourth house and it was also square the progressed IC. The progressed Moon also had a role in this relocation, creating a grand trine with natal Jupiter and the natal Descendant. Val's second house of possessions was active with a progressed Sun-progressed Ascendant conjunction, which is also a marriage aspect, and both were sextile natal-progressed Uranus in the fourth house.

All of these progressed aspects present a strong possibility for relocation (and marriage). Further confirmation comes from solar arc Moon opposition the natal IC.

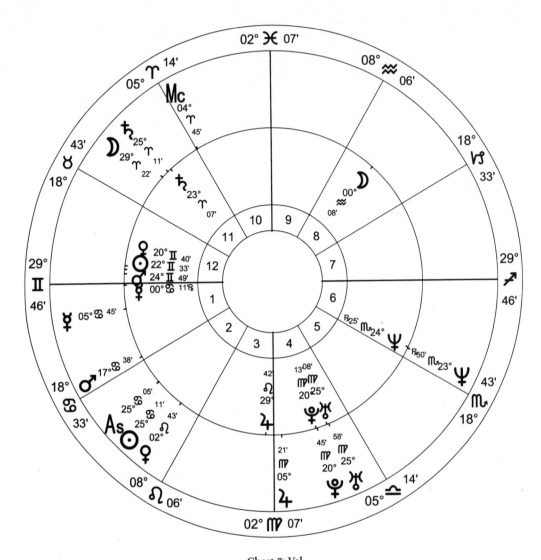

Chart 7: Val
Inner wheel: Birth Chart / June 13, 1968 / 6:01 am PDT / Salem, Oregon
Outer wheel: Secondary Progressed / September 1, 2002 / 8:48:31 am / Salem, Oregon
Placidus House

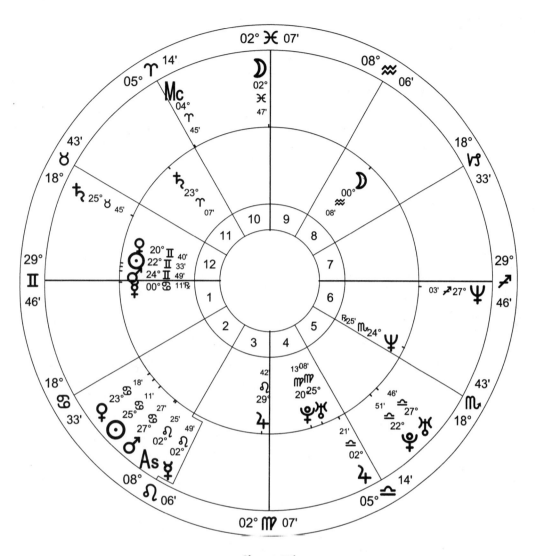

Chart 8: Val
Inner wheel: Birth Chart / June 13, 1968 / 6:01 am PDT / Salem, Oregon
Outer wheel: Directed Solar Arc / September 1, 2002 / 8:48:31 am / Salem, Oregon
Placidus House

PROGRESSED AND SOLAR ARC INFLUENCES IN VAL'S CHART			
Progressed Planet	**Aspect or House**	**Planet**	**Comments**
Mercury	Trine	Prog. Jupiter	Mercury in and ruler of first (self) and ruler of fourth (home, family) trine (ease) Jupiter in fourth; favorable for relocation
Mercury	Square	Prog. IC	Mercury, ruler of fourth (home and family) square (action) IC and fourth (home and family); incentive to move
Sun	Sextile	Uranus	Sun (self) sextile (opportunity) Uranus in fourth (home and family); Sun is in the second (possessions), which also must be relocated
Sun	Opposition	Prog. Descendant	Sun (self) opposition (contact with partner (Descendant); this is an aspect of marriage, which they did about six months later
Moon	Trine	Natal Jupiter	Moon (universal ruler of home and family), ruler of second (possessions) trine (ease) natal Jupiter, ruler of seventh (partners, relationships) conjunction (merging) IC (home and family); relocation to join fiancé
Moon	Sextile / Trine	Natal Descendant	Moon, universal ruler of home and family and ruler of second (possessions) trine (ease) Descendant (partner); relocation to join fiancé
Solar Arc Planet	**Aspect or House**	**Planet**	**Comments**
Moon	Opposition	Natal IC	Dual indication of moving possessions; Moon (universal ruler of home and family), ruler of second (possessions) opposition (separation) IC (home and family) and conjunction (focus) Midheaven (career); relocation required her to seek a new job.

Sun	Sextile	Uranus	Sun (self) sextile (opportunity) Uranus in fourth (home and family); Sun is in the second (possessions), which also must be relocated; same as progressed aspect

Summary: This is a favorable time to relocate, particularly for a romantic relationship, and Val will easily find employment in the new location. She may marry within the next several months if she's currently involved in a serious relationship.

OLD PLANETARY RULERSHIPS

Before the discovery of the modern planets (Uranus, Neptune, and Pluto), astrologers used only the seven visible planets, Sun through Saturn. This approach worked well for several thousand years, and it is still possible to read a chart using only these planets even though the modern planets add much additional information to chart interpretation.

Be sure to consider the old rulerships, especially in predictive charts. They work well, and are often a contributing factor in major events. These rulerships are:

> Mars—Aries and Scorpio
> Jupiter—Sagittarius and Pisces
> Saturn—Capricorn and Aquarius

THREE-ASPECT RULE

Being an astrologer in the pre-computer days took a lot of dedication and commitment. Each birth, progressed, and solar arc chart had to be calculated by hand. But doing it that way had a side benefit: as the charts were calculated and aspects drawn, the astrologer developed an in-depth mental picture of the individual and current trends. These astrologers who did charts the old-fashioned way were adamant about the "three-aspect rule": a potential event or situation will occur only if there are at least three aspects that indicate it. Use it. It works.

PROGRESSED AND SOLAR ARC PLANETS
in House, Sign, and Aspect

PLANETS CHANGING SIGNS OR HOUSES

Although your natal energy remains the same throughout life, your birth planets take on the subtle coloration of each succeeding sign and house they enter by progression or solar arc. Each is a growth opportunity as well as one in which you can experience all the pluses (and minuses) of the new sign or house influence.

In a normal life span, the progressed Moon moves through the entire zodiac two to three times. Once you reach approximately age twenty-eight, you will have experienced the progressed Moon in every sign and house, and this can be valuable information for you to use during the second progressed-Moon cycle. By reflecting on the life events that occurred approximately twenty-eight years before when the progressed Moon was in the same sign or house, you can discover how you might best use the energy during this cycle. Although life circumstances and other influences have changed, your basic emotional responses will be similar.

Your progressed Sun, Mercury, and Venus travel through two or three signs, and progressed Mars usually travels through two (three if natal Mars is in a late degree and remains direct). Venus and Mars, however, can stay in the same sign throughout your lifetime, depending upon their retrograde cycle. Because progressions are based on a day for a year (one day equals one year), the progressed planets also turn retrograde and direct.

For example, if you were born with Venus in an early degree of Gemini as the planet was slowing its motion to turn retrograde at 16 Gemini, and later direct at 0 Gemini, it would not enter Cancer until you were more than 120 years old. These unusual situations represent an opportunity to fully understand and incorporate the energy of a planet in a sign in both retrograde and direct motion.

Solar arc planets can travel through two or three signs in a lifetime, depending on their placement in the natal chart. Since they move at the same rate as the Sun, or about a degree a year, it takes these planets thirty years to move through a complete sign.

Included in this chapter is information about the sign/house changes for the inner progressed and solar arc planets, and hard and soft aspects between planets.

These interpretations should be used only as a starting point, to spark your thinking. Resist the urge to use them verbatim! As with a birth chart, keywords are the best way to develop a forecast.

SUN CHANGING SIGN/HOUSE

Sun keywords in predictive astrology: prominence, creativity, recreation, speculation, children, father, males

Sun in Aries/First House

Fresh starts and new endeavors appeal to you, But don't jump in head-first. List the pros and cons of any endeavor you consider and contemplate how best to invest your energy for maximum personal or professional gain. Impulsive and premature actions can backfire, but you also have the advantage of increased leadership ability.

Keywords: action, energy, initiative, leadership, achievement

Natal Aquarius Sun in Aries: You're challenged to become more of a risk-taker as Aries takes the edge off your fixed nature. Welcome a little spontaneity into your life and boldly chase dreams that were born as your progressed Sun traveled through Pisces or your twelfth house. Be assertive, yet receptive, and open to change.

Natal Pisces Sun in Aries: Born under sensitive Pisces, the impulsive, action-oriented Aries energy is foreign to you. Adapt by viewing it as a breath of fresh air and the chance to further develop initiative and drive in order to create your ideal world. Feel your growing confidence, and focus more on your needs rather than everyone else's.

Sun in Taurus/Second House

Creature comforts take on added importance. Go one step further. Take a practical look at finances and initiate a plan for the long term. You'll have a greater need for financial and material security in coming years. Avoid the tendency to hoard possessions; regularly discard what is no longer useful. Determination and follow-through are assets.

Keywords: determination, security, comfort, stubbornness, inflexibility

Natal Pisces Sun in Taurus: Your Pisces Sun resonates well with Taurus, which is as practical as it is creative. Profit from both by emphasizing a common sense, step-by-step approach to life. Combine the confidence you gained from Aries with the endurance of Taurus to build a secure foundation.

Natal Aries Sun in Taurus: The time has come to finish what you start, to add self-discipline to initiative. Learn patience and determination and refine your impulsive nature to one that's lively yet consistent and dependable. Most of all, move beyond your personal sphere and be more sympathetic to others.

Sun in Gemini/Third House

You feel more light-hearted, and social and mental stimulation appeal to you more now than in the past. Give your curiosity free rein, explore and study what interests you, and strengthen both your communication skills and your network of acquaintances. Make organization a priority.

Keywords: curiosity, restlessness, charm, light-hearted, learning

Natal Aries Sun in Gemini: You experience a new-found sense of freedom, having learned the Taurus lessons of patience and practicality. Now, you're set to search out new adventures, but with a more easygoing attitude. Socialize, network, and expand your information base.

Natal Taurus Sun in Gemini: The energy of the changeable and sometimes frivolous Gemini can be unsettling to your Taurus Sun. Steady and methodical, you're fond of routine, something Gemini shuns. Consider it a chance to break free of self-imposed structures by expanding your mental horizons. Meet people, and learn all you can.

Sun in Cancer/Fourth House

Home and family move higher on your priority list, and you'll find yourself drawn to relatives in addition to spending more time with immediate family. You might have the desire to relocate or remodel your home—welcome domestic change. Now is also the time to free your emotions and to deal with any lingering childhood or family issues.

Keywords: intuitive, sensitive, security, possessive, home, family

Natal Taurus Sun in Cancer: You feel more secure on one level, but not on another. Cancer initiates action where you prefer to fill in the blanks, although both signs are cautious. Home and family offer a built-in safety net for new endeavors and calculated risks. Domestic life centers you.

Natal Gemini Sun in Cancer: Your restless nature is tempered somewhat now that your Sun is in Cancer. You find more value in home, family, and roots, and you make your house a home and a place of retreat where you can get in touch with your feelings. The more emotional baggage you lose, the better. Share your love.

Sun in Leo/Fifth House

Your focus shifts to personal needs and interests, but the best use of this energy is to explore and discover a creative outlet for your energy. Whether you give birth to a child, an idea, or a project, it will be something that's an extension of you. You'll also have more interest in sports, even as a spectator, and socializing away from home.

Keywords: creative, outgoing, popular, ambitious, generous

Natal Gemini Sun in Leo: You're ready to tackle the world, thanks to the confidence boost from Leo. This can be your most creative period, but only if you're committed to producing something tangible. Settle down, focus on a few areas of interest and give them your all. Invite love and children into your life.

Natal Cancer Sun in Leo: Expand your sense of self. Step out of your comfort zone and stretch yourself and your affections because now you can gain the self-assurance you need to be your best. Although praise is important, remember that strength and security come from within. Be generous with yourself and those you love.

Sun in Virgo / Sixth House

The time is right to raise your health consciousness. Get in, and stay in, shape, and tune in and respond to your body's needs. A simpler life attracts you now, as does sharing your talents with others as a volunteer or possibly as a health-care professional.

Keywords: service, health-conscious, worrisome, industrious, methodical

Natal Cancer Sun in Virgo: Details and the practicalities of daily life consume more of your time, and family or parental health issues may also require attention. On a personal level, evaluate your lifestyle. Take action if there's room for improvement in diet or exercise, but try not to be too hard on yourself. Go easy at first and aim for lasting habits and benefits.

Natal Leo Sun in Virgo: Although your strong Leo Sun limits the effects of this Sun-sign shift, Virgo is still influential at times. Emphasis on

details and a practical approach are positive, but the tendency to be overly critical of yourself and others is not. Exercise and a healthy diet are important now to relieve work stress. Share your talents with a good cause.

Sun in Libra / Seventh House

You'll be more people-oriented now and interested in welcoming others into your personal and professional life. Whether you're single or committed, you'll want to spend more time with your significant other (or find one), sensing that two are better than one. But you'll also have a tendency to concede when a firm stand would be to your advantage.

Keywords: cooperation, relationships, strategy, indecisiveness

Natal Leo Sun in Libra: You get more satisfaction from relationships as your affections evolve on a deeper level. Togetherness completes you in a way never before experienced, and partnership efforts can be especially rewarding. The Libra influence also helps you step out of the limelight from time to time in order to give others their due recognition.

Natal Virgo Sun in Libra: Your reserved nature benefits from Libra's social skills. Observe others, learn the art of small talk, compromise, and consensus-building, and expand your social circle. Your eye for detail mixes well with Libra's eye for beauty. Use it to develop a flair for design in home decorating and dress.

Sun in Scorpio / Eighth House

Time alone refreshes and renews you. It's not that other people are less important but that you now look within for strength rather than first turning to others. Use your increased willpower to make self-improvement a goal and establish solid patterns and habits that can benefit you long term. Money motivates you.

Keywords: passion, self-reliance, secretive, financial security

Natal Virgo Sun in Scorpio: Resist the urge to withdraw from the world. Instead, add depth to your relationships by merging resources with those who are closest to you. Financial security also becomes a priority. Use your analytical and research skills to search out the best and most secure path that will lead to long-term financial freedom.

Natal Libra Sun in Scorpio: Although people and partnerships are a driving force in your life, don't be surprised if you experience a growing need for time alone. It helps you get in touch with your emotions and inner voice, both of which add to your depth and magnetism. Strive to open up and get close to people.

Sun in Sagittarius/Ninth House

You emerge into a wider world as your adventuresome side begins to surface. Seek knowledge for fun or profit and learn all you can in a quest for enlightenment. You might also have the urge to delve into your subconscious to better define who you are, what motivates you, and what holds you back.

Keywords: education, enlightenment, religion, self-knowledge, adventure

Natal Libra Sun in Sagittarius: A growing sense of optimism encourages you to explore the world around you. Travel, study, and learning attract you, and you find inspiration in other cultures and viewpoints. Now is the time to pursue further education as a path to advancement or for personal satisfaction. You might also become active in a religious institution.

Natal Scorpio Sun in Sagittarius: Sagittarius is dramatically different from your naturally guarded, internalized Scorpio energy. Yet this transition serves the purpose of expanding your horizons as you gain insights into and build tolerance for human foibles. Experience all the people and ideas you can and explore any life issues or attitudes that could benefit from resolution.

Sun in Capricorn/Tenth House

The urge to excel and elevate your worldly status pushes you to achieve. You want to be seen and heard, and to be valued for your expertise and ideas. As you focus on your career, make it a point to know the people who can aid your efforts, and remember to do the same for others who could benefit from your role as a mentor.

Keywords: ambition, status, reserved, leadership, achievement

Natal Scorpio Sun in Capricorn: You can step into the power seat now and begin to realize long-term goals with solid achievements. Put Capricorn's desire for responsibility, initiative, and ambition to work for you, but go easy. Emphasize the flexibility you learned when your Sun was in Sagittarius, as well as the optimism and openmindedness.

Natal Sagittarius Sun in Capricorn: Although it will stretch you, be smart and rein in your restlessness enough to reap the benefits of conservative, ambitious Capricorn. Learn to be more practical and systematic and show others they can depend on you. Then, your enthusiasm and vision become assets.

Sun in Aquarius/Eleventh House

Your challenge is to free yourself to experience the new and unusual, and to broaden your networking base. Both enhance rather than limit your need for a self-defined lifestyle that recognizes and rewards your achievements. Groups will welcome your leadership.

Keywords: networking, independence, goals, groups

Natal Sagittarius Sun in Aquarius: The free-spirited quality of Aquarius appeals to your independent nature. But Aquarius also challenges you to follow through on commitments. Group endeavors are successful, and friendships become more meaningful. Invite like-minded people into your life, and consider getting involved in a community or humanitarian cause.

Natal Capricorn Sun in Aquarius: Let the influence of Aquarius temper your conservative, structured lifestyle. Take a few more risks, and be open to new and innovative ideas. Change is refreshing if you welcome it. Socialize more, especially with those who can advance your ambitions. Networking is well worth the effort.

Sun in Pisces/Twelfth House

Time alone soothes you and opens up your sensitivities. Get in touch with your feelings, and be receptive to your inner voice, listening to hunches and developing your intuition. A healthier lifestyle could be very beneficial now, and you may be motivated to get involved in a charitable organization where you can improve the lives of others.

Keywords: sympathetic, health, intuition, enabling

Natal Capricorn Sun in Pisces: Although far different from your natal energy, the Pisces lesson is one of inspiration, compassion, and sensitivity. Be receptive to it. Develop your softer emotional side and discover your spirituality and intuition. Doing so can be surprisingly fulfilling and add an entirely new dimension to your practical style.

Natal Aquarius Sun in Pisces: Your altruistic aims fit well with Pisces, a sign that shares your gift of intuition. However, Pisces' emotional and sympathetic traits can be difficult to incorporate into your detached nature. Involve yourself in the lives of others and develop the personal sensitivity that can soften your approach.

MOON CHANGING SIGN/HOUSE

Moon keywords: emotions, home, mother, females, the public, family

Moon in Aries/First House

This influence is all about you and your interests, which is quite effective for self-improvement. You're also more sensitive and impulsive now. This is an asset, but only if your quick temper doesn't yield rash words. Use this influence to learn patience and self-discipline when daily aggravations occur. Listen before you speak, which will help to temper your opinions. Overall, your outlook is more positive and you're passionate about what you do.

Moon in Taurus/Second House

You're more possessive of people and things now. Security, especially financial, becomes more important and has a greater influence on your decisions. Be cautious because both gain and loss are possible. You may spend on home decor and furnishings, but you're unlikely to make major domestic changes. A thrifty mind set can result in wise purchases, and you could gain through a collectible purchased now or in the past.

Moon in Gemini/Third House

You're restless when your Moon is in this sign or house, and fluctuating emotions can make it difficult to define your feelings. As much as you try to apply logic to your thinking, it's tough to do at times, so be cautious about major decisions. Expect meetings and errands to eat up much of your time, and be cautious about taking on too many projects. You'll have increased contact with siblings and neighbors.

Moon in Cancer/Fourth House

Gut feelings, intuition, and first impressions are on target more often than not, but you should also take precautions to protect yourself from the negative energy emitted by people and situations. You're more involved in family and domestic activities, as well as traditions, and you might become interested in researching your family tree. Home improvements are likely, and relocation is possible.

Moon in Leo/Fifth House

Your emotional responses are more dramatic but also heartfelt, and you're more interested in fun and socializing. This influence can be among the best for romance and new romantic opportunities, and you should also find a way to express your creativity through a hobby. If you're a parent, you'll be more involved in your children's lives, but you'll also have a tendency

to spoil them. You can gain or lose through investments, depending upon other active planetary influences.

Moon in Virgo/Sixth House

Service projects give you a sense of satisfaction as never before, and also help to fulfill your emotional needs. This in turn can help to minimize a tendency to criticize others and yourself. Work is more fulfilling now, but keep it in perspective, because you'll want to take on extra responsibilities. Ease stress with a daily walk or exercise. Pets may occupy more of your time and attention at times.

Moon in Libra/Seventh House

Peaceful surroundings balance your emotions, as do soft colors and easygoing, congenial people. You'll have an increased need to reach out to others and will welcome the synergy of love and partnership. Mutually supportive endeavors are particularly appealing to you now, and you can find yourself in the role of peace-maker or consensus-builder. Carefully choose your business and personal alliances.

Moon in Scorpio/Eighth House

Your feelings run deep, and your emotions are passionate and intense. But take precautions and pull back a little rather than let them overpower your usual good judgment. Objectivity is especially important now. You can also initiate positive personal change because you'll have increased willpower. Taxes, insurance, joint possessions, estate planning, and loans are also in focus, and you could benefit through an inheritance.

Moon in Sagittarius/Ninth House

You're drawn to adventure, travel, and learning, all of which can help fulfill your emotional needs now. But be a little cautious. The desire for action can make it difficult to maintain necessary life routines and responsibilities. Insightful dreams open new avenues of personal understanding, as can self-help books and possibly counseling. You may also return to school to complete or begin a degree or advanced training.

Moon in Capricorn/Tenth House

Cautious, controlled responses are a plus in business affairs, and you see achievement as a key factor in emotional security. A more reserved nature can cause you to lose touch with others, however, as you strive for success. So put your ambitions on hold during nonworking hours and connect with friends and family. The desire for status can motivate you now, but don't let it affect your bank account by spending beyond your means.

Moon in Aquarius/Eleventh House

Casual friendships are satisfying, but an air of detachment can make you appear inaccessible at the very time when networking and socializing can help you achieve your goals. This is also a great time to use your leadership skills in a group or teamwork activity or one that involves a humanitarian cause. On a personal level, your thoughts will turn to your goals, hopes, wishes, and what you truly want from life.

Moon in Pisces/Twelfth House

This influence can activate your sixth sense, and you're more sensitive and receptive to people and your environment. But be wary. Appearances are often deceiving, and not everyone shares your good intentions. Help others by helping them help themselves rather than making their problems your own. You'll also have the urge to express your creativity, so find an outlet that appeals to you, one that fosters self-expression.

MERCURY CHANGING SIGN/HOUSE

Mercury keywords: transportation, communication (reading, writing, speaking), learning, siblings, relatives, neighbors

Mercury in Aries/First House

Your mind moves into high gear, with an increased flow of ideas, thoughts, and opinions. But along with that comes impatience and a tendency for snap decisions. Pull back, study the pros and cons, and listen before you speak. Also strive to keep an open mind; you may not have all the facts, even if you think you do.

Mercury in Taurus/Second House

Your focus now is on personal and financial security, but don't mistake an accumulation of possessions as a substitute for a positive self-image. Instead, invest time and effort in yourself to create the inner and outer you that you desire. Common sense, planning, organization, and practicality are strong assets now.

Mercury in Gemini/Third House

Curiosity prompts your desire to learn and you absorb knowledge with ease. But nearly anything and everything will pique your interest now, so be cautious about spreading yourself too thin. Make a pact with yourself to focus your interest on a few areas and then finish what you start. Errands and meetings consume precious time.

Mercury in Cancer/Fourth House

Emotion colors your thoughts more strongly now, and you interact more often with close friends and family. Some of these people are supportive, while other relationships require resolution—something you can do now if you make it a priority. You'll also discover that time at home recenters you, and you may have more interest in domestic activities.

Mercury in Leo/Fifth House

Creativity is one of your assets now, however you express it. Find your natural outlet, whether that's a hobby, workplace projects and ideas, public speaking, or something else that stimulates your mind. You can also be an effective mentor now, finding pleasure in being the spark as well as the flame.

Mercury in Virgo/Sixth House

Details, planning, and analysis are your new-found strengths, along with a growing interest in health and service. You can profit from these traits both personally and professionally as long as you remember that perfection really is an unachievable and unnecessary goal. Fill your mind with positive thoughts every day.

Mercury in Libra/Seventh House

You're attracted to people, and have an increased desire for close, one-on-one relationships. Through these people you gain an appreciation for a wider range of viewpoints and fur-

ther develop your communication skills. You'll be more willing to compromise now, but also prone to indecision, primarily because you see both sides of an issue.

Mercury in Scorpio/Eighth House

You gain the ability to go beyond the obvious, to sense underlying motives and ferret out the facts. Meditation can strengthen your intuition and open access to your subconscious. But guard against a tendency to suspect and look for ulterior motives, as well as a hesitancy to share your thoughts and opinions when appropriate.

Mercury in Sagittarius/Ninth House

Daydreams can sidetrack you, but they also provide the impetus for new horizons. Use visualization to turn them into concrete goals rather than let these ideas drift into the void of wishful thinking. Also take every opportunity to stretch your mind through learning—read, research, and talk with people.

Mercury in Capricorn/Tenth House

Your powers of concentration increase and you find value in a more practical, logical approach. Use it to advantage in your career and to help set long-term goals. This is also the time to seek out opportunities to get acquainted with decision-makers, and to take the lead in projects and presentations.

Mercury in Aquarius/Eleventh House

You're interested in the new, the unusual, and intriguing people. All of these, as well as group and humanitarian activities, are avenues to expand your base of social and networking contacts. Your imagination will benefit from this planetary placement, and your mind will seek innovative solutions.

Mercury in Pisces / Twelfth House

Creative thinking is a plus as long as your ideas and solutions are realistic. Resist the urge to chase rainbows, however. Your intuition is heightened now, which adds perception with people and situations, and your hunches can be on target. Take care to protect yourself from negative people and their energy, which you can subconsciously absorb.

VENUS CHANGING SIGN / HOUSE

Venus in Aries / First House

Impulsive spending sprees are tempting, primarily because you have an increased desire for clothing, jewelry, and all the finer things in life. So develop and learn to live within a budget; save more than you spend. You also can be more impulsive and passionate in matters of the heart, feeling the need for partnership. Think carefully before you commit.

Venus in Taurus / Second House

Steadfast and sensuous in love, you're ready to form a lasting relationship or deepen an existing one. You'll also have a strong desire for creature comforts and upscale clothing and furnishings, and finances take a turn for the better if you conserve resources. This is more easily accomplished now because you're value-conscious and also interested in financial security.

Venus in Gemini / Third House

People see an extra sparkle in you, as well as a charming flirtatiousness that contributes to your rising popularity. Socializing moves up a few notches on your priority list, and if you're single, you're delighted to play the field. Watch your spending, though, because it's easy to put your budget in jeopardy now.

Venus in Cancer / Fourth House

Marriage, family, and home life bring greater pleasure to your life, and you may become a parent or grandparent. Your financial mind-set shifts to one that is more conservative and you're more interested in improving or acquiring property. Real estate purchased during this time can be profitable in the long term.

Venus in Leo / Fifth House

You attract love and romance almost as if by magic, and are drawn to the finer things in life. If you're a parent, you'll want to be more involved in your children's lives, but curb the tendency to be a stage parent. Play, socializing, exercise, sports, hobbies, and vacations refresh and renew your energy more than ever before.

Venus in Virgo / Sixth House

Your challenge is to develop thrifty spending and saving habits, and you may have the urge to search for a more lucrative job opportunity. However, you'll also have a greater desire for order and perfection that could impact relationships with coworkers and loved ones. Go easy on them and yourself, remembering that no one is perfect.

Venus in Libra/Seventh House

You gain an added sense of appreciation for beauty, art, and harmony that refines your taste in people, encouraging you to attract them into your life. Partnerships and close friendships are more fulfilling now, and you have the opportunity to polish your communication and presentation skills.

Venus in Scorpio/Eighth House

Significant financial gains can be yours in the years ahead, so you'll want to plan accordingly to maximize earnings and investments. A significant inheritance is possible under this planetary influence. Love, however, can be stormy, if more passionate, and jealousy and possessiveness could become issues.

Venus in Sagittarius/Ninth House

Your luck is on the upswing. An increasingly independent, free-wheeling attitude in finances and affairs of the heart can make it difficult to hang on to either one. Fuel your desire for adventure with knowledge and inexpensive travel with your partner or close friends, and invest time in learning how better to manage your money for now and the future. Additional education can increase your earning power.

Venus in Capricorn/Tenth House

You're motivated by money, status, and ambition, all of which can be yours in coming years under this Venus influence. The most important factor in achieving your goals will be people. Develop solid relationships with those who can help you achieve your aims, and strive to increase your networking contacts.

Venus in Aquarius/Eleventh House

Mental connections outweigh pure passion in relationships now, and you'll want regular contact with the important people in your life. But you'll also subtly distance yourself from many, and possibly someone close to you, as independence becomes more of a priority for your well-being. Be generous yet economical with money.

Venus in Pisces/Twelfth House

Without even realizing it, you send out the subtle signals that can attract the affection and romance you desire. Try to be practical and objective, though. Love, as well as business relationships, can be deceiving. Don't take risks here. Rather, let things slide for a while if you feel someone tugging your heartstrings. Confusion can surround financial matters.

MARS CHANGING SIGN/HOUSE

Mars Keywords: action, energy, speed, fire, strife, incentive, ambition, passion, leadership

Mars in Aries/First House

You'll experience a taste of pure Martian energy under this influence that will have you in high gear more often than not. Welcome the initiative and drive it adds to your natal Mars and use the combined influence to achieve your goals. Don't dash off without your common sense, however, because speed and a higher risk-tolerance could easily trigger a misstep at any time.

Mars in Taurus/Second House

Your usual high energy is with you, but haste will become less important as you modify your action style to a slower, steadier pace. In many ways, this gives you the best of both because action will now benefit from follow-through. You also become more money-motivated, with an increased desire for financial security.

Mars in Gemini/Third House

Restlessness becomes a factor in your life, although not an overpowering one, and at times you'll feel scattered and disorganized. Counteract the trend with lists and reminders, and get in the habit of dealing with items as they arise. Learning can satisfy your curiosity, and you could develop a talent for public speaking or writing.

Mars in Cancer/Fourth House

Emotional and security needs have a direct effect on your actions now because you have a higher need for both. Although this can have a settling influence on your natal Mars energy, try not to let it become a driving force in your life. This way you can retain your high confidence level rather than let the actions of others affect you personally.

Mars in Leo/Fifth House

Your leadership ability begins to emerge—or is enhanced—and through it comes an increased sense of identity, strength, and willpower. Make your presence known in the wider world, take a few—or a few more—risks, knowing that you have the confidence to succeed and achieve your goals. Be cautious, though, about letting your ego take charge.

Mars in Virgo/Sixth House

You're very industrious now, and work is more satisfying as it becomes more self-defining. Pur-

sue a job or career change if you're dissatisfied with your current path, but put some thought into it first and develop both short- and long-term goals. Health-related fields or the service sector might appeal to you.

Mars in Libra/Seventh House

Cooperative efforts and partnerships can help you realize your personal and business ambitions, and the contacts you develop now can lead to career opportunities in the future. You also have a greater need to invest more of yourself in personal relationships, and in polishing your communication skills. Emphasize compromise.

Mars in Scorpio/Eighth House

Your aura takes on a subtle intensity that reflects your inner will and resolve to see matters through to conclusion. Determination is strong, but this can quickly become an unbending, stubborn attitude that could be your worst enemy. You're also strongly money-motivated, but keep finances in perspective rather than let them consume you.

Mars in Sagittarius/Ninth House

Travel and adventure appeal to you now, and a desire for knowledge compels you to learn. Learning for the fun of it is one option, or you might get a sudden urge to return to school to begin or complete a degree. You'll also be motivated to share your knowledge, and to explore your core beliefs and any lingering issues from the past.

Mars in Capricorn/Tenth House

Mars fuels your ambitions, which benefit from a practical yet decisive approach. Despite the desire to get things moving, plan first. Develop and regularly update short- and long-term career action plans. The correct path will appear when you know where you're going and thus increase your prospects for success and the desired outcome.

Mars in Aquarius/Eleventh House

Groups, friends, and innovative or unusual interests are ideal outlets for your increasing independence, and you can become a leader in any of these activities. In a sense, though, your life becomes more serious now as you define your life priorities. With Mars fueling your

desire, you can accomplish much on your life wish list.

Mars in Pisces/Twelfth House

You're more sympathetic to other people now, but can become mired in their emotional issues. Try to maintain a reasonable distance, and limit your support to helping them to help themselves. Otherwise your stamina and confidence can be adversely affected. However, work with a charitable organization can be fulfilling, and exercise can benefit your energy level. Dreams may be insightful.

SIGN AND HOUSE KEYWORDS

Aries/First: self, new endeavors

Taurus/Second: personal income and debt, possessions, values and ethics

Gemini/Third: transportation, communication (reading, writing, speaking), vehicles, neighbors, siblings, extended family, news, errands, learning

Cancer/Fourth: home, family, domestic and family matters, relocation

Leo/Fifth: children, creativity, romance, speculation, recreation, sports, hobbies

Virgo/Sixth: daily work, workplace, volunteer activities, pets, health

Libra/Seventh: partners, close friendships, cooperative efforts, the public

Scorpio/Eighth: shared resources, debtors, inheritance, insurance, partner's funds, sex

Sagittarius/Ninth: travel, cultural activities, higher education, knowledge, religion, life philosophy, publishing, promotional activities

Capricorn/Tenth: career, ambition, status, fame

Aquarius/Eleventh: friends, groups, humanitarian activities, goals, hopes and wishes, networking

Pisces/Twelfth: charitable organizations, institutions, secrets, health, subconscious, intuition, dreams

---

PLANETARY ASPECTS

During the course of your lifetime you'll experience the majority of planetary aspects, either by progression or solar arc. Except in rare cases, progressed Mercury and Venus will aspect every natal planet in your chart. The progressed Sun and Moon will aspect every natal planet, with the Moon repeating the specific aspect (same sign, house, and aspect) two to three times in a normal life span.

The aspects used in predictive astrology are the same as those used when reading a birth chart, and are classified as hard (difficult) or soft (easy). However, it isn't always this straightforward, because some difficult aspects are necessary to create action. The trine and sextile indicate a smooth flow of energy but do not generally initiate action.

Hard aspects: square, opposition, semisquare, sesquisquare.

The conjunction can be soft or hard, depending upon the planets involved. A Mars-Pluto conjunction, for example, is a hard aspect, while a Venus-Mercury conjunction manifests as more positive than negative.

Soft aspects: sextile, trine, and sometimes the conjunction.

Soft aspects can at times initiate action, such as when a trine activates a natal square. In this case the trine can cause the natal square to operate in its most negative sense, but it also can provide an opportunity to resolve the associated difficulties. Resolution is more possible when, for example, a natal Venus-Saturn square becomes a progressed or solar arc Venus-Saturn sextile.

The progressed Moon travels through the entire zodiac about every twenty-eight years. As it does this, it aspects your natal Moon, providing ample opportunities to experience and learn from its natal placement by sign, house, and aspect. Every seven years, the progressed Moon forms a hard aspect to its natal position, and the same occurs every five years with a sextile or trine. At these times, your natal lunar energy and natal lunar aspects are activated. A progressed Moon square to a natal Moon-Mercury trine could thus prompt action, while a progressed Moon trine to the natal trine would not. Or, a progressed Moon sextile a natal Moon-Pluto opposition could trigger control issues or prompt you to deal with them.

Solar arcs activate your natal planets and angles at various times, depending upon the degrees of the natal planets. Because all the solar arc planets move at the same rate of speed, unlike progressions, the natal aspects are always maintained; that is, a natal square between two planets will always be a natal square by solar arc. The secondary progressed Moon is used with both the progressed and solar arc aspects.

Progressed and solar arc planets in aspect to themselves, such as Mercury-Mercury, activate your natal energy and aspects according to the sign and house position of the planets involved. They also activate the associated planetary aspects.

The interpretations on the following pages are general in nature because they cannot take into consideration the signs, houses, other progressed/solar arc aspects, and the specific birth chart in which they're active. Therefore, use them only as guidelines to spark your thinking. Keywords are the best way to interpret both natal and predictive charts.

For example, a Sun-Mercury conjunction indicates an active (conjunction) mind (Mercury), in large part focused on identity issues (Sun). In the fifth house, it could point to the birth of a child; in the seventh house, a marriage, and in the tenth house, a promotion. To take this a step further, if the Sun rules the natal first house, and Mercury rules the natal tenth, you (Sun) would need to initiate action (first house) by submitting a resume (Mercury) for a promotion (tenth house).

In general, progressed and solar arc planets aspecting themselves have this focus: Sun, ego; Moon, emotions; Mercury, communication, thought process; Venus, relationships, love, money; Mars, drive, initiative.

Jupiter, Saturn, Uranus, Neptune and Pluto do not move fast enough by progression to aspect themselves. By solar arc, their tendencies are: Jupiter, expansion, growth; Saturn, restriction, achievement; Uranus, change, mental stimulation; Neptune, spirituality, confusion; Pluto, change, transformation.

Progressed planets (other than the Moon) aspect themselves in semisquare, sextile, and square, depending upon their rate of movement, and rarely by sesquisquare and trine. The exception is the conjunction, which occurs only if the natal planet is retrograde or turned retrograde after birth.

PROGRESSED RETROGRADE PLANETS

The year a progressed planet changes direction is highly significant, although it may be several years before you fully realize its importance. Because these planets move so slowly (remember, they are stationing when they change direction), it is more of an evolutionary process and almost always in some way a life-changing one. For example, a tenth house planet changing direction could indicate the switch to an entirely new career field and the realization that you are finally on a solid path toward achievement. As another example, marriage often occurs in the year when a retrograde progressed Venus turns direct.

Generally, matters related to the house where a progressed planet turns direct will begin to gain momentum, while interest may wane when a progressed planet turns retrograde. Study the aspects made by the planet changing direction and the house position of the aspected planets and what they rule. These areas of life will also be affected. Again, using the career example, if the tenth house planet turning direct is in opposition to a fourth house planet, you realize the necessity for a more balanced lifestyle that includes more time for family.

Possibly even more significant is the year when a previously retrograde planet moves forward to perfect a natal aspect. The same can happen when a natal direct planet turns retrograde and perfects an aspect. Progressed planets can form these contacts in any aspect. The conjunction yields the most concentrated energy, but the square and opposition are equally powerful, with the other aspects being less significant.

Although a progressed conjunction, square, or opposition as a result of a retrograde pattern often signals an event, its more important on another level. When a planet perfects a natal aspect after resuming direct motion (or turning retrograde), it activates the natal potential,

---

ACTIVE TIME FOR INNER PLANET PROGRESSED ASPECTS

Moon: about two months

Sun: about a year

Mercury: about nine months (if not stationing, or recently stationed)

Venus: about twelve to fifteen months (if not stationing, or recently stationed)

Mars: about two years (if not stationing, or recently stationed)

---

releasing the energy to consciousness. Often the individual will realize a long-wished desire in a specific area of life that he or she was unable to access prior to the conjunction. A planet making a conjunction while retrograde has the opposite effect. It tends to internalize the energy, making it somewhat inaccessible, although the tendency is not as strong as that with a retrograde natal planet.

Watch for these progressed retrograde patterns, which do not occur in every life. Mercury, Venus, and Mars are more likely to perfect natal chart aspects, although Jupiter, Saturn, Uranus, Neptune, and Pluto can do the same if they are in a nearly exact aspect at birth. (The progressed Sun is never conjunct the natal Sun because it's never retrograde; the progressed Moon is conjunct its natal place every twenty-eight years.)

HARD ASPECTS: SQUARE, OPPOSITION, SEMISQUARE, SESQUISQUARE, AND SOME CONJUNCTIONS

Sun-Sun: Your ego is strongly in play and you're inclined to view everything solely from your perspective. Remind yourself to listen and consider what others are saying. This is a time to enlist their support and develop stronger and mutually beneficial relationships. Creative endeavors, sports, and hobbies are good leisure-time outlets.

Sun-Moon: Emotions pull you in one direction, and your self-will in another. Resolving these two energies can be challenging, so expect events to center around your identity, close relationships, and basic life issues. Counteract stress and tension with exercise, leisure time, or other positive lifestyle changes.

Sun-Venus: You're focused on love, partnership, people, and relationships in general. The conjunction is often a marriage or commitment aspect, but the other hard aspects can be positive or negative, resulting in either a separation or the beginning of a serious relationship. You'll also have a greater interest in beauty and fashion; spending could affect your budget.

Sun-Mars: Be careful. A fast pace and an invincible attitude are the perfect setup for an accident. Exercise or other physical activity can help counteract anger, aggression, and sleeplessness, and give you added energy to direct into self-improvement activities and positive goals. Also make it a point to value the opinions of others, and be aware that your strong viewpoints may or may not be accurate.

Sun-Jupiter: You're happy, hopeful, and enthusiastic, ready to grab almost any opportunity that comes your way. But don't go out on a limb. Calculated risks are okay; blind optimism is not, because luck goes only so far. Even so, this aspect can signal a silver lining in what otherwise appears to be a tight spot, and can indicate ultimate good fortune when in the midst of a group of difficult aspects.

Sun-Saturn: This aspect almost always brings exactly what you deserve—gains or losses as a result of past actions. It can pay off handsomely or be a tough lesson. This is also a time when you may feel as though you need to do everything yourself. Not so. Share the load, doing only your fair share. This aspect also can manifest as lowered energy, so get plenty of rest and sleep.

Sun-Uranus: Ready or not, change is coming, along with an independent streak that signals a shift in your perspective. Even if your chart has a fixed-sign emphasis, the best choice is to welcome change or even initiate it. This will increase the odds that this period will be an overall positive and enlightening one. Do, however, take precautions to control your temper and to avoid accidents.

Sun-Neptune: Much of what you view as reality at this time is just the opposite even though your vision seems clear. Used positively, dreams can be insightful and possibly prophetic, and your creative imagination is strong. Listen to your intuition. This is not the time, however, to make important life, partnership, or financial decisions. Only as this aspect separates can you achieve full realization of what occurred while it was active.

Sun-Pluto: Power and intensity are the central theme, whether you're on the giving or receiving end. Be proactive if you feel trapped in a difficult situation at home, at work, or in a friendship or romantic relationship, and don't succumb to manipulation. You can also use this aspect for positive personal transformation, such as a change in attitude and outlook or a healthier life style that includes diet, exercise, and positive self-talk.

Moon-Moon: Emotional responses can be both insightful and enlightening. Take note of them and look for clues that can reveal your hot buttons. With this knowledge you can better understand and manage your feelings and your responses. This aspect could also signify a female who requires your help. This is generally not a favorable time for contact with women and working with the public.

Moon-Mercury: Avoid major decisions and important negotiations because emotions can outweigh logic and common sense. Thus, this is not the time to purchase real estate, investments, vehicles, or furnishings. Walk away if a salesperson pressures you. Minor conflict can occur now, especially with females, so focus on being tactful or say nothing at all.

Moon-Venus: Try to treat loved ones with kindness even if you have mixed emotions. This will help promote harmony and understanding, or at least minimize conflict. Take a similar approach with your home by beautifying it with new decor, handling repairs, cleaning, and organizing. But set a budget for purchases rather than let emotions control spending.

Moon-Mars: Your emotions run high and short on patience, making it possible for people and minor aggravations to easily irritate you now. Try to avoid stressful situations and think calm thoughts if you find yourself in the middle of conflict. Be open to compromise. You can also counteract the effect of this aspect by spending time alone where you can relax and re-center.

Moon-Jupiter: The freedom-loving urge of this aspect could prompt you to, even unconsciously, distance yourself from some close relationships. Opt for another solution, such as travel, learning about another culture or way of life, or taking a hobby or sports class. You might also be tempted to be overly generous with family now; share more of your time than your money.

Moon-Saturn: Loneliness and feelings of guilt or regret can take hold under this influence, possibly because you encounter someone from the past, or are reminded of a past event. Although it will be a challenge to push away these feelings, try to maintain a realistic view of them. Avoid the tendency to isolate yourself. People close to you will be helpful if you ask for their support.

Moon-Uranus: Shifting emotions and moodiness under this aspect can prompt rash actions you might later regret. This makes it important to emphasize patience in all you do, while you also refrain from jumping to conclusions. Recognize the issue for what it is: a desire for change and excitement and the feeling that you need something different in your life. Find a positive, safe outlet to satisfy this need.

Moon-Neptune: You're unusually sensitive to people and your environment now, and both can prompt uncharacteristic emotional reactions, much to your surprise. Try to avoid situations and people you know will be difficult

to handle, and remember that at this time any slights are more perception than reality. You may need to help or care for a female at this time.

Moon-Pluto: Intense feelings can lead to jealousy and the desire to manipulate others, or you could be the target of such actions. Distance yourself as much as possible from those who don't enhance your lifestyle. Also set aside some quiet time to look within yourself in a quest for self-understanding to better grasp your subconscious motivations.

Mercury-Mercury: Your powers of concentration and ability to study and learn can be at their best now. But you'll need to find a way to counteract restlessness and distractions. Quiet music could be more helpful than silence. All forms of communication can steer you off course now, so be selective when you can. Do what's necessary to turn off your mind before bedtime so you don't lose sleep.

Mercury-Venus: This aspect promotes play, laughter, socializing, and happy times. Relationships can be at their best if you emphasize communication. You could meet a potential romantic interest—the conjunction, particularly, can trigger an engagement or marriage. This combination is also useful for working out financial details with a partner. Positive thinking enhances your powers of attraction.

Mercury-Mars: Your active mental energy generates great ideas, but this aspect can also trigger snap decisions and impatience with others that elevates your temper. Coach yourself to slow down; think before you speak and act rather than say or do something you'll regret. Also be careful with tools, ladders, fire, and on the road because this is an accident-prone period.

Mercury-Jupiter: Optimism and uplifting thoughts characterize the positive side of this aspect. However, you could get carried away with wishful thinking, hoping things will be as you want them to be. It's also easy now to overload your schedule without even realizing it—until it all catches up with you. So be selective and promise only what you can deliver.

Mercury-Saturn: This aspect aids concentration, but it also brings out worries and regrets. Try not to dwell on them. Look forward rather than into the past, except as a learning experience, which is where the real benefit of this aspect lies. Your to-do list is also liable to be long at this time, and it could be necessary to deal with mechanical problems. Most of all, focus on positive thinking.

Mercury-Uranus: Be careful what you toss out of your life in your quest for what's new and different. Careful moves, despite your desires, are the best choice now, when accident potential is also high. You can use this energy positively by directing it into learning and innovative ideas in the workplace. Active intuition can lead to flashes of insight at the least expected moment, along with surprising news or events.

Mercury-Neptune: Daydreaming is at its best under this aspect, and you can while away hours as your mind drifts. This can be productive if you have the time for it and want to use it as an aid for your creative talents. But in everyday life, confusion will interfere with communication, and you may have difficulty concentrating on the job. Avoid major decisions, purchases, and contracts, if at all possible.

Mercury-Pluto: Your thoughts are intense and your mind ultimately focused under this aspect. This can be positive or negative, depending upon how you handle personal power issues and pressure from others. The more open-minded and accepting of constructive criticism you are, the better you'll fare. Stay focused on the big picture and beware of tunnel vision.

Venus-Venus: This aspect is favorable for just about anything from love to money to your fondest wish. It's also one that often signifies the start of a serious romance, engagement, or marriage. An indication of a period when you're exceptionally well liked, you can use this to advantage in your professional life to cultivate contacts who might help fulfill your ambitions. Control spending, though.

Venus-Mars: Romance and passion can be at their best when this aspect is active. But animosity is equally possible. You'll probably experience both with various relationships in your life. This is not the time, however, to dash into commitment because you'll be focused on the physical aspects of the relationship rather than whether it's a match of lasting love.

Venus-Jupiter: Rein yourself in a little in money and in matters of the heart. Playing the field can be as fun as spending, but it is possible to have too much of a good thing. Set limits and give yourself a reality check to balance the optimism. If you should receive a windfall, which this aspect often triggers, save and invest rather than spend to your heart's content.

Venus-Saturn: If you're already in a relationship, this aspect can either strengthen it or add a distinct chill. In any case, you will distance yourself from someone now, possibly a close friend or relative. This is not the best timing for a new relationship or a reunion with a former romantic interest, but it can help you assess and realign finances and pay off debt.

Venus-Uranus: New relationships sparkle with love at first sight or an instant friendship, which falls right in line with your need for excitement and change. However, don't leap out of or into a partnership until the aspect passes because you'll change your mind more than once before it does. Instead, find other ways to satisfy your need for independence. A windfall is possible.

Venus-Neptune: This is the aspect of idealistic fantasy that defines romance at its best. But it also comes with a question: is it love or are you in love with love? You won't know for sure until the aspect passes. Also be cautious when hiring any professional such as a contractor or accountant, because self-deception (and deception by others) occurs all too easily now. Watch your budget so money doesn't slip through your fingers.

Venus-Pluto: Even if you're not naturally inclined this way, this aspect encourages jealousy and possessiveness. Not just of people but also of things. You can easily become obsessed with either one, clinging as if for dear life. Instead, use this energy positively by getting in touch with what you value personally, professionally, in life, and in other people as a first step toward defining and resolving the need for control.

Mars-Mars: Slow down! Program regular rest and relaxation time into your busy life even if it means letting things go or passing up an opportunity. You can easily overdo it now and push yourself to the max, which leads to mistakes and accidents. Think before you act and speak, and

be cautious with tools, in the kitchen, and on the road. Impatience can get the best of you.

Mars-Jupiter: Your high energy is great for new ventures and maximum productivity, and calculated risks can turn out amazingly well. But excessive optimism can encourage you to look only at the upside and ignore the potential downside. Take plenty of time to think things through before you act, and be wary about overcommitment. Even you can only do so much.

Mars-Saturn: This is not an easy aspect. It is one that triggers frustration and delays and that requires patience, persistence, and hard work. Despite the periodic desire to walk away, your best option is to keep at it. Eventually, you'll overcome the obstacles and succeed. Resist the urge to take the easy way out, which will only backfire. Live up to your responsibilities.

Mars-Uranus: Even if you're usually easygoing, this aspect can trigger stress and nervous tension, which can lead to haste and carelessness as well as a short temper and accidents. Avoid overscheduling yourself and try to limit contact with high-strung and demanding people. Moderate exercise and quiet music could be helpful now.

Mars-Neptune: Confusion dominates under this aspect. You're unsure which path to pursue and which direction to take, both literally and figuratively. Major endeavors can be sidetracked now despite your best efforts, and it's tough to initiate action or to bring things to conclusion. Try to be patient with yourself and the situation. A creative outlet could help divert the energy.

Mars-Pluto: Positive passions can lead to outstanding achievements, but obsession and power plays—yours or someone else's—can undermine your position. This is not the time to stubbornly resist directives from the boss or other authority figures, because the more you do, the worse the outcome. Instead, tap into the strong willpower you have now. Stay far away from potentially dangerous locations and situations.

Jupiter-Jupiter: Be alert to opportunities, but try not to jump in feet first. Gather the facts and then carefully think things through. Luck is very much on your side now; welcome it but don't count on it. Shift your focus instead to making your own luck by seeking opportunities and then following through on them. Be happy, think positive, learn, grow, travel, and broaden your horizons.

Jupiter-Saturn: It's easy to become overloaded with responsibilities under this aspect. So you'll need to set priorities and tactfully say no when others try to shift their responsibilities to you. Then you can pursue any promising opportunities that pop up, all of which will require effort to earn rewards. Take reasonable risks in career and business, and broaden your knowledge.

Jupiter-Uranus: Known for delivering windfalls and lucky breaks, this aspect can put you at the right place at the right time with little or no effort on your part. Be selective about which opportunities you pursue, and choose the best of the best—whatever has the potential to bring you maximum gain for reasonable effort. Have faith in your decisions.

Jupiter-Neptune: Romance and promises can be the real thing. They also can be pipe dreams, leading you on a merry chase in search of rainbows. Enjoy the fun and laughter that accompanies this aspect and the brief fantasy trip, knowing that in the end it will probably turn out to

be nothing more than smoke and mirrors. Discover your creative self.

Jupiter-Pluto: You can move mountains with this aspect, which can deliver unparalleled success. But you can also be so focused, so intent on your mission, that you miss what else is happening around you. The best approach is to decide beforehand what you want and how to get it. Then combine luck with your strong willpower, and resist the urge for manipulation and control.

Saturn-Saturn: Heavy responsibilities and minimal progress can get you down more than they usually do. If you feel this way, consider it a sign to develop patience and understanding with yourself and other people. Also review past successes rather than dwell on regrets. Then set new goals and aim high. Career success is possible at this time, when you can set things in motion for the future.

Saturn-Uranus: It's time for a change when you realize the old ways no longer work even though there's security in the status quo. Go ahead, take a risk, and let go of the past in order to create a new reality that may be prompted when sudden change is thrust upon you. Through it you can develop new-found independence that sets you free.

Saturn-Neptune: With one foot in reality and the other in a dream world, it's difficult to know where to walk. During this period you learn that life is a matter of perception, beginning with your view of the world. Avoidance of reality may be tempting, but go beyond it even if it means tough decisions related to those you love. Also avoid major career decisions.

Saturn-Pluto: The more you try to control events, the more frustration you experience.

Like other difficult Saturn aspects, this one signifies major change, often career-related. With Pluto involved, events are essentially out of your control. The consolation is that many others are in the same position as you are, so think positive, move on, and re-create your reality.

Uranus-Uranus: The only constant with this aspect is change, as has undoubtedly been more or less the norm in your life. Be prepared for anything and everything, as well as an irresistible quest for independence. Do resist the urge, however, to toss out all of the old in favor of the new before you're completely sure what exactly it is that you want and want to change.

Uranus-Neptune: Excellent for creativity, intuition, and innovation, this aspect (and others involving Neptune)is often found where drugs and alcohol are involved. Irresponsibility is also a factor when the negative side of this aspect dominates. Look around you and take note of what your peers are doing and how they're using this energy.

Uranus-Pluto: A desire for personal freedom and independence can push you to break free of all restraints, but changes made at this time are likely to be irrevocable. This aspect also can turn your world upside down when you're caught in the middle of power plays that are out of your control. The best solution is to adapt, regroup, and restart.

Neptune-Neptune: Get creative and explore your hidden talents that have been waiting for the right time to emerge. That is a positive outlet for this aspect, which can leave you feeling at loose ends with no answers and nowhere to go. Seek a spiritual perspective.

Neptune-Pluto: As in other aspects involving Pluto, there's little you can do to control the events around you. With Neptune, the familiar dissipates, and disillusionment can set in. Seek creative solutions as you move forward within the new paradigm.

Pluto-Pluto: Resist the urge to toss everything and start over, except in a symbolic way. Self-improvement and positive change should be your goals, along with a more complete understanding of your innermost motivations and desires.

SOFT ASPECTS—SEXTILE, TRINE, AND SOME CONJUNCTIONS

Sun-Sun: You and your life are in sync. Assert yourself, find new directions for your talents, and an outlet for your developing leadership. Most of all, this is a growth stage when you reassess your priorities and place more emphasis on your needs and desires.

Sun-Moon: You feel and look good, on an even keel, with emotions and identity in balance. An overall positive aspect, this influence can help you succeed in many areas where good judgment and personal motivation can further your ambitions.

Sun-Mercury: Your thinking is on track, and you make good decisions based on personal needs. Communication is a major asset now, and you should focus on improving or using your writing and speaking skills, possibly through community involvement.

Sun-Venus: Pleasure and comfort are satisfying, as is socializing, but try to limit self-indulgence. You can go overboard in just about anything now, especially spending. Keep your budget in mind and your generosity in control. Share yourself and your time with others.

Sun-Mars: You're in a high energy phase, on the move and on a mission to get or achieve whatever you want. Chances are, you'll be successful. But you also can overdo it and undermine your otherwise admirable efforts. Aim for a measured pace.

Sun-Jupiter: Popularity rises along with optimism and positive thinking, and you could luck into whatever you wish for. Do try, though, to keep events and life in perspective, because you'll have a tendency to do many things to excess. Strive for personal growth.

Sun-Saturn: Patience and slow, steady progress yields results now, when you can be recognized for past achievements. Life may not be exciting at this time, but you do feel grounded and on track, even as responsibilities rise. Help others, but don't take on their work.

Sun-Uranus: You're open to change now, so the time is right to get out of a rut and branch out into the realm of positive personal growth. Opportunities may find you, but you can make the most of this aspect by positioning yourself so they can come your way.

Sun-Neptune: Creativity and intuition are high, and visualization can produce amazing results if you regularly use this technique. Meditation can help you access your inner voice, and dreams can be insightful. Most of all, you'll take daily aggravations in stride.

Sun-Pluto: You have the will, determination, and focus to go after exactly what you want in your personal and professional lives. You'll also come into contact with important people, the movers-and-shakers who can grease your path to success. Do the same for others.

Moon-Moon: You enjoy an easy flow of positive energy with other people, and you're responsive to each other's needs. So it's a good time to ask for favors, socialize, and meet new people. You also can be especially effective if your job or other activities involve working with the public.

Moon-Mercury: If you have something you've wanted to say to someone, now is the time. You can communicate your feelings with relative ease, smooth over rough spots, and gain their support for your endeavors. This is a positive period for public speaking and presentations.

Moon-Venus: Relationships enjoy an easy pace, and contacts with women and partners are especially favorable. But this aspect also inclines to laziness and self-indulgence, which could leave you scrambling to catch up later. Finances are generally positive.

Moon-Mars: You can easily push your own agenda now, and very nicely too. Most people respond favorably and are happy to help you achieve a desired goal. You also can act effectively on your passions, which are backed with a positive flow of emotional energy.

Moon-Jupiter: This ultimate feel-good aspect surrounds you with optimism, luck, enthusiasm, and hope. But as tempting as it is, don't drift along under the pleasant aura this aspect provides. Instead, use effort and opportunity to ensure that things go your way.

Moon-Saturn: Reality and practicality are strong themes under this aspect, which also can benefit your career. This is a good time to deal with stressful emotional situations, including emotional baggage, because you're more in control of your feelings than usual.

Moon-Uranus: The time is right to invite some new people into your life, some of whom may become long-term friends. Others will be valuable networking contacts. Teamwork goes smoothly now as long as you're open to innovative ideas and positive change.

Moon-Neptune: This aspect highlights romance and intuition as you're in sync with your heart and your inner voice. It's also a great time for fantasy daydreams, seeing movies and concerts, and visualizing what you want to achieve when this aspect passes.

Moon-Pluto: You feel strong and powerful and may be inclined to subtle manipulation, especially if this is a pattern in your life. Similarly, you can be on the receiving end, but it will be tough to detect because a smile will accompany any such words and actions.

Mercury-Mercury: Mental energy and communication are major assets now, and you have a strong need to connect (or reconnect) with people. Learning is a breeze if you can curb the restlessness that accompanies this aspect, and public speaking is an ideal way to share your know-how.

Mercury-Venus: An extra level of tact, grace, and charm are yours under this aspect. Relationships particularly benefit from communication, and you get almost everything you ask for, because you're open to compromise. Stay tuned for positive financial news.

Mercury-Mars: Quick thinking aids studies, public speaking, and new endeavors. You'll need to slow down just a little, however, in order to follow through on your great ideas because patience will require effort. This aspect is positive for thoughtful financial planning.

Mercury-Jupiter: Luck is with you now, but you'll need to set things in motion yourself in order to take full advantage of it and to capital-ize on great ideas. You can learn with ease, and positive thinking can be a real benefit as long as you don't gloss over any potential downside.

Mercury-Saturn: Logical thinking and concentration are an asset in business, as are planning and organization. Put all these skills to work for you in your career, in daily life, and on the home front. But also enjoy the light side. You can't be practical all the time!

Mercury-Uranus: Innovative thinking and intuition can lead you in all the right directions from your career to group endeavors, networking, and friendship. Take a class for fun or profit to stimulate your mind, join an organization, or master a computer skill.

Mercury-Neptune: Your sixth sense is on target now, so trust your gut feelings about people, even if you've known them for some time. This aspect gives you the ability to charm almost anyone, so you can pick up lots of information to file away for future reference.

Mercury-Pluto: Your powers of persuasion are at their best, and many people will tell you things they otherwise wouldn't share. All of this can come in handy in presentations and meetings, as well as in the future. You also excel at research now, and can follow the trail to what you need to know.

Venus-Venus: You can attract love and money with little effort now, almost as if by magic. But it also comes with a potential lazy streak and the temptation to kick back, drift along, and spend freely. Resist. When combined with effort, this aspect can multiply your success ratio.

Venus-Mars: Love, passion, and close relationships benefit from this aspect, under which you'll also have opportunities to invite new people into your life. Free spending could impact your budget now, but you're also likely to attract more for your bank account. Save first.

Venus-Jupiter: Fun and socializing are a top priority on your agenda. Go beyond that. Let this lucky combo add success in other areas, but watch your budget.

Venus-Saturn: Solid relationships become more so, but with others you'll finally decide that it's okay to let go and let them fade into the past. This is a favorable time to assess your finances, learn from mistakes, plan for the future, save, and pay off debt. Career gains are possible.

Venus-Uranus: Commitment is the last thing on your mind now, so you can simply enjoy the variety and the sparks of attraction. This also can be a very lucky financial period. Windfalls are possible from unexpected sources, and you might occasionally take a chance on the lottery.

Venus-Neptune: You're at your most charming and above all else, you're in the mood for romance. Find it with your mate, someone new, a steamy novel, or new clothing and lingerie. But monitor your budget because money can slip through your fingers and disappear into the ethers.

Venus-Pluto: You have the power now to attract love, money, and just about anything else you desire. Combine effort with the right mindset to realize your wishes. Loans are usually approved under this aspect, and investments can increase your net worth if you take only calculated risks.

Mars-Mars: Acting quickly and decisively is a snap under this aspect. Acting wisely, however, is more of a challenge during this time of high initiative, because you're impatient and in a hurry.

Slow down, at least on the important things, set clear goals, and capitalize on your talents.

Mars-Jupiter: High energy and good fortune are on your side, so you can accomplish just about anything you focus on. This can be a challenge, however, because events and situations may unfold so quickly that it will be tough to keep up with them. Try not to overdo it.

Mars-Saturn: Although the pace is slower than you wish, it's also a measured one, and steady effort leads to success. Obstacles are manageable if you take your time and use a practical approach combined with knowledge and experience. Delegation can aid your quest.

Mars-Uranus: Opportunities abound, and your sixth sense can help you zero in on those with the most potential. The key is to add your own unique twist to these opportunities and to enlist the support of others through teamwork and networking. Be cautious on the road.

Mars-Neptune: Hunches can pay off if you listen and act on them in concert with solid facts. You're motivated to help others, whether through donations or sharing your skills with good causes. This aspect also adds charm, which is great for promoting yourself and your ideas.

Mars-Pluto: In addition to making it easier to navigate obstacles, this aspect gives you the power to make things happen. Push gently but firmly, convincing others to see things your way, but be cautious of becoming so focused that you miss the big picture.

Jupiter-Jupiter: Luck is with you if you make the most of this time rather than accept only the good fortune that comes your way. Initiate action, look for growth and success opportunities, and capitalize on your knowledge. Travel and education could become priorities now.

Jupiter-Saturn: Optimism and reality balance one another under this aspect, giving you a rational yet hopeful view of any situation. This is a plus for learning and your career, and you could do well with a property or business investment. Education could benefit your career.

Jupiter-Uranus: This aspect adds luck to most any event or situation you're involved in. Or it could be something unexpected that catches you by surprise. Possibilities include a sizeable bonus, a lottery win, a golden opportunity, or someone who smooths your path.

Jupiter-Neptune: Faith and optimism, self-help groups, worthy causes, and spiritual insights can open your mind to new truths. Explore the wider world, other cultures and ways of life, and your own creativity. Most of all, look to the future and all that it can be.

Jupiter-Pluto: Carefully invest your energy and what you wish for. This fortunate aspect can create just the situation or event that can deliver all of that and more if you put your mind to it. Have faith in your abilities and your willpower and believe you are deserving.

Saturn-Saturn: Responsibility and reward go hand-in-hand with this aspect, which especially favors career success and real-estate investments. This is the time to set your sights on career advancement and a plan to achieve it, and possibly to purchase a home or invest in rental property.

Saturn-Uranus: Saturn sets the boundaries now and Uranus encourages you to pursue change within this context. With the addition of innovation and imagination, you could find the ideal career opportunity or, if other factors are favorable, launch an entrepreneurial venture.

Saturn-Neptune: You see structure as just that—a framework within which to create and be inspired. This aspect could thus be an asset in home remodeling, turning a creative hobby into a sideline business, or inspiring others to realize their success potential.

Saturn-Pluto: This aspect helps you set in motion long-term plans in any endeavor, but especially in your career. Use it to plan your rise to success, to get acquainted with decision-makers, or to make a major career move to a more powerful and influential position.

Uranus-Uranus: This is a great time to network, socialize, and get involved in a humanitarian or professional group. Each can be an avenue to unexpected gains and new insights, primarily because you're ready for a life style change that can express your individuality.

Uranus-Neptune: Take the initiative to get in touch with your personal muse under this aspect, which combines creativity and innovation. Write poetry, study metaphysics, volunteer for a good cause, or get involved in a community project.

Uranus-Pluto: Both internal and external events can spark positive personal changes now, and friends and groups will be influential in this process that prompts you to view the world from a different perspective. You could be recognized as a leader in a club or organization.

Neptune-Neptune: Imagination and creativity are at the forefront now, and your thoughts and opinions subtly shift to new personal truths as you discover (or rediscover) yourself and your talents. Your sixth sense also comes alive, and dreams can be prophetic.

Neptune-Pluto: Your spiritual base, as well as many of your beliefs, evolve under this aspect as outside influences alter your world view. Understanding and accepting this shift can be mildly challenging but also achievable if you are open to all possibilities.

Pluto-Pluto: You have the power to make things happen, and you may be in a position to be a mover-and-shaker, the one who revamps current conditions into a more relevant model. This aspect can also be effectively used to reshape your personal image for the better. Change within this context. With the addition of innovation and imagination, you could find the ideal career opportunity or, if other factors are favorable, launch an entrepreneurial venture.

OUTER PLANET TRANSITS

The outer planets—Jupiter, Saturn, Neptune, Uranus, and Pluto—function much like progressed and solar arc planets because of their slow movement. Jupiter is the fastest, transiting a sign about every twelve months, and Pluto is the slowest, moving two or three degrees each year.

These planets, particularly Saturn through Pluto, indicate major life events, usually of long duration and sometimes for as many as three years. Much of this is the effect of their retrograde pattern as they move forward, station, turn retrograde, station, and resume forward movement. The stationary periods, which will be effective for a month or more (with a one degree approaching and separating orb) have the most impact. It is during the stationing period that events often occur because the energy is at its most intense during this time.

An outer transiting planet is almost always within a one-degree orb when an event occurs. Pluto, however, is sometimes the exception, because its influence can be felt from an approaching orb of as many as three to four degrees. It's not uncommon for an outer planet transit to be in an exact aspect to a natal, progressed, or solar arc planet at the time of an event, but it's also not the norm. So don't limit your forecasting time frame to the day an outer planet transit is exact.

What you will see every time a major event occurs is an outer planet transit in aspect to a natal planet or configuration, or in aspect to a progressed and/or solar arc planet that is also in aspect to a natal planet or configuration.

If, for example, transiting Saturn is square a natal Venus-Uranus opposition, relationship difficulties and/or a change in a relationship are likely. What Saturn (restriction) would do in this case is to activate the natal potential for divorce (Venus-Uranus). An individual might, under these influences, end the relationship because he or she would feel restricted (Saturn) and want the freedom and independence represented by the natal Venus-Uranus opposition. The same scenario could play out if progressed Venus were in opposition to natal or progressed Uranus.

In reality, more than one aspect is necessary to indicate such a major event. The guideline is three aspects (plus a lunation, eclipse, or inner planet transit to set them off). Because planets are interconnected by aspect, you could see one outer transiting planet contact one natal (or progressed) planet that is part of a configuration such as a t-square. In effect, the transiting planet would set off the entire configuration and not just the planet with which it is exact or within orb.

Again using the above example, suppose the natal configuration of Venus opposition Mars is part of a t-square with Saturn, with transiting Saturn in opposition to its natal place, but not yet within orb of a square to the other two planets. As an astrologer, you would see the relationship pressure building as Saturn formed an opposition to its natal place before moving on to square Venus and Mars, the other two planets in the t-square. The individual would likely weigh the pros and cons of ending the relationship while transiting Saturn was opposition Saturn, but only cut ties after Saturn had formed an exact square with Venus and Mars. Action could also be triggered by transiting Saturn stationing direct in opposition to natal Saturn even though it did not exactly aspect all three planets.

This is because a stationing planet is more powerful and thus intensifies the energy.

You can often predict how the influence of an outer planet is going to manifest by tracking its retrograde, stationary, and direct motion. An outer planet usually makes three contacts with a natal, progressed, or solar arc planet or angle, although at times it makes only two contacts because one of the contacts is the retrograde or direct station. The usual outcome of this cycle is that the first contact brings the issue to your attention, the second contact prompts you to initiate action or signals further developments, and the third concludes the matter.

The event or life issue will be active as long as the outer transiting planet will return to within about one degree of the natal, progressed, or solar arc planet or angle. The matter might recede into the background, or drop lower on your action list, if the outer transiting planet is out of orb, but it will still be an ongoing part of your life that has yet to be resolved.

Use a one degree approaching and separating orb for the outer transiting planets (one degree on either side of the exact aspect). But be flexible, especially when these planets are stationing retrograde or direct. These stations have more punch and often work with a slightly wider orb. Many events occur within a few days or weeks of a station.

It's important to remember that no two charts are the same, and neither is the combination of outer planet transits and progressed/solar arc planets. During some events, an outer planet transit aspects many progressed, solar, and natal planets, which can make it more difficult to discern the meaning of the influences. In others, the transits and their direct/retrograde/

stationary patterns are narrowly focused and will yield a clear message. To more easily identify the potential outcome, look for the transit connection that repeats the trends seen in the progressed and solar arc aspects.

As with birth, progressed, and solar arc charts, the best interpretations are the result of listing all the aspects and sign/house influences and then using keywords or comments in order to clearly see the trends and patterns.

Because outer planet transits function much like progressions and solar arcs, you should use both together. The easiest way to see the complete picture is to use a tri-wheel chart with the natal chart in the center, progressions or solar arcs in the middle wheel, and transits in the outer wheel. These charts are used in the examples that follow here. Most astrological software also offers the option to create lists of planetary aspects in a user designated time frame, but these can be overwhelming when you're first starting to interpret predictive charts.

If you don't have astrological software, there are two ways you can get the progressed and transiting data. The first option is to simply consult an ephemeris, and the second is to go to an Internet site (see Appendix) that offers free charts and calculate a natal chart for the appropriate number of days after your birth. So if you were born on the first day of the month and are now twenty-five, you would calculate the natal chart for the twenty-fifth day of the month you were born. This would then be your progressed chart. Then calculate another chart for the current planetary positions. Solar arcs are easier. Simply add one degree for each year of your age to the natal position of your planets (for example, twenty years equals twenty degrees).

Keep in mind that each sign has thirty degrees so some planets will change signs. At age twenty-five, you would add twenty-five degrees or days to each planet. A natal planet at 22 Taurus would by solar arc at age twenty-five be 17 Gemini (22 + 25 = 47; 30° for a sign = 17° of the next sign). For a progressed planet, you would look at the next month in the ephemeris.

STEP-BY-STEP ANALYSIS

Using the examples from Chapter 2, let's see how the outer planet transits indicate the events that occurred. Combined with the progressions and solar arcs, they provide additional confirmation of a valid prediction.

AVERAGE TIME FOR AN OUTER PLANET TO TRANSIT A SIGN

Jupiter—1 year

Saturn—2½ years

Uranus—7 years

Neptune—14 years

Pluto—21 years

In succeeding chapters, you'll see how lunations and inner planet transits functioned as triggers for these events, and how eclipses and other predictive techniques also confirm the events that occurred.

PAMELA ANDERSON

The chart for actress Pamela Anderson analyzed in Chapter 2 was for the period when she was discovered while attending a football game with friends. The progressions and solar arcs were related to career and fame, both the beginning of this trend and the succeeding years.

The influence of the outer transiting planets is not obvious unless you look more closely at the chart, which is a good illustration of the importance of minor hard aspects and how the outer planet transits work in tandem with progressions (Chart 9).

One of the major career indicators in the progressed chart is the progressed Moon, which had recently entered the tenth house, and was forming a sextile to the natal Ascendant, an opposition to natal Venus, and a trine to natal Mars. Another career indicator is the progressed Midheaven semisquare the natal Moon. These are the transiting outer planet aspects:

- Jupiter trine progressed Mars
- Saturn semisquare progressed Moon
- Saturn opposition natal Sun
- Uranus semisquare natal Midheaven
- Neptune semisquare progressed Moon
- Neptune sextile progressed Midheaven
- Neptune opposition natal Sun

- Neptune square natal Saturn
- Pluto trine progressed Midheaven

Note that of the two outer planets aspecting the progressed Moon, and thereby activating the natal planets aspected by the progressed Moon, only Saturn, co-ruler of the tenth house, is within the one degree orb. This is an illustration of why you need to be flexible when using orbs: both of these planets were slowing to station direct in September 1989. So already these planets were moving into a more powerful position.

Uranus, ruler of the tenth house, which was about two and one-half degrees from the exact semisquare would also station in September and then move forward to form the exact aspect; it would eventually station within one degree of the natal Midheaven in September 1990, a year later. The point here is that it's always wise to look beyond today to see what aspects are approaching, because they can offer added insights into current trends and how and if they will continue to evolve in the near future. Transits, like progressions and solar arcs, are not static but in constant motion.

Neptune, ruler of the eleventh house of friends, sextile the progressed Midheaven, would also station in September 1989. Pluto, ruler of the sixth house of daily work and in the sixth house, was trine the progressed Midheaven.

Jupiter was trine progressed Mars in the fifth house of sporting events. (Jupiter is the co-ruler of the eleventh house with Pisces on the cusp, and Mars is a co-ruler of the same house because Aries is intercepted there). Along with Neptune ruling the eleventh house, this complements the

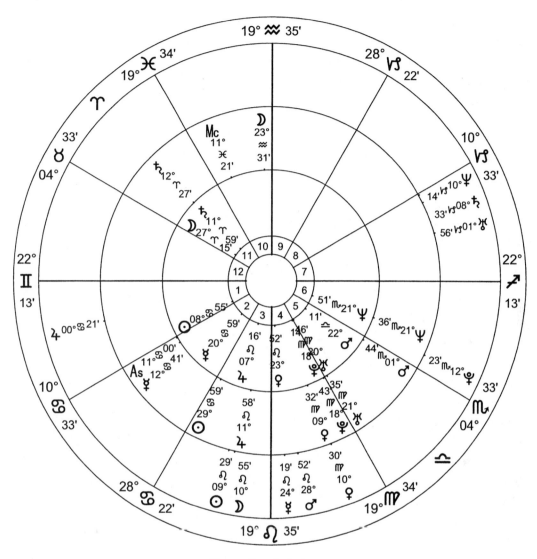

Chart 9: Pamela Anderson
Inner wheel: Birth Chart / July 1, 1967 / 4:08 am PDT / Ladysmith, Canada
Middle wheel: Secondary Progressed / August 1, 1989 / 8:48:31 am PDT / Ladysmith, Canada
Outer wheel: Event Chart / August 1, 1989 / 12:00 pm PDT / Vancouver, Canada
Placidus House

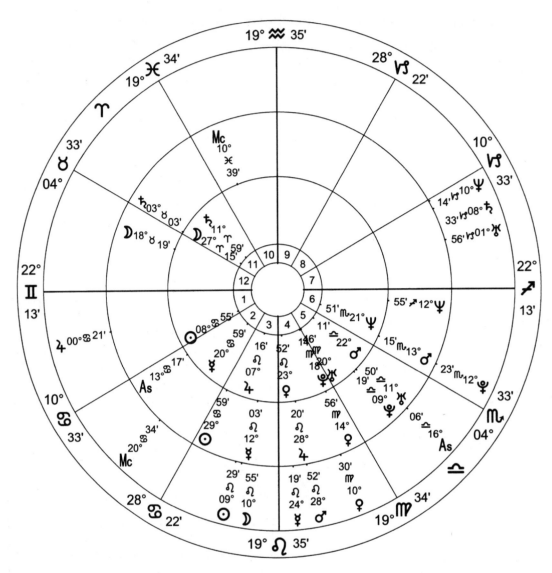

Chart 10: Pamela Anderson
Inner wheel: Birth Chart / July 1, 1967 / 4:08 am PDT / Ladysmith, Canada
Middle wheel: Directed Solar Arc / August 1, 1989 / 3:04:57 pm PDT / Ladysmith, Canada
Outer wheel: Event Chart / August 1, 1989 / 12:00 pm PDT / Vancouver, Canada
Placidus House

progressed Jupiter-natal Saturn trine that indicated luck through friends.

In summary, the natal and progressed Midheavens, which represent career matters, were aspected by four of the five outer planets. In doing so, they indicate on their own a potentially significant career development, and when viewed in combination with the progressions, the outer planets serve as confirmation. The fifth outer planet indicates how this would come about (through friends at a sporting event).

This chart also illustrates another point to look for in predictive charts. Notice how transiting Saturn and Neptune are quite close to each other, fewer than two degrees apart. Whenever outer planets form *any* close aspect such as this,

they operate as one, and you should pay particular attention to any aspects they make to natal, progressed, or solar arc planets.

The outer transiting planets were also active in the solar arc chart (Chart 10), with Saturn and Neptune sextile the solar arc Midheaven and trine solar arc Uranus and Pluto in the fifth house. Pluto was conjunct solar arc Mars in the fifth house (co-ruler of the eleventh) and square solar arc Mercury, ruler of the first and fifth houses, and activating the solar arc Mercury-natal Saturn trine (Saturn in the eleventh).

In order to more easily see the interrelationship between the progressed and transiting planets, below is the listing of progressed planets with the transits in italics:

PROGRESSED AND SOLAR ARC INFLUENCES IN PAMELA ANDERSON'S CHART			
Progressed Planet	**Aspect or House**	**Planet**	**Comments**
Moon	Tenth House		Public, career, fame; rules the second (income) and third (communication) *Saturn semisquare progressed Moon* *Neptune semisquare progressed Moon*
Moon	Opposition	Natal Venus	Venus, a planet of popularity, influences career matters because it is opposition the Midheaven; rules the fifth (recreation and sex appeal) and the twelfth (secrets); progressed aspect activates natal Venus-Mars-Midheaven aspect that indicates potential for fame as an actress and sex symbol *Saturn semisquare progressed Moon* *Neptune semisquare progressed Moon*

Moon	Trine	Natal Mars	Rules the sixth house of work and the eleventh house of friends and goals; activates the same natal configuration as does Venus *Transiting Saturn semisquare progressed Moon* *Transiting Neptune semisquare progressed Moon*
Moon	Sextile	Natal Ascendant	Public attention (Moon) focused on self (Ascendant) *Transiting Saturn semisquare progressed Moon* *Transiting Neptune semisquare progressed Moon*
Moon	Sesquisquare	Natal Sun	Public attention (Moon) focused on self (Sun); rules the fourth, indicating a new beginning and possible relocation *Transiting Saturn semisquare progressed Moon* *Transiting Neptune semisquare progressed Moon* *Transiting Saturn opposition natal Sun* *Transiting Neptune opposition natal Sun*
Midheaven	Semisquare	Natal Moon	Public attention (Midheaven in tenth) involving friends (Moon in eleventh); she attended the game with friends *Transiting Neptune semisquare progressed Moon* *Transiting Neptune sextile progressed Midheaven* *Transiting Pluto trine progressed Midheaven*
Ascendant	Square	Natal Saturn	Ascendant in second (income); Saturn, ruler of the eighth (money) and co-ruler of the tenth, in the eleventh *Transiting Neptune square natal Saturn*
Venus	Square	Progressed Saturn	Popularity (Venus); Saturn, ruler of eighth, co-ruler of tenth; activates natal Venus-Mars-Midheaven configuration, and natal Sun-Saturn square and Saturn-Midheaven sextile (ambition)

| Jupiter | Trine | Natal and Progressed Saturn | Jupiter rules seventh (relationships) and eleventh (friends); perfects natal Jupiter-Saturn trine and activates natal Saturn aspects of ambition *Transiting Neptune square natal Saturn* |
| Sun | Enters | Leo | Sun (self) in Leo (popularity, acting) |

Solar Arc Planet	Aspect or House	Planet	Comments
Mercury	Trine	Natal Saturn	Ruler of first (self) and fifth (recreation and sex appeal); ruler of eighth (money) and co-ruler of tenth (career and fame) in the eleventh (friends); activated natal Saturn aspects *Transiting Neptune square natal Saturn*
Moon	Square	Natal Mid-heaven	Moon (public), second house ruler of income; Midheaven (career, fame, public recognition) *Transiting Uranus semisquare natal Midheaven*

MARTHA STEWART

Entrepreneur Martha Stewart was indicted June 4, 2003, on charges of securities fraud, conspiracy, and obstruction of justice, among others. She was found guilty on four counts on March 5, 2004, entered prison October 8, 2004, and was released March 4, 2005.

As noted in Chapter 2, the natal aspect that indicated the potential for legal difficulties and a prison sentence is Mercury in the ninth house (legal system) semisquare Venus in the tenth house. Venus rules the twelfth house of institutions. So either this natal aspect and/or the progressed and solar arc aspects should be active in her chart from indictment to release from prison. The other important factors here are the Moon and Sun, ruler and co-ruler of the ninth house, and the rulers of the twelfth house:

Venus, Mars (traditional ruler of Scorpio), and Pluto.

Rather than compare the outer transiting planets to the progressions and transits only at the time of the indictment, we'll look at the transits and their aspects for the entire period (Charts 11–14). The goal here is to answer the question of whether she would be found guilty and sentenced to prison, and if so, for how long. This is what someone in her situation would ask an astrologer.

Indictment (Chart 11)

- Transiting Saturn square progressed Moon (ninth house ruler)
- Transiting Uranus semisquare progressed Mars (twelfth house co-ruler)
- Transiting Neptune opposition natal Sun (ninth house co-ruler)

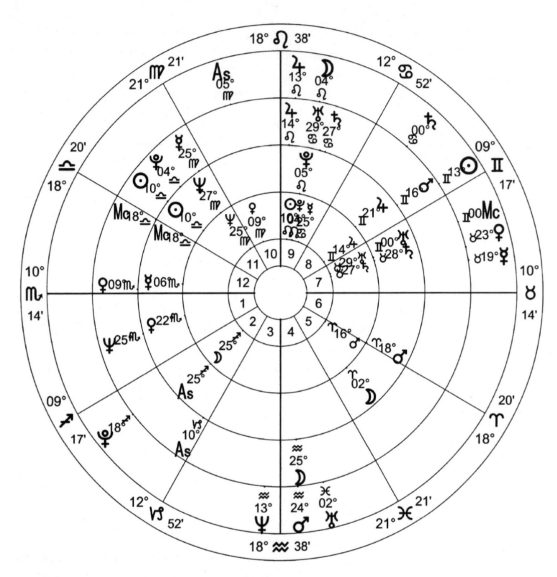

Chart 11: Martha Stewart
Innermost wheel: Birth Chart / Aug. 3, 1941 / 1:33 pm EDT / Jersey City, NJ / Placidus House
Middle inner wheel: Secondary Progressed / June 4, 2003 / 8:48:31 am EDT / Jersey City, NJ / Placidus House
Middle outer wheel: Directed Solar Arc / June 4, 2003 / 8:48:31 EDT / Jersey City, NJ / Placidus House
Outermost wheel: Indictment Transits / June 4, 2003 / 12:00 pm EST / New York, NY / Placidus House

- Transiting Pluto sextile progressed Midheaven (twelfth house co-ruler)
- Transiting Pluto trine progressed Mars (twelfth house co-rulers)

Guilty Verdict (Chart 12)

- Transiting Jupiter square natal Jupiter (natural ruler of the ninth house)
- Transiting Saturn trine progressed Mercury (natal ninth house planet in the twelfth house, Mercury-Venus aspect)
- Transiting Saturn sesquisquare progressed Venus (twelfth house ruler, Mercury-Venus aspect)
- Transiting Saturn sextile natal Venus (twelfth house ruler, Mercury-Venus aspect)
- Transiting Uranus semisquare progressed Mars (co-ruler of the twelfth house)
- Transiting Neptune trine natal Jupiter (Neptune is the natural ruler of the twelfth house, Jupiter is the natural ruler of the ninth house)
- Transiting Pluto semisquare progressed Mercury (twelfth house co-ruler, Mercury-Venus aspect, Pluto stationed direct about three weeks later, so it was moving less than a degree a day)
- Transiting Pluto opposition progressed Jupiter (twelfth house co-ruler, Jupiter is the natural ruler of the ninth house)

Entered Prison (Chart 13)

- Transiting Jupiter semisquare natal Midheaven (natural ruler of ninth house, fame or infamy)

- Transiting Saturn conjunct natal Mercury / semisquare natal Venus (Mercury-Venus aspect)
- Transiting Uranus semisquare progressed Moon conjunct progressed Mars (ninth house ruler, twelfth house co-ruler)
- Transiting Neptune trine natal Jupiter (an applying aspect that was exact while she was in prison, natural ruler of the twelfth house, natural ruler of ninth house)
- Transiting Pluto sextile progressed Midheaven (twelfth house co-ruler, Midheaven in the twelfth house)
- Transiting Pluto sesquisquare natal / progressed Pluto (twelfth house ruler, natal / progressed Pluto in the ninth house)
- Transiting Pluto semisquare progressed Mercury (an applying aspect that was exact while she was in prison, Mercury-Venus aspect)
- Transiting Pluto trine progressed Moon conjunct progressed Mars (twelfth house co-rulers, ninth house ruler)

Released from Prison (Chart 14)

- Transiting Jupiter opposition progressed Mars (ninth house natural ruler, twelfth house co-ruler)
- Transiting Saturn square progressed Midheaven (Midheaven in twelfth house, fame or infamy
- Transiting Uranus trine progressed Mercury (Mercury in twelfth house, Mercury-Venus aspect)
- Transiting Uranus approaching opposition natal Venus semisquare natal Mercury

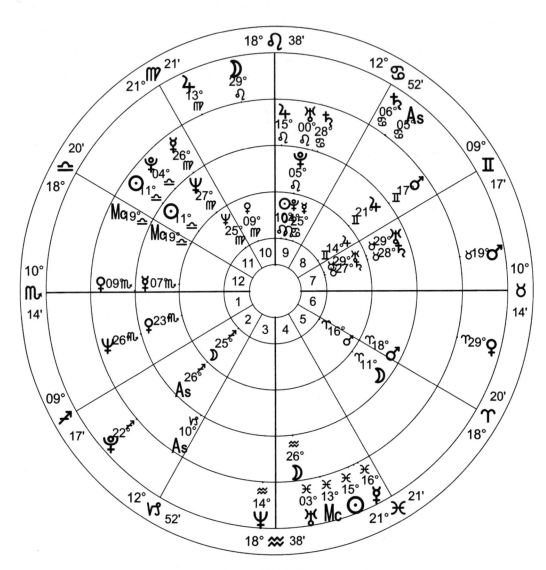

Chart 12: Martha Stewart
Innermost wheel: Birth Chart / August 3, 1941 / 1:33 pm EDT / Jersey City, New Jersey
Middle inner wheel: Secondary Progressed / March 5, 2004 / 8:48:31 am EDT / Jersey City, New Jersey
Middle outer wheel: Directed Solar Arc / March 5, 2004 / 8:48:31 EDT / Jersey City, New Jersey
Outermost wheel: Guilty Verdict Transits / March 5, 2004 / 12:00 pm EST / New York, New York
Placidus House

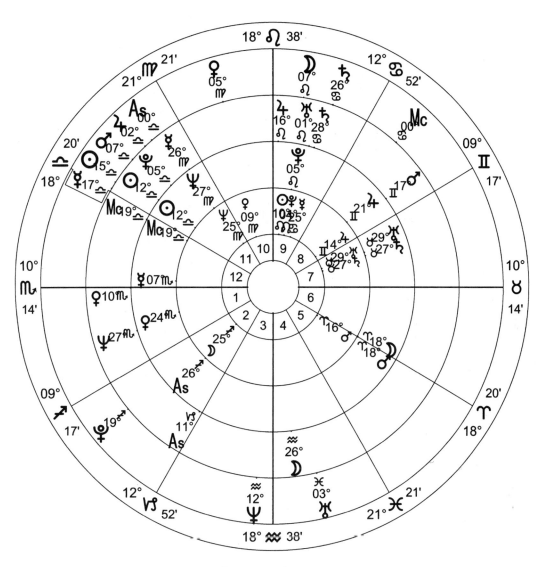

Chart 13: Martha Stewart

Innermost wheel: Birth Chart / August 3, 1941 / 1:33 pm EDT / Jersey City, New Jersey

Middle inner wheel: Secondary Progressed / October 8, 2004 / 8:48:31 am EDT / Jersey City, New Jersey

Middle outer wheel: Directed Solar Arc / October 8, 2004 / 8:48:31 EDT / Jersey City, New Jersey

Outermost wheel: Entered Prison Transits / October 8, 2004 / 16:15 am EST / Aiderson, West Virginia

Placidus House

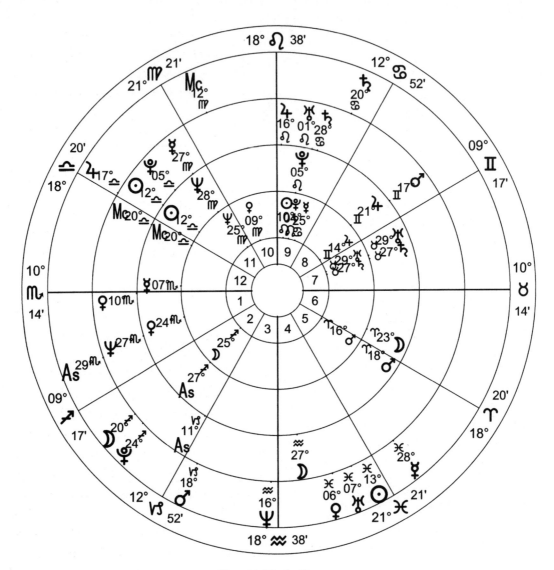

Chart 14: Martha Stewart
Innermost wheel: Birth Chart / Aug. 3, 1941 / 1:33 pm EDT / Jersey City, New Jersey
Middle inner wheel: Secondary Progressed / Mar. 4, 2005 / 8:48:31 am EDT / Jersey City, New Jersey
Middle outer wheel: Directed Solar Arc / Mar. 4, 2005 / 8:48:31 EDT / Jersey City, New Jersey
Outermost wheel: Released from Prison Transits / Mar. 4, 2005 / 0:30 am EST / Aiderson, West Virginia
Placidus House

(Mercury-Venus aspect, this was exact five months later when her sentence of house arrest was completed)

- Transiting Uranus sesquisquare progressed Midheaven (Midheaven in twelfth house, fame or infamy)

- Transiting Pluto conjunct natal Moon (twelfth house co-ruler, ninth house ruler)

- Transiting Neptune sextile natal Mars (twelfth house natural ruler, twelfth house co-ruler)

After reviewing all of these aspects, it is the astrologer's job to answer the client's questions regarding the possibility of a guilty verdict, prison, and prison sentence. The answers are, as would be expected, strongly tied to the natal Mercury-Venus semisquare (and the progressed positions of these planets) because predictive astrology always has its basis in the natal chart.

While it might be tempting (even for an experienced astrologer) to simply count and total the easy and hard aspects, that would be an unwise approach to determine the outcome. Again, hard aspects are necessary for action, so they don't always indicate purely negative events. Yes, there are times when this occurs, such as when traditionally challenging planets form difficult aspects.

In Martha's chart, at the time of the guilty verdict, transiting Saturn (challenging planet) aspected natal Venus (sextile) and progressed Mercury (trine) and Venus (sesquisquare). This doesn't look so bad unless you have first identified the natal Mercury-Venus semisquare. Saturn is also tied to the past (past actions), and it is generally considered a karmic planet. In addition, transiting Pluto (another challenging

planet) was semisquare progressed Mercury, which would suggest that the legal outcome would transform her life. Transiting Pluto was especially powerful because it was moving into a station.

The other aspects active at the time from Uranus, Neptune, and Pluto reinforce this. Jupiter was square natal Jupiter, not a difficult aspect in itself, but transiting Pluto was opposition Jupiter (a negative outcome). Neptune trine Jupiter could indicate disbelief and that she thought she would be found not-guilty (wishful thinking), and Uranus semisquare progressed Mars indicates an element of negative (hard aspect) surprise.

If, after looking at Martha's chart, you determined that she would be found guilty, the next question would be the length of her sentence. The key decision-maker here is to find an outer planet aspect to natal or progressed Mercury or Venus. By looking at the list of outer planet transits when she entered prison, you can see that the stressful aspects to these planets continued. They began to ease when transiting Uranus formed a trine to progressed Mercury, but it was also approaching an opposition to natal Venus. The length of the sentence would have been a tough call because there were other difficult aspects in effect at the time. There were three aspects, however, that could tip the decision.

The first was transiting Saturn square progressed Midheaven (in the twelfth house) and the progressed IC. The second was transiting Uranus sesquisquare / semisquare the same angles. Both of these indicate a potential change of residence. Add to these two transiting Neptune sextile progressed Mars in the sixth house of work and an approaching conjunction to the natal IC. Although transiting Neptune would not conjunct the natal IC until 2006, a year later, a look at the ephemeris reveals that it was approaching a retrograde station at 17 Aquarius 36, which it would make in May.

So the Uranus aspects could indicate that she would be released, and the close but not exact Neptune-IC conjunction would make you question that outcome, despite the approaching station. On the plus side, transiting Neptune's sextile to progressed Mars in the sixth house suggests that she would have the opportunity to return to work.

This example makes another important point in predictive astrology: it is difficult and at times impossible to delineate an accurate forecast without full knowledge of the situation, or in this case the possible sentences she could receive. Martha was indeed released from prison, but she spent the following five months under house arrest wearing an ankle bracelet. She was allowed to leave home to work for a designated number of hours; otherwise, she was required to be at home. With this hindsight, it's easy to see Neptune's (natural ruler of the twelfth house) influence on the outcome as it aspected the IC.

This example also reflects the value of solar arc charts, which can add additional, and in this case, confirming information. Taking a long-term view, solar arc Venus and Mercury would square/ semisquare her natal Sun about the time she was released from prison, when solar arc Mars would sextile the Midheaven (back to business). At the same time, solar arc Moon in the fourth house of home would square natal Saturn in the seventh house. From these and the progressed aspects, you could conclude that she would likely be released from prison in March 2005, but that there would be extenuating circumstances.

If you were forecasting with Martha's chart regarding this specific event, you would have looked at other predictive factors, including the inner transiting planets, lunations, eclipses, and solar and lunar returns. We will see how these factors contributed to the indications in later chapters.

MARILYN MONROE

Although on first inspection it appears that the progressions and solar arcs are the only indications of a potential marriage, a closer look at the transiting outer planets reveals another part of this marriage story (Chart 15). Marilyn married at age sixteen, young even for the 1940s. Rather than a traditional romance, it was reportedly a marriage of convenience—a way for her to avoid being returned to an orphanage when her foster parents declared their intention to relocate to another state. The bride and groom did, however, know each other because Jim Dougherty lived down the street from her foster parents.

So while the progressions and solar arcs are more reflective of traditional marriage indicators, the transiting outer planets strongly color the forecast with the intended purpose: a desire for a more hospitable living situation.

Among the transiting outer planet aspects are several that emphasize the fourth house of home:

- Transiting Jupiter square progressed Mars—optimism and luck (Jupiter) regarding a new domestic situation (progressed Mars, fourth house co-ruler)

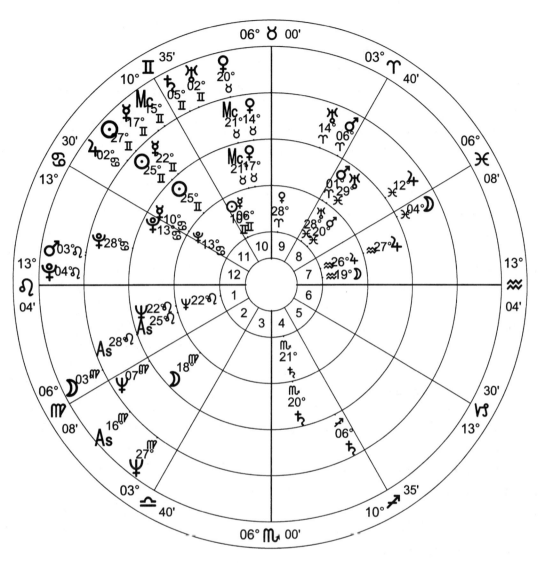

Chart 15: Marilyn Monroe
Innermost wheel: Birth Chart / June 1, 1926 / 9:30 am / Los Angeles, California
Middle inner wheel: Secondary Progressed / June 19, 1942 / 8:48:31 am / Los Angeles, California
Middle outer wheel: Directed Solar Arc / June 19, 1942 / 8:48:31 am / Los Angeles, California
Outermost wheel: Wedding Transits / June 19, 1942 / 12:00 pm PWT / Los Angeles, California
Placidus House

- Transiting Uranus sextile progressed Mars—an opportunity (sextile) for a new living situation (Mars) through marriage (Uranus, seventh house ruler)

- Transiting Pluto sesquisquare natal Mars—this approaching aspect was exact in July and involved the ruler and co-ruler of the fourth house

- Transiting Pluto square Midheaven/IC—this approaching aspect was exact in August and involved the fourth house ruler in aspect to the fourth house

With both transiting Pluto and progressed Mars (in the eighth, the natural house of Scorpio), there was a lot of Plutonian manipulative—but also transformative—energy active in her chart. The marriage did indeed change her life, but the question of manipulation by Marilyn or the foster parents is something we can only surmise. However, transiting Neptune was semisquare/sesquisquare the natal Ascendant-Descendant (marriage axis), preparing to station June 8, just a week after the marriage ceremony. This can be interpreted in one or both of two ways: escapism or deception. Possibly it was some of both because she was escaping a potentially difficult situation (return to the orphanage) and may have been deceiving herself (or been deceived by others) that the marriage would provide a life situation to her current dilemma.

Transiting Saturn was conjunct natal Mercury, ruler of her Sun sign and co-ruler, with Uranus, of her seventh house. So this marriage came with heavy responsibilities of possibly both a practical and karmic nature. She report-

edly said she did not feel like a wife, which corresponds to the July and August Pluto aspects and transiting Saturn conjunction her Sun in August, again in November, and yet again in April 1943, as transiting Neptune continued to move back and forth within orb of aspect to her natal Ascendant-Descendant. It was definitely not an easy or overall happy time in her life. In 1943, her husband departed for the war in the Pacific.

An astrologer consulted prior to the marriage would have immediately identified the probable marriage reflected in the progressions and solar arcs. But the outer transiting planets would have raised some questions regarding the trade-off for happiness. Just because a chart shows strong marriage indicators, it does not mean it will work out as a hoped-for ideal. Because the progressed and solar arc planets do not move quickly, the most telling outcome in the succeeding months is often seen in the outer planet transits.

In addition to the transits already mentioned regarding the marriage, an astrologer would have spotted the possibility of sudden career changes and developments indicated by transiting Uranus in the tenth house, which would soon conjunct her natal Sun-Mercury conjunction in the tenth house and then move on to aspect the rest of her chart as it advanced through Gemini. At the same time, progressed Venus (universal love planet) would move on to square her natal seventh-house Moon about a year and a half later, and to oppose progressed and natal Saturn during the following two years. Reportedly, Jim Dougherty was not at all enamored of Marilyn's career as a model and fledgling actress. An astrologer could thus have questioned the prospective groom's attitude about a wife pursuing a career, especially in 1942, when this was not the norm. They divorced in 1946, as the progressed Venus-Saturn aspect was separating, and as transiting Pluto was crossing Marilyn's Ascendant-Descendant, which an astrologer would also have foreseen.

This example illustrates another important point in forecasting: astrological ethics. An ethical astrologer will never make decisions for a client (or even a friend or family member). Life decisions are the responsibility of the individual. The astrologer's role is to provide information so that the client can, hopefully, make an informed decision. This is the best policy even if you see with one hundred percent certainty that the client will marry, divorce, change jobs, etc. It is up to the individual, not the astrologer, to exercise free will, no matter how much someone pushes for a decision.

VAL

There were a number of progressed and solar arc aspects involving the Midheaven-IC, the second house, and the natal Uranus-Pluto conjunction in the fourth house when Val relocated to a new state in September 2002 (Chart 16). She moved to join her fiancé, and they were married about five and a half months later.

The influence of the outer planet transits are not quite so obvious unless you check their direct, retrograde, and stationary pattern in the ephemeris. Transiting Saturn had a major part in this move and a second one after she arrived in the new location. This planet, which made its first square to natal and progressed Uranus in the fourth house in August (when she decided to relocate), made two more passes: one in early October and another in April 2003, when she moved from one home to another in the new location. Transiting Saturn was also trine to solar arc Uranus three times during the same six-month period.

At the time of the move to the new state, transiting Neptune was sesquisquare the fourth-house Pluto-Uranus conjunction, stationing direct in October. What she initially thought would be the ideal new home was not, thus precipitating the second move the next April. This is reinforced by transiting Saturn (property) opposition solar arc Neptune (illusion). As the Neptune influence passed, the necessity for the second move became apparent in December when transiting Pluto formed a sesquisquare to solar arc Mercury, ruler of her natal fourth house.

Predictably, there were several outer planet transits involving Jupiter. This planet is conjunct the IC in her natal chart and rules her natal seventh house of marriage. Transiting Jupiter was in the second house of possessions, where it was trine the progressed Midheaven-IC, semi-sextile progressed Mercury, and semisquare natal and progressed Pluto in the fourth house. Transiting Saturn was approaching a sextile to natal Jupiter, a particularly strong aspect because Saturn would station retrograde in October conjunct her natal Ascendant-Mercury conjunction and sextile Jupiter. Val thus would not feel completely settled in the new location until the following spring when Saturn made its final pass to the Ascendant, Mercury, and Jupiter.

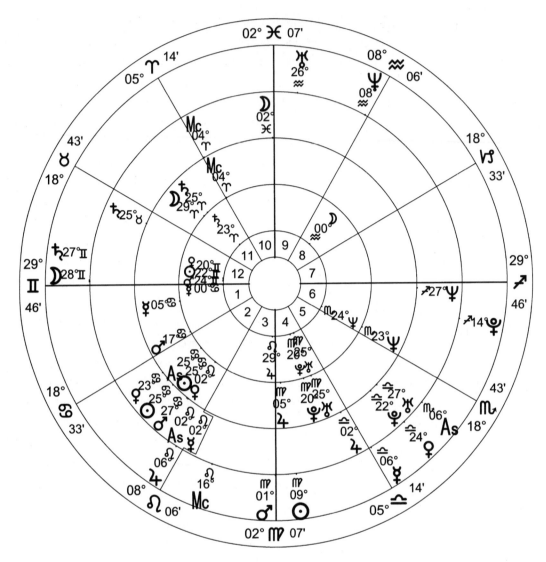

Chart 16: Val
Innermost wheel: Birth Chart / June 13, 1968 / 6:01 am PDT / Salem, Oregon
Middle inner wheel: Secondary Progressed / September 1, 2002 / 8:48:31 am / Salem, Oregon
Middle outer wheel: Directed Solar Arc / September 1, 2002 / 8:48:31 am / Salem, Oregon
Outermost wheel: Relocation / September 1, 2002 / 12:00 pm MDT / Helena, Montana
Placidus House

CONCLUSION

Is it possible to forecast events using only progressions or solar arcs or outer transiting planets? Yes and no.

In some cases, such as Val's, the outer planet transits, especially Saturn, indicate the possible event. Saturn aspecting a planet conjunct the IC and planets in the fourth house increase the possibility of relocation. But the same aspects could indicate major remodeling or someone moving into or out of the home. So how is it possible to determine which of the three would occur?

This is where the progressions and solar arcs are invaluable. In her chart, the progressed Midheaven-IC square progressed Mercury (fourth house ruler) was the strongest indicator of relocation. Remember that it took thirty-four years for this aspect to become exact, which it did only because the progressed Midheaven-IC were moving faster than progressed Mercury. Mercury was retrograde at birth and by progression until she was seventeen, when it turned direct and gradually gained speed until it and the progressed Midheaven-IC were in square aspect. This is a once-in-a-lifetime aspect in her chart and thus an important and strong one that indicates a major relocation.

There are some outer planet transits that are obvious and leave little doubt as to the outcome. Uranus and Pluto are more reliable as predictors because of their nature and slow movement. For example, either of these two planets conjunct the IC can bring relocation, or an often irrevocable change in a close relationship if conjunct the Descendant or Ascendant. Saturn is sometimes a reliable predictor on its own, but because this is the planet of lessons, it can be difficult to forecast the outcome. It would be an erroneous assumption, for example, to forecast the end of a relationship as Saturn transited the Descendant. Saturn there can strengthen a partnership or indicate that the individual ends or distances himself or herself from a close friend but not a partner.

It is well worth your time and effort to list and study all of the progressions, solar arcs, and outer planet transits when forecasting major trends and events in a person's life.

TRANSITING OUTER PLANETS
in Houses and Aspects

JUPITER

Jupiter, known as the greater benefic, is also the planet of expansion. It multiplies whatever it touches, which might or might not be to your liking. As the planet of luck, Jupiter can be associated with a lottery win or another windfall, a major promotion, love, travel, and more. But sometimes it delivers too much of a good thing, or promises you the world, only to leave you wondering how a sure thing failed to materialize.

At its best, Jupiter signals windows of opportunity, the times when you can make your own luck. This is true even when the luckiest aspect seemingly delivers good fortune out of the blue. It's still up to you and your free will to take action, to follow up on a job opening, shop a sale, invite a romantic interest to dinner, or purchase a winning lottery ticket.

Jupiter is also noted for excess, a trait that can cause ironic twists such as when a Jupiter-Neptune aspect brings you new carpeting as the result of a household flood. It also can dangle carrot-like promises, unrealistically raising your hopes that what you wish for will actually materialize.

In general, though, Jupiter does take the edge off difficult aspects, while making beneficial aspects even more so. Just don't count on it to be your guardian angel in every situation.

Jupiter transits the zodiac every twelve years, spending approximately one year in each sign and house.

JUPITER IN THE HOUSES

Jupiter in the First House: This is an overall lucky year, when you can find new avenues of personal expression, experiences, and growth opportunities. Creativity and confidence fill you with optimism and a willingness to move outside your comfort zone. So this is the time to take a few risks, to stretch yourself in areas you've always wanted to explore by learning a new skill or developing a new hobby.

Jupiter in the Second House: Income rises under this transit, but so do expenses as Jupiter expands both sides of the balance sheet. Your challenge is to resist spending sprees, use resources wisely, and get the knowledge you need to establish a path toward long-term financial security. This year is also ideal for self-improvement because Jupiter here reminds you to value yourself. You are your greatest asset.

Jupiter in the Third House: The need for mental stimulation pushes you to learn all you can through reading, talking with people, and taking short-term classes and weekend trips. You'll have more interaction with siblings, other relatives, and neighbors, and now is a great time to take the lead in a community activity or project. Optimism and positive thinking are high, but be sure not to overlook any potential downside.

Jupiter in the Fourth House: A growing interest in the domestic scene can motivate you to purchase property, relocate, or redecorate, possibly because of an addition to the family. This is a great time for do-it-yourself skills, home improvement projects, and entertaining, and Jupiter here is favorable for family relationships. Do be cautious, though, about taking on more than you can realistically accomplish.

Jupiter in the Fifth House: Creativity is high, and you're in a social, fun-loving period that favors romance and meeting new people. You'll delight in spending time with your children now, although take care not to over-indulge them, and if you're hoping to become a parent, Jupiter luck could be with you. Investments can be profitable if you resist the urge to gamble; base decisions on fundamentals, not hope.

Jupiter in the Sixth House: Your work life is upbeat and satisfying now, and conditions favor job-hunting. But you also have a tendency to take on too much, truly believing you can accomplish all you set out to do. That may or may not be true, despite your optimism, so promise only what you're positive you can deliver. Volunteer activities can be especially rewarding, and motivation is high to adopt a healthier life style.

Jupiter in the Seventh House: Close relationships, including romantic and business partnerships and close friendships, benefit from this Jupiter transit. You can also make some lucky contacts now with the potential to pay off within the next several years. Knowledge and favors are easily traded, and people are willing to share their expertise with you. Marriage is possible, but congenial relationships are more likely.

Jupiter in the Eighth House: This year-long financial trend is generally positive, putting you in a position to attract money from many sources, including a sizeable wage increase, an inheritance, or a windfall. You also could gain through an insurance settlement. Loans are usually easy to get now, but that can encourage you to overspend on credit. Think twice before you do that, and emphasize saving instead.

Jupiter in the Ninth House: With Jupiter here, the goal is to increase your knowledge and broaden your perspective. This can be accomplished through many avenues, including classes, teaching, and travel. Metaphysical studies can be especially enlightening now and lead to a greater depth of self-understanding. It's possible you could be summoned for jury duty this year, or be involved in a legal matter.

Jupiter in the Tenth House: Increased confidence in your career skills and talents can result in a promotion, increased status, and awards. You'll also be in the right place at the right time to take advantage of any of the many career and attention-getting opportunities and lucky breaks that can come your way. This is the time to reinforce your position with decision-makers who could benefit you in the future.

Jupiter in the Eleventh House: With the influence on your sector of friends and groups, your goal is to widen your circle of personal and business contacts. Get involved in a good cause or a professional organization, both of which also offer networking possibilities. People you meet now will bring you luck and help you redefine, even indirectly, your evolving life and career goals.

Jupiter in the Twelfth House: Jupiter here functions much like a guardian angel, arriving in the nick of time to assist you when you need it most. Not that you should depend on it, but more often than not Jupiter will come through for you. This transit also encourages you to look within as a means of defining your subconscious needs and desires, as well as to free your sixth sense.

JUPITER HARD ASPECTS: SQUARE, OPPOSITION, SEMISQUARE, SESQUISQUARE, AND CONJUNCTION

Jupiter-Sun: This is an aspect of opportunity and good fortune, but it's still wise not to push your luck. Any form of excess, including financial extravagance and foolish schemes, is inadvisable, but well thought out new endeavors can do well if you consider all the pros and cons. Mostly, though, life perks along and this is a happy time.

Jupiter-Moon: You're upbeat, optimistic, and generous under this aspect. Keep things in perspective, however. Otherwise you could easily slip into a self-indulgent pattern of spending and eating. Your emotional needs will be better satisfied by sharing yourself with close friends and family members and bringing cheer into their lives.

Jupiter-Mercury: Positive thinking and a wide range of information coming your way can generate big ideas. But be sure they're practical before you proceed because it's easy to see only the positives now. Fortunately, you now also have access to people who can offer knowledgeable input and feedback. Listen closely to what they say and seriously consider their advice. Relationships with siblings and neighbors are upbeat.

Jupiter-Venus: Relationships bring you pleasure, and most are at their best during this transit, especially business and personal partnerships. You could meet a new romantic interest or celebrate an engagement now. But monitor your budget because you'll be in the mood to spend freely. Also be realistic about investments and credit, and use this transit to learn more about money management.

Jupiter-Mars: Your high energy and ambitious attitude are assets as long as you don't push yourself and other people. Because you want everything now, it's all too easy to act prematurely and to expect others to operate on your time line. Think first, and take only calculated risks rather than let overconfidence undermine potential gains. Also be cautious on the road and when working with tools.

Jupiter-Jupiter: The conjunction marks the start of a new twelve-year cycle. It's a generally lucky year for new endeavors and personal directions, although it's wise to plan first and look to the future. What you set in motion now with an emphasis on common sense rather than blind optimism can grow for years to come. Finances can be up or down during this time, depending upon other influences and your decisions; have a safety net.

Jupiter-Saturn: This combination challenges you to balance expansion and contraction, growth and caution. Think big but realistically, and resist any tendency to be either too conservative or too optimistic. Strive instead to blend both energies, using knowledge and experience as your guidelines. Further education can be a good investment in your career and lead to advancement. Expect matters to unfold slowly.

Jupiter-Uranus: This is potentially one of the luckiest periods during Jupiter's transit, particularly the conjunction. Much depends upon your natal chart and other predictive factors, but sudden opportunities and windfalls can appear at the least expected moment. Your need for excitement, however, can prompt careless actions that undermine the potential for major gains. Make networking through groups and friends a priority.

Jupiter-Neptune: You're on a spiritual, idealistic plane that can put you at a disadvantage in everyday affairs and certainly with major life decisions. Because you're more trusting now, seeing the good in almost everyone and everything, you can more easily be deceived and accept false promises. Be particularly cautious with money matters. This aspect, however, is among the best for volunteer activities and promoting charitable causes.

Jupiter-Pluto: Ambition drives you. That's advantageous as long as you keep your power in perspective, which will be difficult in some situations. Even if you're not usually controlling, that's likely to emerge to some extent now simply because you're deeply invested in your goals. So try not to push your agenda too strongly; do try to let things evolve at their own pace. This is also an aspect that indicates power struggles, so be aware of what's going on around you.

JUPITER EASY ASPECTS: SEXTILE, TRINE, AND CONJUNCTION

Jupiter-Sun: You're surrounded with good luck during this fortunate period that features supportive relationships, an even flow of money, and overall happiness. An upbeat attitude results from optimism, but it's also easy to kick back and let life float along. Do more. Put this time to constructive use in personal goal setting.

Jupiter-Moon: Your optimistic mood attracts pleasant, uplifting emotional contacts and experiences, and you'll especially enjoy time with your partner, close friends, and loved ones. Women can be especially fortunate for you now and be your link to opportunities. This transit also favors working with the public.

Jupiter-Mercury: Communication, business matters, and learning benefit from this aspect that accents positive thinking and easy access to information and knowledge. This is usually an excellent time to sign contracts, negotiate, and network because you're in sync with most people, who are also likely to grant favors. Travel is also favored, particularly weekend trips or visiting relatives.

Jupiter-Venus: It's easy to slip into self-indulgence mode under this aspect, simply because you're lazy and crave comfort. That's fine to a point. But too much of a good thing can cause you to miss the potential upside of this period. You could benefit financially. If so, turn a desire to spend into a mission to find the best bargains, and then save the difference. Relationships are upbeat, and love can be at its best.

Jupiter-Mars: This aspect accents a period of high energy, drive, leadership, and confidence that is best used to further your goals or desires. What it needs is a finite, productive outlet such as improving a skill or taking the lead in a project. Exercise is also positive as long as you don't overdo it, and this is an excellent time to smooth over any lingering conflicts with people.

Jupiter-Jupiter: Life perks along, and it takes little effort to fulfill your desires during this lucky phase. You can use this easygoing time to catch up with life and yourself and do what you most enjoy. This is also a generally good time for travel, time off, learning, and social events. Legal matters usually have a favorable outcome.

Jupiter-Saturn: During this time you have an opportunity to reap career rewards based on your past efforts. It may not be a huge leap forward, but more of an incremental step on the path. You also can easily meet and even exceed job-related responsibilities now because you can maintain a steady, measured pace that yields solid output. Rely on your knowledge and experience and that of others.

Jupiter-Uranus: Sudden opportunities are a perfect match for your innovative ideas during this period as you welcome change. All of this can come about through education, travel, and group endeavors—whatever can satisfy your need for mental stimulation and what is new, fresh, and different. A windfall is possible with this aspect if other chart factors are in agreement.

Jupiter-Neptune: This aspect emphasizes spirituality and intuition, both of which can be strong now. But it will also be easy to get lost in a world of illusion and wishful thinking, so give yourself a periodic reality check (or bounce your ideas off someone close to you, and then listen to the advice). A worthy cause is a good outlet for your idealism.

Jupiter-Pluto: Your ambitions come alive, but it will take focused effort to direct and capitalize on them now. Used at its best, this aspect can enhance your leadership skills and possibly help you achieve a major goal. You also can benefit financially as long as you don't put too much faith in luck.

SATURN

Saturn represents restriction, setbacks, and the past. It also rewards effort, responsibility, and playing by the rules. Saturn provides structure, the framework within which we shape our lives and the foundation on which we build long-term gains. It is also the planet of life experience and lessons learned.

Saturn can frustrate and delay what we hope to achieve, because it teaches patience and the importance of hard work and follow-through as the path to achievement. Although it can take much of a lifetime to truly appreciate and understand its rhythm, careful observation of its cycles and related events can speed up the learning process.

Saturn moves through the entire zodiac about every twenty-eight years, forming major hard aspects (conjunction, square, opposition) to its natal place and to all other planets and angles in your chart every seven years. Check the ephemeris for the dates these have occurred and then reflect on events and your responses at the time. You will be able to identify a common theme(s) and thus be better prepared at the next Saturn transit. This knowledge will give you a general idea about how you respond to Saturn as well as ways to minimize its negative traits and capitalize on the positive ones.

In general, Saturn is the career planet and suggests delays, limitations, tough lessons, hard work, and older people. Saturn is also associated with security, authority, status, self-discipline, depression, patience, responsibility, achievement, restriction, and pessimism.

SATURN IN THE HOUSES

Saturn in the First House: This is an ideal time to take stock of yourself. Identify your strengths and weaknesses, what you have accomplished in your lifetime, and what you still want to achieve. This self-evaluation can be enlightening if you're honest with yourself and lead to new personal directions. Let them evolve and emerge at their own pace because this is a time for planning rather than one for new endeavors.

Saturn in the Second House: Although this transit can limit income, there is no reason to fear that it will. Think of this transit instead as an opportunity to balance your budget and to learn thrifty habits. The main lesson, however, is values. What is really, truly important to you in life? What do you value most about yourself? What is your attitude about possessions?

Saturn in the Third House: Your mindset is likely to be more serious during this transit, with thoughts about the past as memories surface. Because your concentration level is high, this is an excellent time to begin a degree or certification program. You may also have a tendency to distance yourself from siblings, other relatives, and neighbors, one or more of whom could be difficult.

Saturn in the Fourth House: Family responsibilities increase during this transit, and you may have to care for a parent or elderly relative. You also could relocate, or have an adult child or another relative move in or out of your home. The need for domestic repairs could arise at any time. If other factors are in agreement, this could be a good time to purchase or remodel property.

Saturn in the Fifth House: Your children are more of a responsibility now, possibly because you're a new parent, dealing with teens, or heavily involved in their schooling or activities. This can limit your free time to the point where you feel all the fun has gone out of life. Think of yourself and attend to your needs. Although romantic interests are generally limited with

Saturn here, they may be more rewarding. Be cautious with investments.

Saturn in the Sixth House: You're in a period of hard work and increased responsibilities on the job. Unfortunately, you're unlikely to get the recognition you deserve now. That will come in time, most likely in about three years. It's also wise to pay attention to your health now. Minimize stress, eat a healthy diet, and try to get regular, moderate exercise. Pets and volunteer efforts can be rewarding.

Saturn in the Seventh House: People demand much of you and much of your time during this transit. Some relationships will end by your choice or theirs, and others will be strengthened. This is a time to consciously distance yourself from people who no longer have a positive role in your life, and to expand your knowledge of human nature. If other factors are in agreement, marriage is possible.

Saturn in the Eighth House: This is a time to trim your budget, pay off any existing debt, and avoid new loans, regardless of your overall financial status. Also remind yourself to regularly check your (and your immediate family's) credit report for errors. Your partner's income is more likely to be restricted than is yours, and there could be delays or difficulties surrounding inheritance or insurance.

Saturn in the Ninth House: This transit can trigger extensive business travel, more interaction with in-laws, or legal matters, including jury service. It's most effective use, however, is higher education, so consider returning to school for a degree or additional certification. You also could have an opportunity to teach others, or learn about other cultures and ways of life.

Saturn in the Tenth House: This can be a career pinnacle, bringing the success you've dreamed of and worked hard to earn. Or, it could be just the opposite. Much of the outcome is dependent upon how you lived up to your work responsibilities during the previous seven to fourteen years. So don't be tempted to take the easy way out on your way up because it's likely to catch up with you. Relocation is possible.

Saturn in the Eleventh House: You may be asked to accept a leadership position in an organization or group endeavor. Although this will contribute to your overall life and career success, be sure to emphasize delegation and teamwork rather than try to do it all yourself. At this time, friends can help you redefine and achieve personal and professional goals, and you could reconnect with people from the past.

Saturn in the Twelfth House: Time alone can be satisfying and productive with Saturn here, and so much so that you may at times bypass social events in order to enjoy your own company. Use this time to evaluate and learn from the past, as well as to complete unfinished projects. Also pay attention to your health and your body's signals. You probably will need extra rest and sleep now.

SATURN HARD ASPECTS: CONJUNCTION, SQUARE, OPPOSITION, SEMISQUARE, AND SESQUISQUARE

Saturn-Sun: This is a time of hard work, when you should finish what you start and fulfill all responsibilities. Although you won't see immediate rewards, they will come in time, so be prepared to be patient. Relationships can be trying now, mostly because you approach life with more seriousness. Make rest, sleep, and relaxation daily priorities because this aspect can affect vitality.

Saturn-Moon: Depression, loneliness, guilt, and isolation often occur with these aspects. Realistic or not, you can feel as though you're going it alone without the emotional support of others, and this can affect close relationships. As difficult as this sounds, and can be, this is also a time to reassess your life, out of which can come fresh ambitions and the enthusiasm to achieve them. Treat yourself with kindness.

Saturn-Mercury: Your thoughts drift to the negative under this aspect and you can be overly concerned with details and critical of others. This can naturally affect communication and relationships. You can turn pessimism into at least acceptance if you replace the negative with the positive, and from there you can realistically assess challenges and take action to resolve them.

Saturn-Venus: Some relationships end under this aspect, while others will be strengthened. Which end and which are strengthened depends mostly upon your perspective and attitude. You could meet a soul mate during this time, and it's possible you'll need to take on more responsibilities in a business or personal partnership. This transit also provides a lesson in thriftiness, whether because of tight finances or your desire for financial security.

Saturn-Mars: Frustration is your chief stressor now, and no matter how hard you push, it's tough to make much progress. This all increases the potential for accidents and relationship challenges. Find a way to relieve the tension, beginning with accepting what is and the need to work within the existing structures. Moderate exercise can also be helpful, but take care not to overdo it.

Saturn-Jupiter: This period provides you the opportunity to learn how to best deal with life restrictions. Although you see the need to maintain a conservative approach and operate within the established structure, you also want freedom and expansion. Resolving these two factors is the learning experience of this aspect. Even if you're unsatisfied with your current job, a search for another is unlikely to produce results. Be patient.

Saturn-Saturn: This aspect represents a life turning point as you review the past and confront security and confidence issues. There also could be difficulties with authority figures. But this period could also bring you a major achievement, such as a promotion or reaching a long-anticipated goal. As you see this aspect approaching, think about what was going on in your life seven years ago; the events are likely to be related.

Saturn-Uranus: You have the urge to break free of perceived restrictions, yet life circumstances or security needs hold you back. Resolving these two conflicting energies is not a simple task, but common sense and a positive outlet such as a hobby or exercise can help minimize the effects. This conflict will likely be centered in career or relationship matters, where you'll feel trapped with no escape hatch.

Saturn-Neptune: Doubt and confusion add an illusive quality to life as stability fades and you debate reality versus the ideal. Career difficulties can arise as a result, and you'll feel as though your security is evaporating without really knowing why. You could be involved in misunderstandings and the blame game, without any effective means of recourse. A creative or spiritual outlet can help temper the energy.

Saturn-Pluto: This aspect, which signals endings and major changes, almost always produces difficulties when personal planets or the angles are involved. Financial trouble, a job layoff, power struggles, and control issues are all possible. Unfortunately, you feel—and probably are—mostly powerless to fight back. The solution is to believe in yourself, accept life as it is, and move on, looking toward the future.

SATURN EASY ASPECTS: SEXTILE, TRINE, AND CONJUNCTION

Saturn-Sun: Past efforts can yield current rewards under this transit, particularly with the conjunction, which will bring you what you deserve. This is also a great time to take on additional tasks in order to demonstrate your value in the workplace, because what you do now can help set things up for future gains.

Saturn-Moon: Your emotions are steady under the sextile and trine, and you're attuned to family responsibilities. Use this phase to solidify your life foundation and set new career goals. Real estate deals can be positive. With the conjunction, however, you're likely to feel somewhat depressed and lonely.

Saturn-Mercury: Communication, concentration, and clear, analytical thinking are among your best assets now. You also can reap career rewards as long as you can detach yourself from old habits and work methods that are no longer

effective. Guard against negative thinking with the conjunction, as well as dwelling on the past and regrets.

Saturn-Venus: Relationships and money are stable, and important people favor you. If other factors are positive, this aspect is auspicious for marriage, business partnerships and relationships, and a modest yet well-deserved salary increase. During this time you can strengthen ties with family members, and may reunite with people from the past.

Saturn-Mars: Slow, steady progress appeals to you, and hard work is as satisfying as it is productive. Even the most daunting tasks are no match for the extra determination you enjoy at this time. But with the conjunction, take care not to push others in order to fulfill your own agenda, and also go easy on yourself, with an occasional step back to view the big picture.

Saturn-Jupiter: Be alert for career opportunities during this period, and don't hesitate to do a little self-promotion with decision-makers, when appropriate. Education can also lead to current or future career gains, even if you take a short-term class to learn or improve skills. Business matters are generally positive because you can see the positives as well as the negatives.

Saturn-Saturn: Under the sextile and trine, you feel secure and on track with your life and career. But it's still a good time to give your goals a check-up and then revise as necessary for maximum potential gain. With the conjunction, you may feel as though you're getting nowhere fast. Consider it instead a turning point and aim for more.

Saturn-Uranus: New opportunities can appear seemingly out of nowhere in the form of an unexpected job offer or promotion. Don't leap. Take the time to analyze whether this is the best move for you rather than succumb solely to the need for change. The conjunction can bring a sudden job change that is really an opportunity in disguise.

Saturn-Neptune: Set aside time for solitude and meditation during this transit. Both will help you re-center and thus encourage new personal and professional insights about your overall direction. This is generally not the best time for a job change because there can be hidden factors, and you see only what you want to see.

Saturn-Pluto: You're focused, ambitious, and methodical as you strive to achieve. Ambitions are more easily realized under the sextile and trine, but tread lightly and make it a policy to lead by example and be a team player. Power struggles, career difficulties, and personality conflicts with supervisors are likely under the conjunction.

URANUS

Uranus is *the* planet of the unexpected. And it never ceases to amaze astrologers as well. Just when you think you know what a Uranus transit will do, it surprises you with something entirely different, something that never occurred to you. It's definitely the universe's wild card.

As the planet of the unexpected, Uranus triggers change through internal and external events. It can change your thinking or your life path as easily as your residence, your job, or a relationship. Uranus loves surprises.

Uranus is an accurate timer, with events often occurring when aspects are exact or within a few minutes of exact. An intuitive planet, its energy is linked to flashes of insight, those "light bulb" moments when what was

previously unseen is suddenly apparent and fully understood.

Change can be difficult during the best of times. Some people cope well with it, while others, especially fixed signs, fight change unless they initiate it. Whatever your natal mindset, try to be open to change during Uranus transits, particularly those involving hard aspects. Life will be easier, and you can benefit from the sense of freedom and independence that result.

Uranus is often involved when people make what seem to be sudden major decisions such as divorce, marriage, and job/career changes. Although such events sometimes appear spontaneous to outsiders, the internal rumblings have been in process for some time. Retrograde patterns are often the key to timing, with the second or third contact triggering action.

Uranus transits the zodiac every eighty-four years, moving through a sign/house in approximately seven years. The conjunction, square, and opposition signal life turning points.

URANUS IN THE HOUSES

Uranus in the First House: Your mission is to break free, to redefine yourself and become the "real" you, without the inhibitions of the past. But as you discover (or rediscover) your independence, be careful what you toss out just to satisfy the urge of the moment. Relationships are particularly at risk now because you crave freedom and everything that is new and different. Remember, though, that changes made now will be permanent.

Uranus in the Second House: Unexpected income can offset sudden expenses during this transit, but don't count on it working out that way every time. Instead, take advantage of unexpected gains to build a nest egg that will see you through leaner times. A change or addition in income is also possible, such as a new job or career, a second job, or a sideline home-based business that could grow into a much larger enterprise.

Uranus in the Third House: Open your mind to new attitudes, information, technology, and innovative ideas and concepts as Uranus transits this house. Take classes and polish your communication skills. You should expect the unexpected in daily life, where there are likely to be unusual events from time to time involving siblings, relatives, and neighbors.

Uranus in the Fourth House: Relocation, renovation, and other major domestic changes are likely as Uranus forms a conjunction to the IC and then transits this house. On another level, you can use Uranus to help you break free of old childhood influences that hold you back. If you're a parent, a young adult could leave the nest, or if the reverse, a need for independence could motivate you to establish your own home.

Uranus in the Fifth House: This can be one of the most highly creative periods of your life, so explore options until you find the outlet for you—anything from writing to crafts to painting or gardening. A sudden but not necessarily lasting romance is possible under this transit, or there could be an unexpected pregnancy. If you're a parent, be prepared for your children to test their independence.

Uranus in the Sixth House: Unexpected events can trigger a job change, or you may decide it's time to find a more stimulating position. You'll also have little patience for hovering, hands-on supervisors now; in fact, the freedom to plan

and monitor your workload will be vital to job success. Anything else can create stress that can affect your health. You may unexpectedly acquire a pet during this transit.

Uranus in the Seventh House: Relationships, including partnerships and close friendships, undergo a period of change during these years, in part because of your need for excitement. Or, it may be your partner who has this need and thus initiates a change. Separation and divorce are possible as Uranus transits the Descendant and this house. A union formed at this time could be short-lived.

Uranus in the Eighth House: This transit often triggers sudden financial developments, including an inheritance. But they're not always positive, so plan ahead and create a nice nest egg in case you need it. Joint resources can be affected as a result of an income shift for you or your mate, or you could discover that insurance doesn't cover a loss. Avoid incurring new loans and credit if at all possible.

Uranus in the Ninth House: The world beckons you. Explore it in person or via books, TV, and the Internet. You also should further your education in some way, either by traditional means or online, to earn a degree or certification. Or, study metaphysics or other cultures and ways of life. Legal matters can be disruptive with an unsure outcome, so you should avoid initiating lawsuits if possible.

Uranus in the Tenth House: Career and status are subject to change, whether to your advantage or disadvantage. Cover your bases and remain alert, listening to the rumor mill as to your company's future health and prosperity. If your job feels restrictive and lacks growth, it might be time to search for a new position or career. Be sure the need is real, however, and not just your desire for change and freedom.

Uranus in the Eleventh House: During this transit, you're involved at various times in group activities, clubs, organizations, and good causes that interest you. Each is a great source of new friends and networking contacts, and many of them can have a positive influence in your life. Some will link you to opportunities. Your life goals are likely to change now and take you in unexpected directions.

Uranus in the Twelfth House: Secrets you thought safe can be revealed, and other hidden factors may come to light. The best policy throughout this transit is to share nothing you don't want repeated. Tune in to your sixth sense, which can bring sudden insights about yourself, your life, and other people. Also be sure to relax because nervous tension will be high at times.

URANUS HARD ASPECTS: SQUARE, OPPOSITION, SEMISQUARE, SESQUISQUARE, AND CONJUNCTION

Uranus-Sun: This aspect is all about freeing yourself to be the real you. If you think you've already achieved that, take a deeper look. This can be an exciting period of personal change, but be cautious about tossing out your current life just to satisfy your need for independence and something different. A relationship can undergo a major change, especially under the opposition.

Uranus-Moon: Expect fluctuating emotions, along with periodic upsets and mood changes.

Security issues may arise, and domestic changes are possible, including relocation and family members moving in or out. Be especially cautious with electronics and electricity. A female friend or acquaintance could spark an opportunity, and the same could come through a group or organization.

Uranus-Mercury: This aspect can bring innovative ideas and flashes of insight, and also sudden news (welcome or unwelcome). Most especially, you need to guard against impulsiveness and snap decisions, either of which you could quickly regret. Also find the stress reliever that works for you, because nervous tension can be high now. Listen to your intuition.

Uranus-Venus: Relationships begin and end suddenly under this transit, which also can spark love at first sight. However, it might or might not be the real thing, so don't elope, at least not until this transit passes. Existing close relationships can benefit from positive change, however, if you and the other person welcome the idea. Plan ahead to save some money before this transit that can trigger a windfall as easily as extra expenses.

Uranus-Mars: You can be impulsive and short-tempered now, even if you're not fully aware of it. The root cause is likely a desire to assert your independence and individuality. Think calm thoughts before you speak, and also find a positive outlet for this energy. Just be sure it's one that isn't high-risk, especially of the physical variety. This is an accident-prone aspect.

Uranus-Jupiter: This aspect can be one of the luckiest, bringing sudden opportunities. But what looks like a positive personal, career, or financial move may or may not be what you hope for. Slow down and gather information before you act, and then blend positive thinking with common sense. Faith in others and the universe can be advantageous as long as it's realistic.

Uranus-Saturn: Some, and possibly many, of the constants in your life are subject to change during this transit. Although your goal should be to move past restrictions and let go of what you no longer need, resist the urge to completely cut ties, and be especially cautious in career matters. The challenge is to work within the existing structure, modifying it to better suit your current needs.

Uranus-Uranus: One way or another, your quest for independence marks this period as one that can send you in positive new directions. But it can do just the opposite if in your desire for freedom you completely toss out your current life in exchange for a new one. Instead, seek positive outlets to satisfy your urge to be different as you take this growth step and ultimately become more true to yourself.

Uranus-Neptune: This transit can be enlightening if you don't enter the realm of illusion and confusion of the changing conditions that surround you. Question what's real and what's not, and remember that any imagined ideal is most likely only what you wish for. Creativity and intuition can be strong now, but drugs and alcohol could be a problem for you or someone close to you if such a tendency exists.

Uranus-Pluto: External change prompts internal change under this aspect that requires you to adapt to a new reality. Conditions are what they are and beyond your control, so think positive and take yourself in a different direction or one that's an offshoot of current activities. Even though this process can be difficult,

you will ultimately value the new you and the new life that emerge.

URANUS EASY ASPECTS: SEXTILE, TRINE, AND CONJUNCTION

Uranus-Sun: This is a marvelous time to connect and network with friends and groups and to welcome new acquaintances. Each can add excitement and new experiences to your life and bring opportunities to maximize your skills and talents. You also find self-expression easier now in the sense that you're more comfortable with the real you, secure in your identity.

Uranus-Moon: Socializing, meeting people, and making new friends are priorities now, and opportunities can come through females and working with the public. This is also the time to make positive relationship changes because you can freely express your emotions while maintaining a healthy detachment. Your sixth sense is active, offering fresh insights and intuitive hunches.

Uranus-Mercury: Your curiosity comes alive and you're open to new ideas as well as generating your own, thanks to an active imagination during this period. Spend time with siblings and relatives, take a class, learn a new skill or hobby, or enhance your job skills. Each can provide the added benefit of connecting with stimulating people in your community, where you could be more involved.

Uranus-Venus: Friends increase your luck and can be the catalyst for a windfall or romance. This is also a great time for social events and activities, especially if you step out of the norm and try new venues. Almost anything that's new and different appeals to you, including interesting people, art work, and food. Use your imagination if you plan to redecorate, with an eye for the eclectic and unusual. Bargain shop.

Uranus-Mars: Energy is high, but you'll want to monitor your nervous system because tension can rise during this period. Spontaneous activities and events and exercise are good ways to relieve stress, which in turn gives you the chance to slow the pace a little to reflect upon recent events. You also can shine as a leader now in teamwork situations.

Uranus-Jupiter: Learn, grow, add some sparkle and excitement to your life during this lucky period. Travel, teaching, and study are excellent avenues, whether for pleasure or to boost your career skills. A windfall is possible if your money houses are activated, or this could manifest as an opportunity through someone you meet or through a group or organization that taps you as a rising star.

Uranus-Saturn: Your most effective course of action is to work for change within existing structures. You can change the corporate culture by using originality on the job, although it's wise to ease into any new approach so that decision-makers have time to embrace the idea. This is also a favorable time for planning and organization as well as home improvements.

Uranus-Uranus: Although you have a need for change, it's not overpowering. Rather, it's the time to explore what catches your interest and to enjoy new experiences and people as a way to provide stress relief from the daily grind. Friends and group activities are especially enjoyable now. You could be a leader in a humanitarian effort by organizing an action group.

Uranus-Neptune: Charitable causes attract your interest, especially as a hands-on volunteer. You'll feel good about your efforts and reap the side benefit of widening your circle of acquaintances and networking contacts. Meditation can be effective now, both as a tension reliever and to access your subconscious and free your sixth sense. Hunches can be on target. But be cautious if someone tries too hard to convince you that their path is the right one for you.

Uranus-Pluto: Expect far-reaching change to touch your life, mostly on an internal level. Your shift in perspective can come through other people or the study of metaphysics, and this new-found knowledge will add depth to your life and your life path. Move outside your normal avenues of thought, as well as your life approach, if you're caught in a cycle of major change that is out of your control.

NEPTUNE

Neptune, planet of illusion, confusion, and deception, is also inspirational, creative, spiritual, and romantic. Sorting out what's what with Neptune can be a challenge if you're under its influence, and only after the aspect passes do you see what was obvious. With hindsight, all is clear when it comes to Neptune.

When Neptune is active, you see what you want to see, hear what you want to hear. Reality is the furthest thing from your mind. Depending upon current circumstances, this can be a plus or a minus. It's marvelous for creativity, but dangerous in money and matters of the heart. These transits can also make it difficult to be understood or trigger impossible-to-define conflicts with other people.

Neptune is also associated with water, chemicals, substance abuse, and medication. These problems occur more often with hard aspects, but not always. Difficult career aspects in combination with, for example, a progressed or solar arc Mars-Neptune trine can suggest alcohol abuse as the root cause of a job loss.

Neptune moves so slowly through the zodiac that you are unlikely to experience any aspect beyond the opposition, which occurs in the lives of people who are in their mid-eighties.

NEPTUNE IN THE HOUSES

Neptune in the First House: You question your identity, who you are and what you want. Don't hurry this potentially positive process out of which can evolve a new and more confident you. Give yourself time to explore your life and your skills and talents in tune with this energy, which can reveal many sides of yourself never before realized. Be patient with yourself because false starts and reversed decisions are all a part of the process.

Neptune in the Second House: Avoid major financial decisions and risks, such as investments, especially when Neptune is aspecting other natal, progressed, and solar arc planets. In day-to-day transactions, money can slip through your fingers, leaving you wondering where it went. Have faith that what you need will come, which Neptune here is noted for, while also reassessing what you value in yourself, your life, and possessions.

Neptune in the Third House: Misunderstandings can occur frequently with Neptune here, and you easily slip into daydreams and wishful thinking. However, you're also attuned to the unseen and are sensitive to people's feelings. Inspiration can come through poetry, art, and music. Be especially cautious with contracts, which can be misleading, and be sure to clarify what you write or speak.

Neptune in the Fourth House: Family affairs are confusing at times, and it can be tough to get a straight answer from relatives. Use your intuition to look beneath the surface for the true motivation. Also take precautions to avoid water-related domestic problems, be sure your property is well insured, and be cautious with real-estate purchases. Home decorating benefits from this transit.

Neptune in the Fifth House: You attract love and romance, but matters of the heart can be colored with dreamy idealism. Protect your heart and your resources. This is a poor time for investment decisions, but excellent for creative endeavors. If you're a parent, keep a watchful eye on your children, who could get involved with the wrong friends or activities.

Neptune in the Sixth House: Health diagnoses are often difficult under this transit, and you can be sensitive to medication. Job disillusionment can drag you down, but the energy won't change if you seek a new position that seems ideal. It won't be. So find an alternative to make positive use of Neptune by developing your creativity or getting involved in a project for a good cause.

Neptune in the Seventh House: Connections with other people are blurred at times and you feel out of sync with them as understanding eludes you. Love can capture your heart now, but ask yourself (and someone close to you) whether it's real or merely an illusion. Business partnerships and professional contacts can suffer from the same illusions, and drugs or alcohol can be part of the picture.

Neptune in the Eighth House: You could be a victim of fraud or a significant misunderstanding in money matters, particularly if Neptune forms difficult aspects to natal, progressed, or solar arc planets. Check your credit report at least annually, and don't assume you and your partner are in financial sync. This is an excellent time to study metaphysics and to develop your intuition.

Neptune in the Ninth House: You seek answers to life's big questions during this transit, with an interest in faith and spirituality motivating your quest. Travel, study, and dreams help reshape your attitudes so they're more in tune with the person you are today. You can also discover new creative outlets such as photography and writing, and inspire others through your spoken and written words.

Neptune in the Tenth House: You may feel a growing sense of dissatisfaction with your career and your place in the world, although it's difficult to define exactly what you want or need. The answers will appear in time if you give yourself the gift of patience. In the meantime, keep close tabs on your current career situation, where the reality may be far different from what you observe and hear.

Neptune in the Eleventh House: Choose your friends and group activities carefully. Well-intentioned or not, both can drain your energy and resources. Some will inspire new goals, but others will disappoint or deceive you. Protect yourself by not being too trusting, especially of new people who enter your life, and help friends help themselves rather than being an enabler.

Neptune in the Twelfth House: Solitude is beneficial as long as you don't completely withdraw from the world, which will be tempting at times. You can achieve the same positive result through daily meditation or quiet time that also opens your intuitive channels to the power of visualization. Use it to heal your spirit and to let go of what holds you back.

HARD ASPECTS: SQUARE, OPPOSITION, SEMISQUARE, SESQUISQUARE, AND CONJUNCTION

Neptune-Sun: With this aspect, you question your life direction and experience some confusion about what and who you are and the avenues you should pursue. Be careful of deception, initiated by you or someone else. There could be periods of disappointment and disillusionment. However, this can be a positive time for creativity and intuition.

Neptune-Moon: Emotions can be confusing, and this aspect often generates moodiness and tears. You're very sensitive now, so protect yourself from negative psychic energy, which can affect you in unseen ways. Other people will also be able to more easily trigger your sympathies, but you should put yourself, your family, and your needs first. Water problems in your home are possible.

Neptune-Mercury: Major decisions are difficult because your thinking is fuzzy. An even bigger challenge can be the belief that your thoughts are on target when they're well off the mark. Be cautious, and ask someone trustworthy for an opinion. Misunderstandings are also common with this aspect, and you could be deceived by someone who appears to be well-intentioned.

Neptune-Venus: The ultimate romance aspect, this planetary duo also enhances your creativity and imagination. Try not to idealize love, however, because disappointment is the probable result, or you could fall into the trap of trying to "save" someone. Be cautious with money matters. What appears to be a fabulous deal could leave you poorer but wiser, despite the guarantees you hear.

Neptune-Mars: Your energy and efforts are diluted under this aspect, and you're unsure at times what action to take. This is not the time to begin a new endeavor that involves a major commitment. You also could become a scapegoat or unknowingly fall prey to an underhanded scheme. Replenish yourself with plenty of rest, sleep, water, and healthy foods.

Neptune-Jupiter: You're idealistic and prone to false hopes and promises, both your own and those from others. As much as you want to help people, do it with caution because some will try to take advantage of you and your good will. Instead, satisfy the need by donating your time and talents to a well-recognized charitable organization. Your faith is strong and an asset if balanced with reality.

Neptune-Saturn: It's easy to slip into a pattern of self-doubt and worry during this aspect as your feeling of security diminishes. The structures in your life, such as career, relationships, and family, can be affected by disillusionment, and you feel powerless to effect positive change. Go with the flow and adapt as necessary, while using recreational activities and hobbies to bolster your confidence.

Neptune-Neptune: An uneasy feeling of dissatisfaction begins to surface in your life as this aspect comes into effect. It's as tough to get a handle on the problem or issue as it is to find a solution. The best option is to let matters take their natural course, listen to your intuition, take note of your dreams, and wait it out. Answers eventually begin to emerge. This can be a highly creative time.

Neptune-Uranus: This transit activates your sixth sense, leading to fresh insights about life and your role in the world at large. But this is not the time to stretch the truth or to entrust friends, groups, or really anyone with secrets. Sooner or later, they will be revealed and at the least opportune moment. Changes are likely in the area in your chart influenced by Neptune.

Neptune-Pluto: Change is baffling, and the more you try to understand it, the less you succeed. This is, in part, because powerful people—possibly hidden enemies—may try to undermine your efforts and mislead you. Be wary of forming alliances because it will be difficult to identify true supporters. Peer pressure can also be an issue now. Protect yourself.

NEPTUNE EASY ASPECTS: SEXTILE, TRINE, AND CONJUNCTION

Neptune-Sun: This is a peaceful, spiritual time in your life, and you're receptive to the needs of others, guiding them toward viable resources for assistance. Music aids visualization, which can turn your daydreams and fantasies into reality as this aspect separates. You could attract much positive attention through your career or leisure-time activities.

Neptune-Moon: You're sensitive to the feelings of people and can easily sense the mood when entering a room. This aspect increases your sixth sense, but it also can open you up to negative energy in your environment. Be aware of this and avoid those situations and people that can drag you down. Time at home and with family and close friends can be especially rewarding.

Neptune-Mercury: You can combine intuition, imagination, and creativity in a unique combination that helps you sense what people are thinking and what they're not saying. It also aids you in learning because you easily absorb the information. Use this positive to take a class for fun or to benefit your career, or begin a daily journal to explore your innermost thoughts.

Neptune-Venus: Love is lovely and so is romance when these two planets align. Enjoy both even if you know you have an idealistic view of the relationship. Stop short of mixing love and money as well as any investment that appears to be a sure winner, because it may or may not be what you hope it will. Money can also evaporate as if into thin air with nothing to show for it.

Neptune-Mars: This isn't the best time for new endeavors despite your enthusiasm and belief in success. The better choice is to maintain the status quo because your ambitions aren't as focused as you believe them to be. Use this aspect instead to reorient yourself to the softer side of life and your close relationships. Take it easy for a change.

Neptune-Jupiter: High hopes guide you. That's great as long as you accurately assess the risks involved in any undertaking, which can be difficult to do now. Turn your attention instead to romance, travel, learning a new hobby, or volunteering for a charitable cause or organization. This is also an aspect of faith and spirituality, both of which could enhance your life.

Neptune-Saturn: You can use this time to envision a new reality that incorporates your most idealistic side with your practical one. Balancing the two diverse aims will be easy with the sextile and trine, but the conjunction can cause you to question your ambitions. Knowledge gained and shared can help answer your questions and foresee the path you need to take.

Neptune-Uranus: Whether you touch one person or thousands, you can make a difference in someone's life under this aspect that also can awaken your intuition. Friends will value your input, and a charitable organization will welcome the gift of your time and effort.

Neptune-Neptune: You can use this aspect to enrich your life in ways you've never before imagined. Explore your ideals to determine what works for you and what doesn't and to discover new truths that can broaden your world view. Your intuition is active now, as is your creative energy.

Neptune-Pluto: This is the time to tap into your subconscious through meditation, music, nature walking, or quiet time. Use it to learn what makes you tick as you explore hidden urges and motivations, and don't be surprised if you discover unknown talents just waiting to be revealed. Dream big and act on those dreams.

PLUTO

Pluto goes beyond mere change to another level—transformation. It challenges any planet or angle it contacts to move beyond an event and into its core meaning. Then, out of understanding comes transformation, the process that replaces old, outworn structures, conditions, and ideas with new, viable ones.

Pluto represents power, obsession, and events beyond your control, such as job layoffs and natural and man-made disasters. It also can signify Plutonian people in your life. Control freaks—those who manifest Pluto's energy negatively—are usually easy to spot. Positive Plutonians can be more difficult to identify because they are the catalysts who work subtly as agents for constructive change.

Pluto moves so slowly through the zodiac—two to three degrees a year—that it will transit half or less of your chart in your lifetime. The years when it forms action aspects to your natal, progressed, and solar arc planets and angles are memorable for their intensity and sweeping change. As is true with the other outer planet transits, your willingness to work with the planetary energy can spell the difference between success and failure. The more you fight it—and in the case of Pluto, try to control it—the more difficult conditions become.

You may begin to feel Pluto's influence when it's as many as four degrees from exact, and only rarely will an event occur when it is exact. In a sense, because of its slow movement, it forms the backdrop for the changing conditions that precede and ultimately bring about the transformation process. Other outer planet transits, progressions, and solar arcs fill in the lessons and more specific details about what the Pluto transit signifies.

For example, in the case of a job layoff, the transformative issues involved could be security, the need for education, or family responsibilities. It is these issues the individual must deal with; the actual layoff—the event—was the mechanism to initiate the transformation process. Such knowledge can be very valuable as the cycle unfolds, and its effect will most often be positive once the process is complete. On a practical level, steps toward resolution will invite new—transformed—energy that will benefit the ensuing job search.

PLUTO IN THE HOUSES

Pluto in the First House: A strong will gives you the power to make things happen. Use it wisely and for your own gain rather than for manipulation or control of others. Confidence grows as you test your personal limits in search of a new you, but intensity can undermine your efforts. Step back, widen your perspective, and let at least some things evolve as they will.

Pluto in the Second House: Because this is the house of values, you can benefit from this transit in two ways. Use it to clean out junk and clutter and to generally reorganize your space at home and work. Through it you will learn more about your material values. Then turn your attention to your personal philosophy and initiate changes that will benefit your self-worth

Pluto in the Third House: Deep thinking characterizes this transit. That's positive and useful in exploring your psychological motivations and needs. However, it will take some effort to maintain objectivity and an open mind.

Relatives can be manipulative as they attempt to pressure you with guilt, and you could experience difficulties with a neighbor or neighborhood association.

Pluto in the Fourth House: Change centers on home and family. Relocation, remodeling, or major repairs are likely, and parents or other relatives can be a concern at some point during this long transit. This is an excellent time, however, to address and resolve childhood issues through counseling. Be sure property insurance is up to date, and also periodically check your home for damage.

Pluto in the Fifth House: Love matches can be intense, obsessive, or both, and constant turmoil can end a dating relationship. Creative projects and exercise are good stress relievers, but avoid extreme sports. If you're a parent, expect your children to test your limits and theirs, knowing that the situation will often be a contest of wills. Be cautious with investments.

Pluto in the Sixth House: Job conflicts and power struggles with supervisors and coworkers can prompt you to do the same. Don't. It's unwise to burn bridges, because this transit can trigger a job loss, whether through a layoff or conflict with a coworker or supervisor. Use it instead to do something positive for yourself: live a healthy lifestyle from diet to exercise to time for yourself.

Pluto in the Seventh House: Relationship tension can build as ongoing resentments surface or reach the breaking point, and a close tie can be severed as a result. You should avoid entering into any partnership as Pluto crosses your Ascendant-Descendant axis or makes difficult aspects from the seventh house; the other person may turn out to be someone you never imagined, far different from your perception.

Pluto in the Eighth House: Although the process can be painful, this transit can be effective and positive if you use it to consolidate or pay off debt. If you're debt-free, maintain that path and avoid financial risk. Finances can change at any time, for better or worse, depending upon the aspects Pluto makes to the rest of your chart. Be cautious and read the fine print if you need a loan or mortgage.

Pluto in the Ninth House: Religion and spirituality may take on added importance as you search for in-depth knowledge and understanding of yourself and your world. Higher education and exploring other cultures can also fulfill the goal of this transit. Seek competent advice if legal problems develop during this time, which is unfavorable for initiating legal action.

Pluto in the Tenth House: Your career reaches a pinnacle as Pluto transits the Midheaven and moves into this house. With careful attention you can use your drive and ambition to succeed, but resist any urge to challenge those above you. You also could get caught up in a power play without even realizing it until it's too late and thus lose what you have spent many years trying to achieve.

Pluto in the Eleventh House: Transformation comes through friends and groups, but be cautious. Align yourself with people who can be a force for positive change, rather than steer you down the wrong path. The challenge here is to maintain a healthy distance because it's all too easy to become consumed by a cause. Throughout this transit you will meet at least a few influential people who can enhance your life.

Pluto in the Twelfth House: Your subconscious releases long-buried memories as Pluto in this house urges you to resolve life issues. Work through them with therapy, a self-help group, or reading on your own. Also tune in to your sixth sense, which can offer valuables clues to self-understanding. With Pluto here, you also have maximum willpower and the ability to change yourself for the better.

PLUTO HARD ASPECTS: SQUARE, OPPOSITION, SEMISQUARE, SESQUISQUARE, AND CONJUNCTION

Pluto-Sun: Drive and ambition can bring success, but also power struggles with those who perceive you as a threat to their own aims. Emphasize fairness, compromise, and teamwork even if you'd rather take charge and control. The lesson here is to develop your leadership skills, guiding others to success as you learn to tactfully handle conflict.

Pluto-Moon: Intense emotions, relationship changes, and subconscious urges can upset your equilibrium during this transit, when it's wise to avoid difficult, controlling women and relatives. Although your feelings are real, your perspective may be too narrow, so try to view situations realistically. Relocation and household repairs are possible, and the most positive use of this transit is to clean out clutter and junk.

Pluto-Mercury: This aspect can manifest as conflict with authority figures, manipulation, and obsessive thinking. It also can reflect depression. At its best, however, this planetary influence is excellent for research, study, deep thinking, and persuasive communication. You can also program your mind with the willpower to accomplish whatever you set out to do.

Pluto-Venus: Some relationships reach a crisis point as stresses and strains, jealousy, or possessiveness surface. The most difficult are likely to end, while others will be transformed. You may be attracted to people who are married or otherwise unavailable. Be cautious with investments because anything high-risk can result in a loss. Use the influence to save and pay off debt.

Pluto-Mars: This time frame is one of either major success or failure. Although your drive and determination are high, it can be tempting to cross the line into ruthlessness even if that's out of the norm for you. Sidestep power plays and protect your interests, while resisting the temptation to push yourself too hard, mentally or physically. Drive with care.

Pluto-Jupiter: Ambition promises success or results in failure if you take on more than you can deliver. Keep your limits in perspective even though you're highly optimistic, and see this as an opportunity for gain. This transit can also signal legal problems, and it is a poor time to initiate legal action. Keep an open mind; it will expand your awareness.

Pluto-Saturn: The more you hang on to the past and existing structures, the more difficult change becomes. As tough as it is, the best option is to let go and move on to a place where you can embrace personal and professional growth. A financial downturn at this time could be the result of a layoff or company restructuring that reflects global conditions rather than an individual situation.

Pluto-Uranus: You're in the mood to toss out all those elements of your life that no longer work, or that you perceive as no longer viable. Stop before you act. Wholesale change is rarely a good idea, especially when it's prompted by the need to rebel against authority, an individual, or the world at large. Sort through your issues, examining them carefully for the motivation.

Pluto-Neptune: Your world is changing in the global context, as it is for most people born in your generation. Keep an open mind and adapt, because what was will never be again. You can gain understanding through metaphysical studies or by developing or reinforcing your spiritual foundation.

Pluto-Pluto: This aspect prompts you to examine your basic wants and needs, your power and effectiveness in the world, and how you deal with authority and conflict. Take the initiative to revamp your approach, if necessary, before someone forces the issue. The houses influenced by Pluto show the areas where change is needed.

PLUTO EASY ASPECTS: SEXTILE, TRINE, CONJUNCTION

Pluto-Sun: You have the power to make amazing things happen in your own life, the lives of others, and possibly in the world. Focus the energy on yourself first and make self-improvement your main objective. That will bring you the added confidence to aim for career achievements and make the most of your leadership ability.

Pluto-Moon: You can easily connect with your emotions now and work through issues that hold you back and limit success. Clean out your physical house too by remodeling, renovating, and clearing out what is no longer useful. Doing this will free your space as much as your feelings. A female can have a profound effect on your life.

Pluto-Mercury: This aspect is an asset in research and the serious study required in higher education or for advanced certification. It also gives you insight into human nature, which may actually teach you more about yourself than you learn about others. Communication is also a powerful tool for you, and you should take advantage of public speaking opportunities.

Pluto-Venus: Love is intense, and so much so that it generates the deepest of feelings, care, and concern. This is beneficial to both new and established relationships, as well as long-time friendships. Finances can also benefit from this aspect because your powers of attraction are especially strong now. However, use common sense and don't take financial risks.

Pluto-Mars: High energy, drive, and ambition propel you toward new successes, possibly among the best of your life. Use your power wisely as a motivator who leads by example. Also do something good for yourself: begin an exercise program, learn a new sport, or join a weekend athletic team as a great way to ease workweek stress.

Pluto-Jupiter: Luck allows you to achieve more without expending maximum effort, although be careful not to take on too much. Legal and financial affairs also can benefit from this fortunate aspect, and confidence is high because you believe in yourself and your abilities, skills, and talents. You may also travel or return to school.

Pluto-Saturn: Determination and staying power can aid your every endeavor and help you rise above others who are less industrious. This can be the time when you earn a major promotion or take a step up through a new position. Thrift and moderate caution can help you make the most of personal and financial resources. Think long term.

Pluto-Uranus: Move out of your usual world and seek the mental stimulation of new people, new ideas, and new experiences. All can have a profound effect on you and your life in different yet equally effective ways. You also can initiate

positive change in the areas of life associated with Uranus and Pluto in your chart.

Pluto-Neptune: You're motivated to examine your spiritual beliefs as a means of learning what works for you and what doesn't. This revamped philosophy is then easily incorporated into your everyday life because it's your own and not a product of your family or your environment. The study of metaphysics can add additional insights and depth.

Pluto-Pluto: Subconscious urges prompt subtle changes that ultimately can have a major impact on your life direction. Listen closely to them and think about how best to merge them into your current life and framework as additional building blocks of strength for the future.

NEW MOONS, FULL MOONS, AND ECLIPSES

NEW MOONS AND FULL MOONS

A New Moon, also called a lunation, occurs about every twenty-eight days, when the Sun and Moon are in the same sign and at the same degree (a conjunction of the Sun and Moon). A Full Moon also occurs about every twenty-eight days, about two weeks after the previous New Moon. The Sun and Moon are in opposite signs at the same degree at the Full Moon (an opposition of the Sun and Moon). There are twelve New Moons and twelve Full Moons during most years, but in some there are thirteen instead of twelve, with two in the same month.

Essentially, a New Moon initiates an event that then culminates or takes a step forward with additional information at the Full Moon. Interpretation begins with the house placement of the New Moon and any aspects the New Moon and the transiting planets at the time of the New Moon make to natal, progressed, and solar arc planets. A three to five degree orb can be used for the New and Full Moon and the faster-moving inner planets, but a one to two degree orb is a better choice for the outer planets.

New and Full Moons do not always indicate an event. If there are no aspects to your chart, the month will be mostly routine and uneventful, with an emphasis on the house where the New or Full Moon occurs. For example, home life is emphasized with the fourth house, relationships with the seventh, money matters with the second, etc. But more often, a New or Full Moon will activate trends established by the progressed, solar arc, and outer transiting planets.

New and Full Moons usually, but not always, occur in opposing houses such as the first and seventh, second and eighth, third and ninth. This can work one of two ways: the New Moon occurs first in, for example, the second house, followed by a Full Moon two weeks later in the eighth house. Or, the Full Moon can be first, followed by the New Moon in the opposing house.

The energy is different, depending upon the order. If the New Moon is first in, for example, the second house, this could increase income but also spending. When it's followed by the Full Moon in the eighth, you might discover you have overspent your budget because of the extra income, or you could choose to pay off existing debt instead of spending. In the reverse situation, with the New Moon in the eighth house, you could realize you need to take control of debt and then add to savings rather than spend at the Full Moon.

If a New Moon and Full Moon are not in opposing houses, activity is focused on two different areas of life. For example, if an expected salary increase does not occur around a New Moon in the second house, the following Full Moon in the ninth house could provide the incentive to broaden your skills in order to qualify for a raise.

Take careful note of the natal, progressed, and solar arc planets that are aspected by the New or Full Moon and transiting planets at the time of the New or Full Moon. Then check the ephemeris for the date(s) when a fast moving transiting planet (Sun, Moon, Mercury, Venus, Mars) will aspect that planetary alignment in your chart. This is when you can expect an event, or subsequent related event, to occur.

For example, if you're anticipating a decision regarding a loan application during a month when the New Moon is in your eighth house, look first for an aspect between the New Moon and the ruler of your eighth house. The ruler can be the natal, progressed, or solar arc planet. Then check whether the transiting planet that rules your eighth house aspects a natal, progressed, or solar arc planet in your chart. Also look for aspects at the New Moon to any natal, progressed, or solar arc planets in your eighth house. For further confirmation, look for transiting aspects that involve Mars or Pluto, the natural rulers of the eighth house. Do the same with the next Full Moon (two weeks after the New Moon), which in this case would often be in the second house (Moon in second, Sun in eighth). If the transiting aspects at the time of the Full Moon are favorable and favorably aspecting the pertinent eighth-house related planets in your chart, you can expect the decision within a few days of the Full Moon. If they're unfavorable, there may be a delay, additional information may be required by the lender, or the loan could be denied.

Using the same example, you can check the ephemeris for when the transiting planets during the four weeks following the New Moon are in aspect to your eighth-house related planets. There will be developments when these contacts occur.

Amanda's Chart: New Moon Example

Although Amanda is a college student with a part-time job (Chart 17), she had no credit because her parents provided her car and co-signed for her apartment rental. She discovered this, and the realities of not having a credit history, when she applied for an account with a cell phone company. When she was denied, she

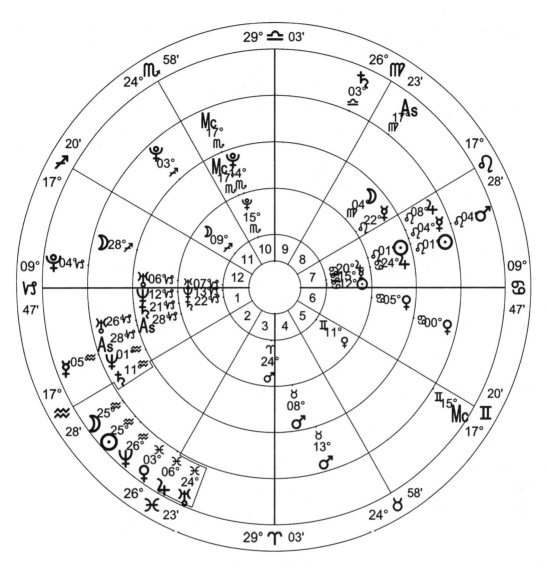

Chart 17: Amanda

Innermost wheel: Birth Chart / July 4, 1990 / 7:25 pm MST / Good Samaritan Hospital
Middle inner wheel: Secondary Progressed / February 13, 2010 / 10:27:13 am MST / Good Samaritan Hospital
Middle outer wheel: Directed Solar Arc / February 13, 2010 / 10:27:13 am MST / Good Samaritan Hospital
Outermost wheel: New Moon / February 13, 2010 / 7:51 pm MST / Phoenix, AZ
Placidus House

applied for several credit cards, with the same result. Even though the New Moon is a good time to begin an activity or launch a new project, if the natal, progressed, and solar arc charts don't indicate success, the effort is fruitless.

The New Moon occurred in her second house of personal money and income (she had the income to pay for the phone). The Sun rules her eighth house of joint resources, including lenders, and the progressed Moon and progressed Mercury were in the eighth house. The aspects at the time of the New Moon were not favorable. The New Moon was opposition progressed Mercury, and transiting Venus was opposition the progressed Moon. Note also that transiting Neptune (confusion) was conjunct the New Moon and also opposition progressed Mercury (she couldn't understand why she was denied because she had a job).

Also at the time of the New Moon, transiting Pluto (natural ruler of the eighth house) was opposition progressed Venus (money), and transiting Mars (natural co-ruler of the eighth house) was retrograde and conjunct solar arc Mercury and trine solar arc Pluto. Transiting Mercury was opposition solar arc Mercury and transiting Mars. (Mars would station in early March conjunct the progressed and solar arc Sun.) Transiting Saturn was square progressed Venus, forming a t-square with transiting Pluto.

Could she have found a worse time to apply for credit? Probably, but not much more so. This is an outstanding example of how predictive astrology can be used to forestall difficulties: forewarned is forearmed. All the Mercury aspects, and Saturn in the ninth house, suggest that this would be a learning experience and

that she needed more information and knowledge before applying for credit. This is what an astrologer would have told her, had she consulted one. The problem ultimately had a positive outcome later that summer, when she applied for and was a given a secured credit card with which to build a credit history. The August New Moon was in the eighth house cusp at 15 Virgo and trine solar arc Mars (a money planet) in the fourth house (the money came from her father), which was sextile natal Pluto (natural eighth house ruler) and trine natal and progressed Neptune (co-ruler of her second house of personal resources).

ECLIPSES

Eclipses coincide with New or Full Moons and are similar in impact, although stronger and with a longer lasting effect. Their influence lasts from six to twelve months. Eclipses (at least four per year: two solar and two lunar) are particularly useful in predictive astrology when they echo major trends. An eclipse at a critical point in the chart, such as a solar arc or progressed planet conjunct a natal one, is added confirmation that a long-term event or development is in process.

Eclipses tend to have a negative connotation among the public, and even some astrologers, possibly because for centuries they were viewed that way by people who didn't understand the astronomy behind the phenomenon. Like all else in astrology, however, they are neither positive nor negative. It all depends upon what transiting, natal, progressed, and solar arc planets they aspect. The house, planet, or angle aspected by an eclipse is highly energized and a focal point for other factors in the chart. Eclipses can also help you refine an annual forecast (just as the New and Full Moons do on a monthly level).

As an example, there was an eclipse in August 1989, the month Pamela Anderson was discovered at a football game and subsequently skyrocketed to fame. That lunar eclipse at 24 Aquarius was conjunct her natal Midheaven and progressed Moon in the tenth house.

In Marilyn Monroe's chart, there were two eclipses in August 1942, both in her seventh house. Note the timing. She was married in June 1942. It's always wise to look forward a few months to see where the eclipse emphasis will be, because sometimes they act early.

Like New and Full Moons, solar and lunar eclipses usually, but not always, occur in opposing houses. For example, a solar eclipse in the tenth house could trigger a promotion or job offer that required relocation at the following lunar eclipse in the fourth. In the reverse, a lunar eclipse in the fourth house could trigger relocation in order to seek employment at the following solar eclipse. Eclipses in non-opposing houses are interpreted in the same way as New and Full Moons in non-opposing houses.

Bev's Chart: Eclipse Example

Although you should never forecast based on eclipses alone, by looking at them and their influence in Bev's chart (Chart 18) as a first step, you can begin to focus on the active themes in her life in 2009 and 2010. Bev is married, owns her home, and does quite well financially as a bartender employed at the same restaurant for more than fifteen years. She also designs jewelry.

Here are the eclipses and aspects to her chart from July 2009 to June 2010:

- July 7, 2009, lunar eclipse, 15 Capricorn 24, in the fifth house of creativity; sextile natal IC-Mercury-Venus-Saturn conjunction in the fourth house of home; conjunct solar arc Venus in the fifth house; Saturn rules the sixth house of work; Venus rules the natal Midheaven; Mercury rules the second house of money

- July 22, 2009, solar eclipse, 29 Cancer 27, in the twelfth house; conjunct the lucky natal/progressed Jupiter-Uranus conjunction; trine natal Sun in the fourth house; square natal/progressed Neptune in the third house; Jupiter rules the fifth house of creativity and co-rules the eighth of money; Uranus rules the seventh house of partnership; Neptune rules the eighth house

- August 6, 2009, lunar eclipse, 13 Aquarius 43, in the sixth house; square natal IC-Mercury-Venus-Saturn conjunction in the fourth house; trine natal Moon in the third house; Moon rules twelfth house

- December 31, 2009, lunar eclipse, 10 Cancer 15, in the eleventh house of friendship and goals (eclipse Sun in fifth house); trine IC-Mercury-Venus-Saturn conjunction in the fourth house; square natal Moon; opposition solar arc Saturn in the fifth house

- January 15, 2010, solar eclipse, 25 Capricorn 01, in the sixth house, conjunct progressed Sun; opposition natal/progressed Jupiter-Uranus conjunction; sextile natal

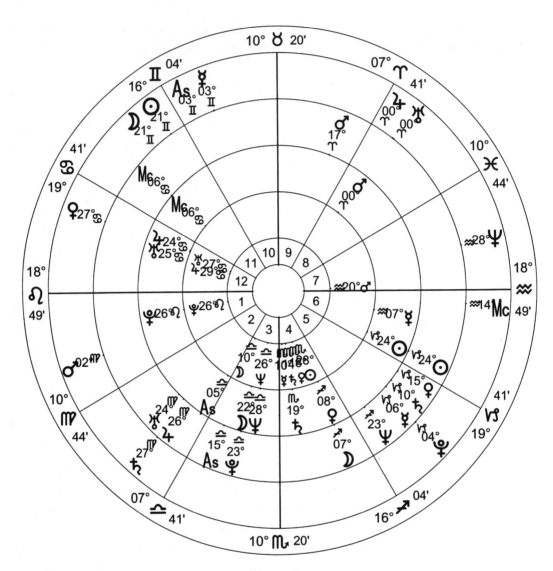

Chart 18: Bev

Innermost wheel: Birth Chart / November 20, 1954 / 10:37 pm EST / Reading, PA
Middle inner wheel: Secondary Progressed / June 12, 2010 / 1:39:17 pm EST / Reading, PA
Middle outer wheel: Directed Solar Arc / June 12, 2010 / 1:39:17 pm EST / Reading, PA
Outermost wheel: New Moon / June 12, 2010 / 4:15 am MST / Phoenix, AZ

Placidus House

Sun; square natal/progressed Neptune; trine solar arc Jupiter-Uranus conjunction

- June 26, 2010, lunar eclipse, 4 Capricorn 46, in the fifth house; opposition progressed Midheaven

Looking at these house positions and aspects, it's easy to sum up the themes active in her life at the time: home, job, career, creativity. What all these eclipses reflect is her desire for a new job, one that involved creativity that she could do from home. In other words, quit or cut back on her job hours in order to have more time to create and develop her home-based jewelry business—and of course to make more money.

The eclipses really only signal the desire and the opportunity to do what she wanted to do. The progressions, solar arcs, transiting outer planets, and New and Full Moons had to come together to create a triggering event that would launch this home-based business into the wider world.

The most outstanding aspect in her chart is the progressed/solar arc Sun in the sixth house opposition progressed Jupiter in the twelfth. In many respects, this was the opportunity she had been waiting for her entire life even if she was unaware of it. Here, the natal Sun trine to the Jupiter-Uranus conjunction is unfolding, and because the natal energy is a positive trine, the progression/solar arc will be the same. Notice how the progressed/solar arc Sun will move forward and aspect progressed Uranus and then natal Uranus and Jupiter during the following four years. So this was not just a small window of opportunity but an ongoing one. Remember: always look at the predictive chart in motion,

with the planets continually advancing in forward or retrograde motion.

Also among the progressions is a sextile between progressed Mercury (ruler of the second house of income) and Venus (Midheaven ruler). Another aspect, whose significance could easily be overlooked, and which is a key part of the triggering event, is the progressed Midheaven sesquisquare natal Mars, ruler of the ninth house and co-ruler of the fourth house.

Solar arc Mercury was opposition the solar arc Midheaven, indicating the possibility of earning money (second house ruler Mercury) through a creative venture (fifth house) that could be a new career direction (Midheaven). Also of interest is solar arc Mars in the ninth house trine the natal Ascendant.

The transiting outer planets made many contacts to her chart. Of major significance was the transiting Jupiter-Uranus conjunction conjunct progressed Mars (in the eighth house and ruler of the ninth), which can be interpreted as a surprisingly unexpected windfall. Transiting Pluto was conjunct solar arc Mercury and opposition the progressed and solar arc Midheavens. Sixth-house ruler, Saturn, transiting the second house, was conjunct solar arc Jupiter (fifth house ruler and eighth house co-ruler) and sextile the natal Jupiter-Uranus conjunction.

So, what happened? At the June 12, 2010, New Moon in Gemini in her eleventh house, a friend told her she'd read about another designer whose jewelry was featured in the *Sports Illustrated* annual swimsuit edition. Two days later, on June 14, Bev sent samples of her jewelry to the magazine for consideration. She tracked the package and knew it arrived at its destination on June 17. Several days later, on June 23, she received an e-mail and phone call to let her know her jewelry had been selected.

The New Moon was trine her progressed Moon in the third house of communication (mail, e-mail, phone call). In the New Moon chart, Mercury (in the tenth house and second house ruler) was square Mars (ruler of the ninth house of publishing, and co-ruler of the fourth house), and both planets were aspecting her solar arc Mars in the ninth house (semisquare/sesquisquare). Additionally, Venus in the New Moon chart was conjunct natal Uranus-Jupiter, sextile transiting Saturn, and square natal/progressed Neptune. It was a perfect setup.

She sent the jewelry to the magazine on June 14, with transiting Venus (Midheaven ruler) trine progressed Mars in the eighth house. Transiting Venus was also trine the transiting Jupiter-Uranus conjunction. On that date, transiting Mercury was at 7 Gemini, trine progressed Mercury in the sixth house.

Why did she hear the positive news when she did? Again, looking at the New Moon chart, the Sun had advanced to 2 Cancer on the 23rd, where it was sextile Mars at 2 Virgo, setting off the New Moon chart Mercury-Mars square and its contacts to her chart. Venus in the New Moon chart had moved forward to 10 Leo, where it was square her natal Midheaven, and Mercury was then at 26 Gemini, square solar arc Jupiter in the second house and ruler of the fifth. Mars, which moves more slowly than the other two planets, was at 8 Virgo on the 23rd, square progressed Venus and semisquare progressed Jupiter.

The Moon is often the final trigger, so you should look to its position for timing and when the other already identified aspects might be activated. In this case, the Moon was in late degrees of Scorpio when she received the e-mail, conjunct natal Sun and trine the natal Jupiter-Uranus conjunction.

What this example illustrates is the importance of:

- Eclipses as indicators of trends when aspecting natal, progressed, and solar arc planets
- Progressions and solar arcs as trends and the natal chart unfolding
- Transiting outer planets as trends, especially when aspecting progressions and solar arcs
- Multiple aspects confirming the event
- New Moon and its aspects that indicate an eventful month according to the trend indications
- Transiting planets as triggers for all of the predictive tools

TIMING EVENTS WITH NEW MOONS, FULL MOONS, AND ECLIPSES

New Moons and solar eclipses generally relate to ego and identity, while Full Moons and lunar eclipses have an emotion-based component. Because the Sun and Moon are conjunct at the New Moon/solar eclipse, these events are symbolic of increased focus and unified effort. At the Full Moon/lunar eclipse, however, the Sun and Moon are opposite each other, bringing a relationship emphasis into events, which is common with the opposition aspect. At the outset, a New Moon/solar eclipse concentrates its energy in one house/sign, while the Full Moon/lunar eclipse involves two opposing houses.

You can use the guidelines below as a starting point when interpreting these events in the houses, while remembering that the influence of an eclipse is much longer than a New or Full Moon. In order to get a true picture of what the event might indicate in your chart, you should also look at these factors:

- Aspects made to your natal, progressed, and solar arc planets and angles and their house positions

- Aspects to the ruler of the house where the New Moon, Full Moon, or eclipse occurs, e.g., if Gemini is on the cusp of the house, look for aspects to natal, progressed, and solar arc Mercury, and aspects from transiting Mercury to these charts

- Aspects to the ruler of the sign of the New Moon, Full Moon, or eclipse, and aspects from that transiting planet to the natal, progressed, and solar arc planets and angles

- The house or houses ruled by any natal, progressed, or solar arc planet that is aspected by the New Moon, Full Moon, or eclipse

- The houses with planets to which aspects are made by New Moon, Full Moon, or eclipse. For example, if a New Moon occurs in the second house and is square a natal, progressed, or solar arc planet in

the fifth house, you could have additional expenses involving a child or social event. If the New Moon were trine a planet in the sixth house, you could receive a raise or bonus that month

- Any transiting outer planets aspected by the New Moon, Full Moon, or eclipse, and their house positions, particularly if any of the outer planets aspect your natal, progressed, or solar arc planets or angles

- A t-square involving the New Moon, Full Moon, or eclipse and natal, progressed, or solar arc planets often indicates a change in plans. For example, a seventh house New Moon involved in a t-square with planets in the fourth and tenth houses could indicate a change in a domestic project or event because of your partner's career commitments

- Retrograde inner planets (Mercury, Venus, and Mars) that will aspect the New Moon, Full Moon, or eclipse degree during their retrograde cycle

Camilla Parker-Bowles: Timing Example

Camilla Parker-Bowles (Chart 19) and Prince Charles were married April 9, 2005. The wedding had been scheduled for April 8, but because Charles attended the funeral of Pope John Paul II held on the 8th, the ceremony was delayed by one day. The Pope died April 2.

Charles and Camilla announced their engagement February 10, two days after the New Moon at 20 Aquarius 16 in Camilla's seventh house of partnership, representing the marriage and Charles. The wedding would not

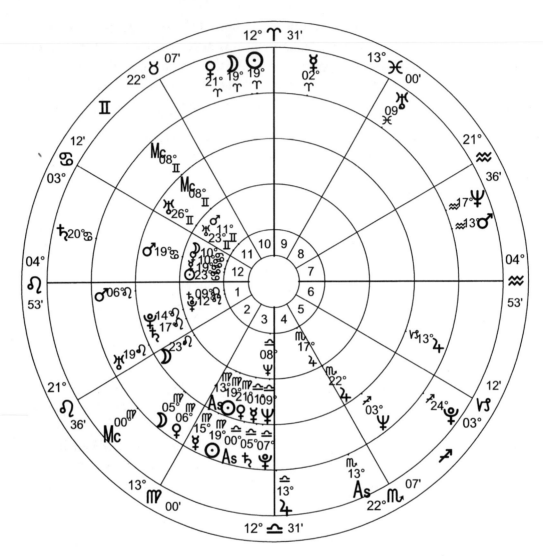

Chart 19: Camilla Parker-Bowles
Innermost wheel: Birth Chart / July 17, 1947 / 7:10 am BDST / London, England
Middle inner wheel: Secondary Progressed / April 8, 2005 / 1:00:10 BST / London, England
Middle outer wheel: Directed Solar Arc / April 8, 2005 / 1:00:10 BST / London, England
Outermost wheel: Event Transits / April 8, 2005 / 9:32 pm BST / London, England
Placidus House

have been the following month, when the New Moon was at 19 Pisces 53 in her ninth house. Both of these New Moons aspected natal Uranus, ruler of her seventh house. The February New Moon was trine natal Uranus, and the Pisces New Moon was square natal Uranus. The March New Moon in the ninth house of travel was square (difficulty) Uranus (Charles), and opposition (separation) Camilla's progressed/ solar arc Sun (self) and progressed Venus (partner) in the third house of quick trips. Given these indications, you could predict that her fiancé would travel unexpectedly sometime during the four weeks following the March New Moon. When he would travel is the question, and for that, we look to the next Full Moon.

The March 25 Full Moon at 5 Libra 18 in Camilla's third house (Sun in the ninth house) was conjunct solar arc Saturn, co-ruler of her seventh house. This configuration with Saturn indicates responsibilities involving travel, and Saturn is also the planet of delays. Although the trip could have occurred at the Full Moon, better indicators are the rulers of Camilla's third and ninth houses.

Mercury, the third house ruler, was retrograde at the time of the Full Moon. Looking forward in the ephemeris, it shows Mercury at 5 Aries (opposition the Full Moon position) on April 2, the date the pope died, and April 3. Jupiter and Neptune rule the ninth house, and on April 2 and 3, Neptune was opposition Camilla's progressed Saturn and square natal Jupiter. But a further trigger is necessary: the transiting Moon. The decision to postpone the wedding was likely made after the transiting Moon entered Camilla's seventh house in the early afternoon of April 3. The announcement of the postponement was made the next day as the transiting Moon was square natal Jupiter (and conjunct transiting Neptune).

There are also indications of a delay in the New Moon/solar eclipse chart of April 8. This New Moon at 19 Aries 05 in Camilla's tenth house of status was square transiting Saturn, co-ruler of her seventh house. The Sun-Moon conjunction was conjunct transiting Venus, also square Saturn. Because the Sun and Moon are in a degree earlier than Saturn and thus approaching the aspect, is a strong indication of a delay. Going through the list of guidelines above, these are other indications:

Mars, as ruler of Aries, is the ruler of the house of the New Moon, and this New Moon was square her progressed Mars.

Mars, as ruler of Aries, is also the ruler of the sign of the New Moon, which was square her progressed Mars.

At the New Moon, transiting Mars (ruler of the house and sign of the New Moon) in the seventh house of Camilla's chart was opposition her progressed Pluto (frustration, and possibly a disagreement about the delay).

The New Moon in the tenth house was square transiting Saturn, co-ruler of Camilla's seventh house (delay due to her fiancé's official role and responsibilities), but also trine natal Saturn (she recognized and accepted the need for delay).

At the time of the wedding on April 9, the transiting Moon was just past a sextile to Camilla's progressed Uranus, transiting Venus was sextile natal Uranus, and the angles of the wedding chart were almost exactly the same (within a degree) as the natal angles in Camilla's chart.

NEW MOONS, FULL MOONS AND ECLIPSES IN THE HOUSES

A New Moon, which is a Sun-Moon conjunction, represents personal initiative, and its house placement is where you will invest more of your energy in the following four weeks. The effect is stronger and longer lasting with a solar eclipse—six to twelve months. In addition to the house location of the New Moon/solar eclipse, look for aspects to planets in your natal, progressed, and solar arc charts. The house placement of these planets as well as the houses they rule in your natal chart will offer further insights into possible events.

Events that occur in your life or that you initiate at a New Moon begin to move toward completion at the following Full Moon. The same happens with a lunar eclipse, but like a solar eclipse, the effect is stronger and longer lasting. Because a Full Moon is a Sun-Moon opposition, events usually involve other people (a relationship) who have a role in concluding the matter that occurred near the New Moon/solar eclipse. As in all opposition aspects, the objective is to find a middle ground, the solution that is agreeable to all involved.

For example, your energies will be focused on career matters during the month with a New Moon in your tenth house. However, two weeks after the New Moon, when the Full Moon occurs in your fourth house, you could realize that you've been neglecting your home or family—or have that pointed out by a family member. Because the time frame is short, it probably won't become much of an issue as it will quickly pass. With the stronger and longer influence of a solar/lunar eclipse, however, a family relationship could go through serious difficulties and possibly end if you are unable to achieve a healthy balance between the two areas of life. Equally possible with the eclipse is career-related relocation that disrupts family life.

First House

New Moon/Solar Eclipse: You may make changes in your appearance and habits, and also begin new personal ventures such as an exercise program or hobby project. This influence also often indicates a rise in popularity. It's main emphasis, however, is to encourage you to define your strengths and weaknesses and how best to develop and use them to become the best you can be.

Full Moon/Lunar Eclipse: You seek emotionally satisfying people and mutually supportive relationships under this influence. A partnership or close relationship could end because it no longer fulfills your emotional needs, or because your expectations were unrealistic. This is an unfavorable time for negotiations or serious discussions, because there is an overall lack of cooperation.

Second House

New Moon/Solar Eclipse: This energy emphasizes material values, financial status, and possessions, and urges you to examine your overall attitude about money. Your income may increase and you can add to savings and possibly receive a gift. But ego needs could cause you to go into debt to get what you want. Banking and budgeting are practical outlets for this influence.

Full Moon/Lunar Eclipse: Your emotional security is linked to financial security under this influence that advises against spending beyond routine purchases. There can be extra expenses or delays in expected income, and it can be difficult to get credit or a loan. Your goal is to learn how to stabilize your finances through budgeting, saving, and financial planning.

Third House

New Moon/Solar Eclipse: Activities surround siblings and neighbors as well as community events, projects, and involvement. You also can expect a higher volume of calls, mail, social-media contacts, and e-mail. This is generally a favorable time for test-taking, reviewing documents, and errands and weekend trips. Your goal is to share ideas and knowledge, and to gain practical, everyday information.

Full Moon/Lunar Eclipse: This time frame can be unfavorable for travel, contact with in-laws, and matters related to education. You also should be cautious about what you put in writing because your words can be misinterpreted, and important information may not be received or conveyed. Legal matters can be stalled or surrounded with difficulties. Much of your thinking is colored by your feelings.

Fourth House

New Moon/Solar Eclipse: Events are related to domestic matters, including the possibility of relocation, home improvements, parental responsibilities, and a roommate or relative moving in or out of the home. Conditions or circumstances may require household changes. You can successfully deal with life and family issues at this time and better understand your family members and your role within the family.

Full Moon/Lunar Eclipse: Emotional overtones color family life during this time when domestic and family security and stability are all-important. Despite the effort, there may be difficulties between parent and child, or with a roommate. It can be a challenge to balance family and career responsibilities, and it may be necessary to change a home office or to relocate for employment.

Fifth House

New Moon/Solar Eclipse: During this time many events are related to children, romantic relationships, sports, socializing, investments, creative endeavors, and generally anything that brings you pleasure. Growth can come through all of these ego-satisfying activities. A child could leave home for college or to live independently–or move back to the family home.

Full Moon/Lunar Eclipse: Your desire now is to achieve the feeling of satisfaction that comes from positive activities with children, a romantic relationship, sports, creative endeavors, or other leisure-time pursuits. Your children may need extra attention now, and they or other people can upset social plans or cause difficulties in a romantic relationship. There can be conflict with friends.

Sixth House

New Moon/Solar Eclipse: This is a good time to apply for or begin a job, and relationships with coworkers and supervisors are generally favorable as long as you keep your ego in check. You also could begin an exercise program now, acquire a new pet, purchase appliances, or handle repairs. This influence is primarily centered on job and service, however, and being helpful to others.

Full Moon/Lunar Eclipse: Your work environment, including relationships with coworkers, is directly linked to your health and emotional well-being now. This influence can also indicate involvement in gossip or rumors on the job, as well as an attempt by someone to sabotage your efforts or play the blame game. Keep personal information to yourself even if you feel secure with a coworker relationship.

Seventh House

New Moon/Solar Eclipse: Partners and close relationships are in focus now and you have a strong need to interact with people. But you'll also have contact with competitors who could try to sidetrack your hopes and aspirations. Negotiations can be effective if you're open-minded and inclined to cooperate with others, and find the ideal compromise. Engagement or marriage is possible.

Full Moon/Lunar Eclipse: Make it a priority to listen to other viewpoints and to compromise when necessary, both of which will benefit your emotional connection to other people. There could be challenges with others regarding important issues when someone opposes your plans, which you will take more personally at this time. This influence can also result in an engagement (or marriage) that was delayed for some reason.

Eighth House

New Moon/Solar Eclipse: Family funds are in focus, as are joint resources, spousal maintenance, taxes, debtors, and your partner's money, income, and property. An inheritance is possible (more likely with an eclipse) under a New Moon, which can increase family funds in other ways,

such as a raise, tax refund, or small windfall. Do be cautious with loans, however, and resist the urge to borrow more than you can afford.

Full Moon/Lunar Eclipse: You should save for unexpected expenses prior to this event, which could trigger an increase in insurance premiums, income, or property taxes. This is an unfavorable time to apply for or co-sign for a loan or sign related documents, and news of an audit could be received. Decline financial requests and offers that sound too good to be true, despite the emotional tug you feel.

Ninth House

New Moon/Solar Eclipse: This is an ideal time to look to the future and formulate long-range plans. You may hear from people at a distance, travel, experience other cultures, be involved with in-laws or legal matters, or be called for jury duty. This influence also emphasizes ethics, and challenges you to assess your personal life philosophy in a search for truth and knowledge.

Full Moon/Lunar Eclipse: Difficulties with in-laws are possible, and travel plans could be delayed or cancelled, possibly because a partner is unable to make the trip. Be cautious about what you promise now, and don't put too much faith in what others promise you. This is an inopportune time to be involved in legal matters. Look inward. Spirituality (or religion) can provide emotional support.

Tenth House

New Moon/Solar Eclipse: What you seek and need most at this time is solid evidence of advancement in the wider world. Your focus is on career and status issues under this influence, which can trigger a promotion and bring praise, honors, or recognition from supervisors. Contact with government entities is also possible, and you could be more involved with a parent.

Full Moon/Lunar Eclipse: Your greatest sense of emotional satisfaction now comes from career-related events. A job change is possible. You also could have extra parental responsibilities or obligations (for your children or your parents), and it can be difficult to find a balance between career and domestic matters. This can trigger workplace or domestic conflict, and difficulties can also arise regarding home ownership or rental property.

Eleventh House

New Moon/Solar Eclipse: This can be one of the lighter months or periods in your life, filled with social events and time with friends, as well as networking opportunities. Groups, teamwork, and organizations are in focus, as are humanitarian endeavors. Take this influence a step further and set aside some time to review and update your short- and long-term goals.

Full Moon/Lunar Eclipse: You feel strong bonds with some friends now. But others may ask too much of you in the way of favors, or expect you to carry more than your fair share of the load in group and organizational activities. There can be a clash with a friend and/or romantic interest, or your parental responsibilities could interfere with time for your own interests.

Twelfth House

New Moon/Solar Eclipse: Confidential information is often communicated with this placement that also encourages you to review events during the past several months as preparation for the New Moon in your first house, which will occur following this one. You also may be involved with someone who is hospitalized or otherwise confined in an institutional setting. Your hidden side, including intuition and suppressed desires and talents, may come forth now.

Full Moon/Lunar Eclipse: This position often triggers rumors and gossip, and hidden matters and unknown enemies can come to light. You should be cautious with medication and chemical substances, and also make rest and relaxation priorities. It's possible you may be required to care for someone who is ill, and your job can be demanding with people trying to pressure you to handle their responsibilities. Awareness can come through intuition and subconscious thoughts.

SIX-MONTH TIMING

Every year, from about October through the next March (or April, depending upon the date of the New Moon) the monthly New and Full Moons are at about the same degrees. Only the sign changes. So, from the Libra-Aries New Moon-Full Moon in October through the Aries-Libra New Moon-Full Moon in April, nearly the same degrees of the signs are repeated. This can be an important forecasting tool when studying the trends in your life. If you have a natal, progressed, or solar arc planet at the degrees of the New Moons and Full Moons during these months of the year, that planet will be activated month after month. This, along with the other forecast indicators, can show you how events will unfold as the New and Full Moons progress through your houses.

As an example, consider an October Libra New Moon in the sixth house conjunct natal Venus in and ruling the same house. The October New Moon brings a job offer. In the next month, with the Scorpio New Moon in the seventh house, you get better acquainted with coworkers, but because this is a semi-sextile to natal Venus, it also represents a period of adjustment to varying personalities.

In November, the Sagittarius New Moon in your eighth house is sextile natal Venus, indicating an opportunity to make more money. December brings the Capricorn New Moon in your ninth house, where it is square natal Venus; this could indicate issues surrounding requested time off for holiday travel. January's New Moon in Aquarius, your tenth house, is trine natal Venus, indicating an easy flow of energy between your daily work (sixth house) and your career (tenth house); in essence, you've reached a comfort level with the new job and people recognize your skills and talents.

February's New Moon is in your eleventh house, forming an inconjunct with natal Venus, prompting you to assess and update your job/career goals and possibly stretch yourself by taking charge of a group project. March then brings the New Moon in opposition to natal Venus, when you'll be ready to slow the pace after having given the new job your all in the past months. This is also a time to reassess what you have accomplished since beginning the job.

Remember that the Full Moons in each of these months are also at nearly the same degree (although different from the New Moon degree and thus possibly aspecting other planets in your chart) month after month and occupying the opposite houses from the New Moon. Through this six-month time frame, you will experience your new job from the perspective of every house in your chart.

SOLAR, LUNAR, AND PLANETARY RETURNS

Return charts are excellent supplemental predictive tools. Used in conjunction with progressions, solar arcs, outer planet transit, and eclipses (and, of course, the natal chart), these charts also show trends. Their period of influence varies from a month for the lunar return to a year for the solar return to decades for the outer planet returns. The most effective trend setters are the inner planets (Sun, Moon, Mercury, Venus, and Mars) because their influence is measurable within a period from a month to about two years. A Saturn return occurs only every twenty-eight to thirty years, and it takes Uranus about eighty-four years to complete its cycle.

A return chart is simply a chart for the moment that the transiting planet returns to its natal position. The lunar return occurs twelve (and sometimes thirteen) times each year, or once a month, because the Moon travels through the zodiac about every twenty-eight days. The solar return is an annual event, and for Mercury it can be anywhere from eleven to thirteen months, depending upon its retrograde cycle. A Venus return occurs about every eighteen months, and Mars returns to its natal place about every two years.

These charts are read much like natal charts, applying the same principles of interpretation, such as house placement, quadrant and hemisphere emphasis, the Ascendant sign, and aspects. Most astrology calculation software will automatically generate return charts.

There has been much debate among astrologers as to whether the return charts should be calculated for the birth place (as you would a progressed or solar arc chart) or for your current place of residence. The consensus is the current place of residence, but you should try both to see which works better for your chart and your life. If you live close to where you were born, there will be little difference between the two charts.

Some people erroneously believe they can alter the universe by going to a new location just for their birthday. This does not work, and you would quickly see that the solar return chart for the year has no resemblance to what is happening in your life. So don't be pulled into thinking that by manipulating the chart location you can create a year that's good for romance, career, money, or anything else.

Solar and lunar return charts are the most commonly used, although you can gain additional insights by studying the other planetary return charts. The energy, activities, and influences represented in all of these charts can be activated by transiting planets, New and Full Moons, and eclipses during the time they are in effect. This is especially true with any major configurations in the return chart (stellium, t-square, grand cross, etc.) and with planets conjunct the angles.

SOLAR AND LUNAR RETURNS

When working with solar (and other) return charts, it's useful to look at them on their own and also with the natal chart, while keeping in mind any significant progressions, solar arcs, and eclipses that are in effect at the time. Also check the positions of eclipses during the time the return chart is in effect and where they fall in the natal and return charts.

You can get a general idea of the year's emphasis by looking at the quadrant and hemisphere emphasis (those with the most planets) in the solar return chart. The modes of the houses (angular, succedent, cadent) indicate the approach to activities and how they will evolve. Here are some guidelines:

- Southern Hemisphere (top half of the chart, houses seven through twelve): The emphasis is on the outer world, other people, relationships, recognition, career, and leadership. This hemisphere represents an outgoing nature and an interest in interacting with people.

- Northern Hemisphere (bottom half of the chart, houses one through six). This hemisphere represents a more introspective and self-reliant approach out of the public eye with an emphasis on home, family, work, job, service, and the community and neighbors.

- Western Hemisphere (right side of chart, houses four through nine). The emphasis is on other people (family, partner, coworkers) and interacting with them, and you're responsive to their wants and needs.

- Eastern Hemisphere (left side of chart, houses ten through three). A majority of planets here represents self-awareness, self-reliance, and self-motivation, as well as an emphasis on career and friendship.

- First Quadrant (houses one through three). With this quadrant emphasized, the emphasis is on independence and action, and personal needs, desires, and interests take priority.

- Second Quadrant (houses four through six). Although this quadrant indicates self-direction, there is also an emphasis on relationships with family, children, and coworkers.

- Third Quadrant (houses seven through nine). Many planets here emphasize a focus on other people, including partners, debtors, teachers, counselors, and clergy.

- Fourth Quadrant (houses ten through twelve). This quadrant represents self-motivation and teamwork, and can indicate status and recognition; introspection is also emphasized.

- Angular Houses (first, fourth, seventh, tenth). This emphasis indicates new endeavors, but trying to do it all can result in little being accomplished.

- Succedent Houses (second, fifth, eighth, eleventh). Many planets in these houses emphasize completion of endeavors, but there can be resistance to change.

- Cadent Houses (third, sixth, ninth, twelfth). The emphasis is on changing conditions with many planets in these houses, as well as intellectual activity, but forces can be scattered.

Keeping the big-picture factors in the chart in mind, the next step is to look at the solar return angles. You can determine more trends for the year ahead by noting whether the signs on the angles are cardinal, fixed, or mutable. Sometimes the signs will be in the same category, and at others you will see, for example, mutable on the Ascendant-Descendant and cardinal on the Midheaven-IC.

- Cardinal signs (Aries, Cancer, Libra, Capricorn) indicate new endeavors and a high level of activity with a focus on self, home

and family, relationships, and career. But premature action is also associated with these signs.

- Fixed signs (Taurus, Leo, Scorpio, Aquarius) are related to personal and joint finances, recreation, children, and friends. These signs dislike change, however, and prefer stability, so the tendency is to maintain the status quo, or to remain stuck in a rut.

- Mutable signs (Gemini, Virgo, Sagittarius, Pisces) on the angles indicate a year focused on work, service, education, communication, knowledge, information, and travel. However, with these signs on the angles, it can be difficult to focus on goals.

Take particular note of a solar return chart with the last few or first few degrees of a sign on an angle. The last few degrees indicate a year during which something is coming to an end or being concluded, while the first few degrees signal a year for a new endeavor. A planet in the last few degrees also reflects a door closing or the completion of a cycle.

It's also important to note where in the natal chart the solar (or other planetary) return Ascendant falls. This adds additional information about the year's focus of activity. The natal chart house cusp closest to the solar return Ascendant can also be significant if it falls in a house different from the solar return Ascendant. Follow the same procedure with the planet appropriate to the return, such as Mercury for the Mercury return, and Venus for the Venus return. The house(s) ruled by the planet is one where much of the activity represented by that planet will occur.

The first planet to rise in the return chart (the one closest to the Ascendant, beginning with the first house, often carries added significance. It can indicate, along with the Ascendant sign, the main emphasis for the year. Any major configurations involving this planet, the house it (and the other planets in the configuration) rules, and where it falls in the natal chart add additional details and depth to the interpretation. You also should look at the house in the natal chart ruled by the rising planet, being sure to check whether it is being aspected by progression, solar arc, or outer transiting planets.

A return chart with the same rising sign (Ascendant) as the natal chart often indicates a momentous year in addition to being one focused on the individual. This is even more true if the Midheaven is also the same. When the angles are the same, the natal chart planets can fall in the same houses in the return chart. Take special note of any conjunctions between natal and return planets, because there will be extra emphasis in that area of life in that year.

You also can glean much information by considering the polar opposite house. For example, if the Sun is in the third house, incorporate ninth house influences in your interpretation.

When studying a return chart, look at the planets in the return chart houses, their aspects, the houses they rule, where they fall in the natal chart, and how they aspect natal planets. Although these interpretations are much the same as when reading a natal chart, they do need to be blended with the natural inclinations shown in the natal chart. For example, if you have a natal Capricorn Sun and Virgo Ascendant, with Leo on the solar return Ascendant, you won't suddenly step into a star-studded life.

Rather, the natural leadership qualities of Leo can enhance your ambitious Capricorn Sun and hard-working Virgo Ascendant.

Use a smaller orb for return chart aspects than you would for a natal chart–about five degrees. Also look for planetary configurations such as a t-square, grand cross, or grand trine. These can help pinpoint key areas of activity for the year.

Sometimes the obvious choice for a return chart doesn't reveal what you expect it will. If, for example, the other forecasting tools indicate the possibility of a marriage, don't rely solely on the Venus return chart in addition to the solar return. Also look at the Mercury and Mars return charts. They may show the expected event more clearly, depending upon when the return occurs. Return charts that occur closer to the birth date are often more accurate.

JIMMY CARTER

Jimmy Carter was elected United States president in 1976 but lost his reelection bid in 1980. The solar and lunar return charts illustrate the interpretive techniques used for these charts, and it's easy to see how each set of solar and lunar returns for different years and months indicates a different outcome to the election.

Before looking at Jimmy Carter's solar and lunar returns, it's important to first study some of the other predictive factors in his chart in the time leading up to the election (Chart 20).

He was in a period of good fortune with a progressed Venus-progressed Jupiter sextile, and because it involved the second house (Jupiter in this house) and the eighth (Venus rules the eighth), he had plenty of money to finance the

KEYWORDS FOR THE HOUSES

First House: Self-expression, initiative, self-development, personal interests, overall personal viewpoint and direction, self-projection

Second House: Finances, values, income, assets, possessions, self-worth

Third House: Communication, neighbors, relatives, errands and quick trips, learning, intellectual interests and general mindset

Fourth House: Home, family, property, endings, beginnings, domestic environment

Fifth House: Children, creativity, recreation, investments, romance

Sixth House: Work, service, health, pets, workplace environment and coworkers

Seventh House: Partnership, cooperation, compromise, competitors, admirers, the public

Eighth House: Joint resources, debtors, loans, insurance, inheritance

Ninth House: Travel, knowledge, higher education, life philosophy, legal matters, spirituality, religion, foreign affairs

Tenth House: Career, status, recognition, authority figures, government, honors

Eleventh House: Friendship, groups, organizations, humanitarian activities, goals, teamwork, supporters

Twelfth House: Secrets, gossip, institutions, solitude

KEYWORDS FOR PLANETS

Sun: Ego, central focus, honors, creativity, children, recreation, romance, personal accomplishments, self-confidence

Moon: Change, emotions, restlessness, family, the public, domestic activities

Mercury: Communication, learning, work, health

Venus: Love, partner, beauty, attraction, comfort, social events, fun

Mars: Action, energy, conflict, challenges, risk, courage, impatience

Jupiter: Good fortune, expansion, knowledge, higher education, the future, legal matters, travel

Saturn: Ambition, restriction, responsibility, authority, government, limitation, insecurity

Uranus: Innovation, independence, freedom, the unexpected, enlightenment, change

Neptune: Illusion, vision, imagination, idealism, creativity, secrets, inspiration

Pluto: Transformation, power, control, stress, intensity, the subconscious

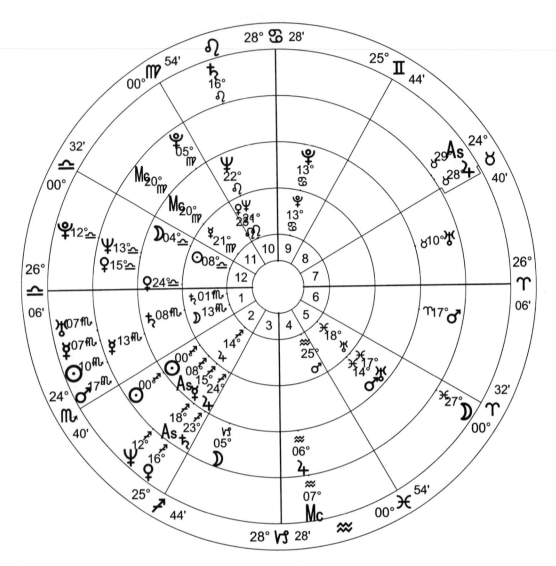

Chart 20: Jimmy Carter
Innermost wheel: Birth Chart / October 1, 1924 / 7:00 am CST / Plains, Georgia
Middle inner wheel: Secondary Progressed / November 2, 1976 / 8:48:31 CST / Plains, Georgia
Middle outer wheel: Directed Solar Arc / November 2, 1976 / 8:48:31 CST / Plains, Georgia
Outermost wheel: 1976 Election Transits / November 2, 1976 / 6:00 pm EST / Washington DC
Placidus House

campaign and was surrounded by supporters. Overall, because Venus is his Sun and Ascendant ruler, he was in a period of high self-confidence and self-worth—a definite advantage for a candidate. On election day, transiting Jupiter in the eighth house was sextile his natal Midheaven. Mars, ruler of the sixth house of work was sesquisquare the natal Midheaven.

The most telling influence, however, was Saturn in the tenth house, a transit that brings great rewards or a plunging downfall and loss of status. Saturn was slowing to station retrograde at the end of November, and thus was trine progressed Mercury and natal Jupiter (wider orb permitted with a stationing outer planet) for about two months. Transiting Uranus in his first house was conjunct progressed Saturn (a relocation aspect, because Saturn rules Carter's natal fourth house). He also benefitted from an October 23 solar eclipse at 29 Libra 56, conjunct his natal Ascendant and square his natal Midheaven. November 6 brought a lunar eclipse at 14 Taurus 41 that activated the natal Moon-Uranus-Pluto grand trine in his chart. The Moon rules his natal Midheaven. He was in the right place at the right time with the right message and aspects to appeal to the voters and the media.

In Jimmy Carter's 1976 solar return chart (Chart 21), the planetary emphasis is on the southern hemisphere (seven planets), western hemisphere (eight planets) and the third quadrant (seven planets). At first glance, it might be surprising that someone could be elected president without a group of planets in the southern hemisphere, fourth quadrant, and the tenth house of career, but there are other indications, including solar return aspects, progressions, solar arcs, and transits.

In the context of a presidential *candidate*, the hemisphere and quadrant emphasis is logical. Anyone in this position would be in continual communication with campaign advisors, and in his case, there was also much media attention directed toward his brother and daughter. Contact with the public is represented by the Moon (the public) in the third quadrant (relating to other people).

It's also important to remember that this solar return was in effect during about the first eight months of his term of office, where it would have had the longest influence. As the solar return indicates, Jimmy Carter and his aides and associates were dubbed the "Georgia Mafia"—Washington outsiders who followed their own agenda and shunned long-established political "rules and regulations." In essence, they did not play the Washington game. This also fits with the solar return's emphasis on hometown people close to him.

The house activity emphasis is evenly distributed with three planets in angular houses, four in succedent houses, and three in cadent houses. Succedent house emphasis is slightly stronger, indicating completion of his goal, but also his unwillingness to change and adapt to Washington ways.

Jimmy Carter's 1976 solar return chart has mutable signs on the angles, indicating the central themes of communication, service, and travel, all of which are fitting for a presidential candidate and president. The Ascendant at 27 Gemini 49 is one of the last few degrees of this sign, and can be interpreted as his completing a personal quest. The Midheaven is in early

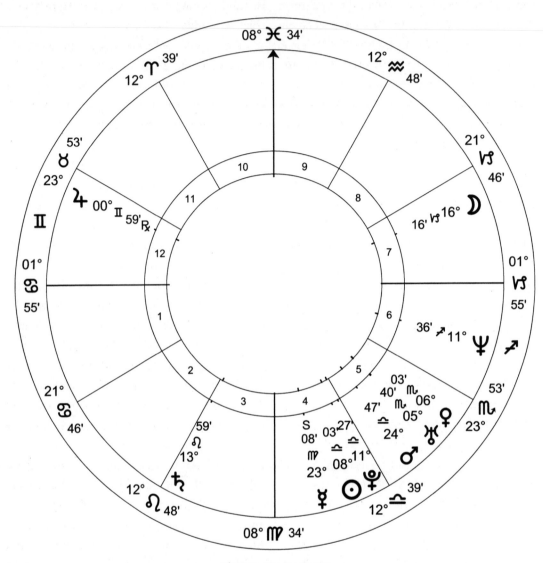

Chart 21: Jimmy Carter
Solar Return / September 30, 1976 / 10:56:55 pm EDT / Washington DC / Placidus House

degrees of Pisces, reflective of his new endeavor. The solar return Ascendant is in the natal ninth house of travel, and sextile natal Venus and Neptune in the natal tenth house, and trine progressed Venus and the natal Ascendant.

The ruler of the Gemini solar return Ascendant is Mercury, which is in the solar return fourth house, emphasizing home and family (the Georgia Mafia), and relocation to a new residence (the White House). Mercury is retrograde, so the move would be a temporary one. It also indicates that his actions and words could be misunderstood and his decisions subject to change–a trend that could amplify any tendency of his natal Libra Sun and Ascendant for indecisiveness. Jimmy Carter's natal Mercury in Virgo in the eleventh house of friendship, groups, and teamwork is only two degrees from the solar return Mercury in the fourth house. Mercury in Virgo can be the ultimate micro-manager, which was often cited in the media, and the placement of these two Mercurys in the fourth house suggests he should have relied more on himself than on the hometown people that accompanied him to Washington.

This solar return chart is particularly interesting in that the fourth house is the house of endings as well as beginnings, and Mercury, ruler of the late-degree Ascendant (endings) is in that house. He was ending one phase of his life and beginning a new one, although the retrograde Mercury indicates it would be a bumpy transition.

Since we know Jimmy Carter was elected president in 1976, there should be strong career indications in the solar return chart. Saturn, the universal career planet, is in Leo (leadership, recognition, popularity) in the third house of communication. It rules the solar return eighth house of other people's resources, which he surely needed as president, and co-rules the ninth house of travel and foreign affairs. Saturn's house placement, and co-rulership of the ninth house, and sextile to the solar return Sun-Pluto conjunction (Sun rules the solar return third house) also reflect his popularity with the media at the time of his election.

Neptune, ruler of the solar return Midheaven (career) is in the sixth house of work. This placement and rulership indicates that service rather than power was his main motivation in running for office. (He was a strong proponent of human rights and establishing a national energy policy.) But Neptune in the sixth house also reflects his idealism about his job and the potential for illusion and deception by coworkers (his key staff members). Jupiter, co-ruler of Neptune, is in the twelfth house of secrets and solitude. Because Jupiter rules the Descendant, his closest key advisors were well-intentioned. But there were undoubtedly difficulties with some of these people because the solar return Moon is in Capricorn (restriction) in the seventh house and square (conflict) Pluto (power, control), ruler of the sixth house. Possibly the advice he received from some of these people affected his image with the public (Moon).

There is a strong element of change in Jimmy Carter's solar return chart, beginning with the mutable sign angles and Mercury (Ascendant ruler) and Neptune (Midheaven ruler) in mutable signs. Indeed, he ran on a platform of government reorganization. The solar return Venus-Uranus conjunction (change) in a fixed sign (Scorpio) is trine the solar return Midheaven. He saw government (tenth house) change (Uranus) as his mission (Venus rules his Sun sign).

The powerful position to which he was elected is seen in the solar return Sun-Pluto conjunction, both of which are sextile Neptune in the sixth house, and Saturn—the universal career planet— is in the third.

Turning to the natal chart, there are a number of interesting contacts with solar return planets. Solar return Mars conjunct the natal Ascendant in the twelfth house is sextile his Venus-Neptune (charm and popularity) in the natal tenth house. Mars rules his natal sixth (work) and seventh (partners) houses, and the solar return eleventh (goals, supporters). This placement indicates that there was much behind the scenes activity with advisors and key staff members regarding his lofty goals (Venus in the natal tenth ruling the natal twelfth and first houses)–and probably conflict as well (solar return Mars in the natal twelfth). Solar return Mars is also trine natal Mars in the fourth house (Georgia Mafia).

The solar return Moon in the natal third house is opposition natal Pluto and sextile the natal first-house Moon. Rather than interpreting this as a difficult aspect, it's one that activates the powerfully deep emotions of the natal Moon-Pluto trine in mutual reception (the Moon in Pluto's sign, and Pluto in the Moon's sign). And, the Moon rules his natal Midheaven. The solar return Moon is also sextile natal Mercury in the eleventh house of goals and supporters, and ruler of the ninth (travel) and eleventh houses. These aspects also reflect his commitment to his mission for his presidency and the country.

Lunar returns are equally insightful, and sometimes more so because of their short time frame of effectiveness–about twenty-eight days. While Jimmy Carter's solar return is more indicative of his first eight months in office, the lunar return is more pertinent to the election (Chart 22).

The lunar return prior to the election is similar to the solar return in many respects. The Midheaven at 01 Aries 35 clearly reflects a new career endeavor, and Cancer is on the Ascendant, the same sign as his natal Midheaven. Lunar return Venus (popularity) is trine the lunar return Midheaven, and there is a lunar return Moon-Mars conjunction (Mars rules the Midheaven, Moon rules the Ascendant and the public).

Even the lunar return reflects his platform of change, with the Sun-Uranus and Uranus-Mars-Moon conjunctions. With four planets in the fourth house, including the Sun, relocation is highly probable.

The Saturn-Neptune trine shows that in addition to support from the public, he had the support of the media (Neptune rules the ninth) and his advisors and close supporters (Saturn rules the seventh); Neptune, ruler of the ninth house of media, is trine Saturn, ruler of the seventh house of partnership.

Jupiter in the twenty-ninth degree in the eleventh house suggests that he would complete his goal of securing a new job (Jupiter rules the sixth house.) Venus, ruler of the fourth and eleventh houses, and trine the Midheaven, provides more confirmation of achieving his goal and relocation.

In 1980, Jimmy Carter lost the presidential election in a landslide to Ronald Reagan. Comparing the differences in the solar and lunar

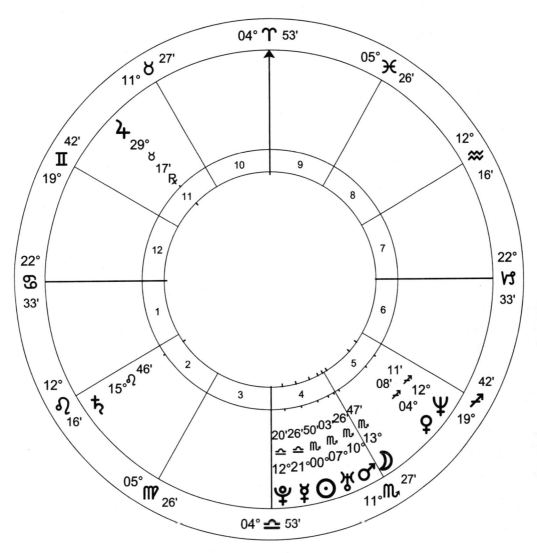

Chart 22: Jimmy Carter
Lunar Return / October 23, 1976 / 11:03:25 pm EDT / Washington DC / Placidus House

returns for both elections illustrates how the first shows success and the second defeat. But first, we will look at some of the other predictive influences to see how they changed in the four years between elections (Chart 23).

Transiting Saturn had advanced into his twelfth house, where it was joined by Jupiter. Saturn was approaching a conjunction to his natal Sun, where it would station retrograde in January on the date he left office. This can indicate a period of discouragement and depression, and in his chart, with Saturn ruling the IC, it also indicated relocation. Jupiter would station at about the same place a week later. These two planets in the twelfth house conjunct his Sun indicate a time of isolation, solitude, and soul searching. Transiting Uranus trine the Midheaven also indicated the potential for change, and its retrograde pattern would take it back and forth in aspect to his natal Sun by semi-square.

Where the first solar return chart has mutable signs on the angles, the second solar return chart (Chart 24) has mutable signs on the Ascendant-Descendant and fixed signs on the Midheaven-IC. Mutable signs reflect change, while fixed signs are associated with an unwillingness to change. Aquarius (1980 solar return Midheaven), unlike Pisces (1976 solar return Midheaven), can be distant and unapproachable, and the late degrees on the Aquarius Midheaven indicate an ending versus the early degrees on the Pisces Midheaven.

The strongest indicator of disfavor with the public and the resulting loss is the solar return chart Mars-Uranus conjunction in the sixth house of work square the solar return Midheaven. This is reinforced because Mars is ruler of Aries, intercepted in the eleventh house of

goals, and Uranus rules the tenth house. Mars is also a co-ruler of the sixth house. All these factors combined have a unified message: job/career change. This time, the press did not promote him (Uranus rules the ninth house).

Where the Venus-Neptune trine to the Midheaven helped him charm the voters in 1976, Neptune worked against him in the 1980 solar return. Its placement in the seventh house (public) conjunct the Descendant made it difficult for him to connect with the public, and people were disillusioned with him. Solar return Venus at the bottom of the solar return chart opposition the Midheaven also made it difficult to attract public support. The sole positive aspect, Pluto trine the Midheaven, was not enough to overcome the negative factors.

The October 11 lunar return prior to the 1980 election (Chart 25) is not as negative as the September 20 solar return, but it nevertheless has some difficult placements. That it would be a momentous month is obvious from the angles, which duplicate the signs on his natal chart angles. In this chart, the Sun rises conjunct Pluto, an aspect of intense inner focus and major change out of his control. Both these planets are square the lunar return Midheaven.

Mars, ruler of the seventh house, is at twenty-nine degrees, indicating the end of his relationship with the public. The Moon-Mercury conjunction provides a positive influence with its trine to the Midheaven, so he still had some supporters among the press (Mercury rules the ninth house) and people behind the scenes (Mercury rules the twelfth house). Jupiter and Neptune, co-rulers of the sixth house, with Jupiter in the twelfth and ruling the third, repeat the solar

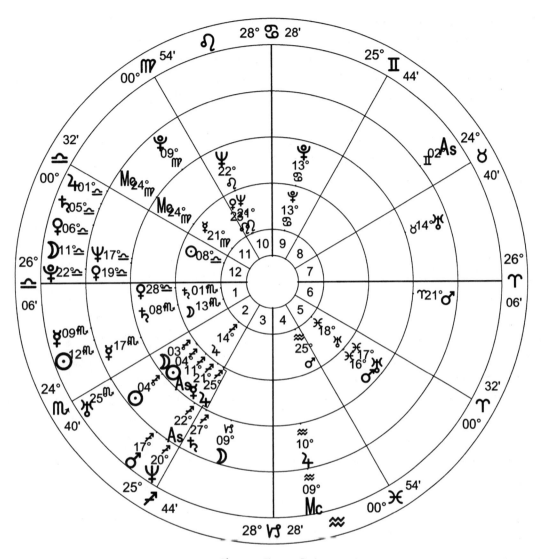

Chart 23: Jimmy Carter

Innermost wheel: Birth Chart / October 1, 1924 / 7:00 am CST / Plains, Georgia
Middle inner wheel: Secondary Progressed / November 4, 1980 / 8:48:31 am CST / Plains, Georgia
Middle outer wheel: Directed Solar Arc / November 4, 1980 / 8:48:31 am CST / Plains, Georgia
Outermost wheel: 1980 Election Transits / November 4, 1980 / 6:00 pm EST / Washington DC
Placidus House

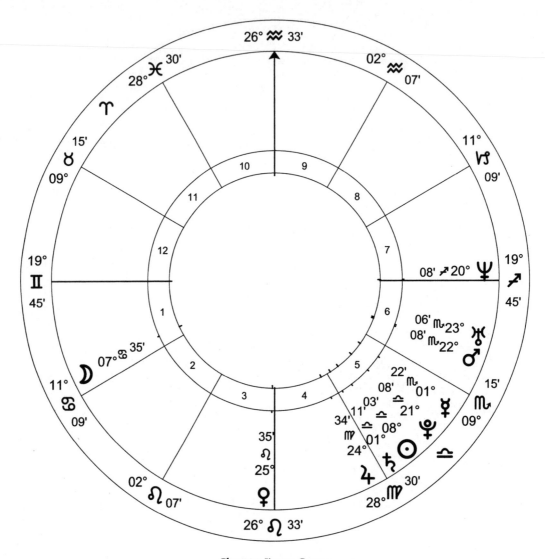

Chart 24: Jimmy Carter
Solar Return / September 30, 1980 / 10:23:24 pm EDT / Washington DC / Placidus House

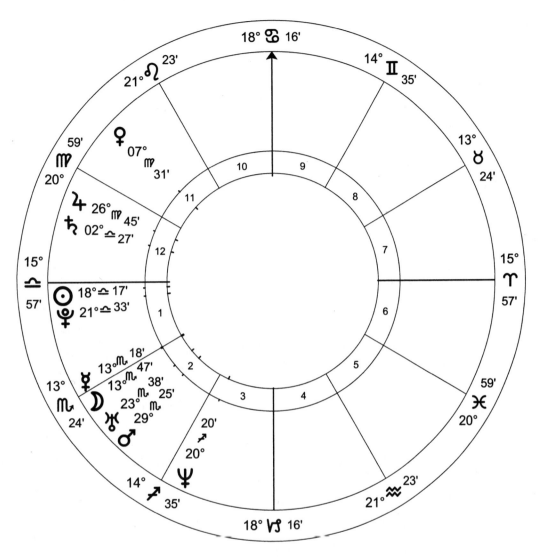

Chart 25: Jimmy Carter
Lunar Return / October 11, 1980 / 7:06:33 am EDT / Washington DC / Placidus House

return indication that it was difficult to deliver a clear message (Neptune in the third house).

Although Jimmy Carter left the White House under a cloud, at least in the public's view, he has regained a great degree of his former popularity in the succeeding years. In 2002, he was awarded the Nobel Peace Prize "for his decades of untiring effort to find peaceful solutions to international conflicts, to advance democracy and human rights, and to promote economic and social development."

His solar return for 2002 (Chart 26) presents a far different picture from his 1980 solar return. In the 2002 chart, Saturn is notably in the tenth house of achievement, signifying the reward he earned for his untiring efforts. It is in a trine with Uranus in humanitarian Aquarius in the sixth house of service. Interestingly, Mercury, ruler of the first and tenth houses of the solar return chart, is retrograde. This suggests he may receive additional recognition in the future and possibly also that he felt his work was unfinished. Indeed, he has continued to promote peace.

On the date the Nobel Peace Prize was announced on October 11, 2002, transiting Jupiter was in Carter's natal tenth house and trine his natal Moon, ruler of the tenth house. Progressed Mercury was sextile the natal Moon, and transiting Saturn in the ninth house of foreign affairs was square progressed Mars, ruler of his natal sixth house of service.

In his 2010 book, *White House Diary*, Jimmy Carter admits his presidential mistakes but also cites his accomplishments, including normalizing relations with China and having more of his programs passed by Congress than any other recent president. He also said he left the White House "in despair."

Jimmy Carter's 2010 solar return chart (Chart 27) reflects the publication of excerpts from the daily diary he kept while in the White House. A fortunate Jupiter-Uranus conjunction in the eighth house indicated the book would be profitable. With Uranus involved, and the conjunction in opposition to Mercury, it was also full of revealing surprises. The Sun-Saturn conjunction in the second house indicates income from past events associated with Carter's (Sun, ruler of the Ascendant) job (Saturn, ruler of the sixth house).

This chart also has a Mars-Venus conjunction in the third house of writing, with Mars ruling the ninth house of publishing and Venus ruling the third house (communication) and the tenth house (fame). The Moon (the public) trine the Mars-Venus conjunction shows that the book would be well received and bring him favorable attention. As the ruler of the twelfth house and in square aspect to the Sun-Saturn conjunction, the Moon reflects the nature of some of the content: secrets from the past being revealed.

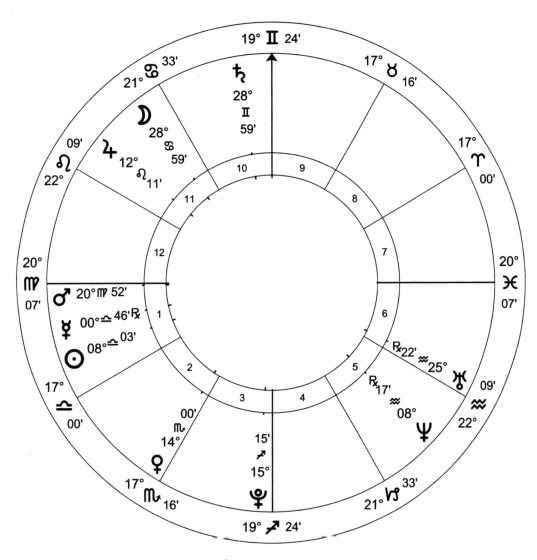

Chart 26: Jimmy Carter
Solar Return / October 1, 2002 / 4:11:35 am CST / Plains, Georgia / Placidus House

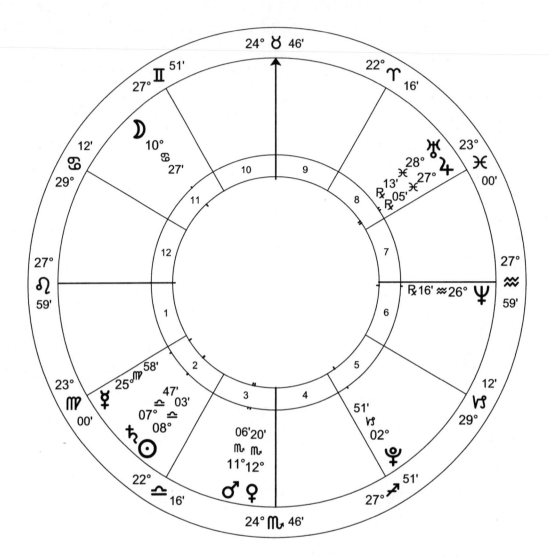

Chart 27: Jimmy Carter
Solar Return / October 1, 2010 / 2:27 am EST / Plains, Georgia / Placidus House

VAL

Val's chart was used as an example for relocation. Her solar return for that year (Chart 28) graphically shows that possibility. The angles all have mutable signs, indicating change. Four planets in angular houses and four planets in cardinal signs signal new endeavors.

The reason she moved to another state was to join her fiancé. This is reflected in solar return Neptune, ruler of the seventh house, in the fifth house of romance and trine/sextile the solar return Midheaven-IC. Solar return Pluto, planet of transformation, is in the fourth house of home and square the Ascendant-Descendant, indicating a major change and relocation because of a partner.

Of course, relocation necessitated the search for a new job, shown by the solar return Sun-Saturn conjunction in the tenth house, and solar return Uranus, planet of change, in and ruling the sixth house of work. Ascendant ruler Mercury in the ninth house indicates she would travel. This planet also rules the solar return Midheaven, and she found a new job with a printer (Mercury rules printing).

The move can also be seen in the lunar return (Chart 29) in effect for the time she relocated. Here, lunar return Jupiter, ruler of the fourth house and co-ruler of the seventh, is opposition the Moon (home) and Neptune (partner) in the fifth house of romance. Lunar return Venus in the second house of possessions, is sextile lunar return Pluto in the fourth.

There are two planets in the lunar return twelfth house, Mars and the Sun, both opposition Uranus in the sixth. The planets involved in this opposition are sextile/trine Saturn in the tenth house, suggesting that she would be able to find a job in the new location even though she regretted the need to resign from her current position.

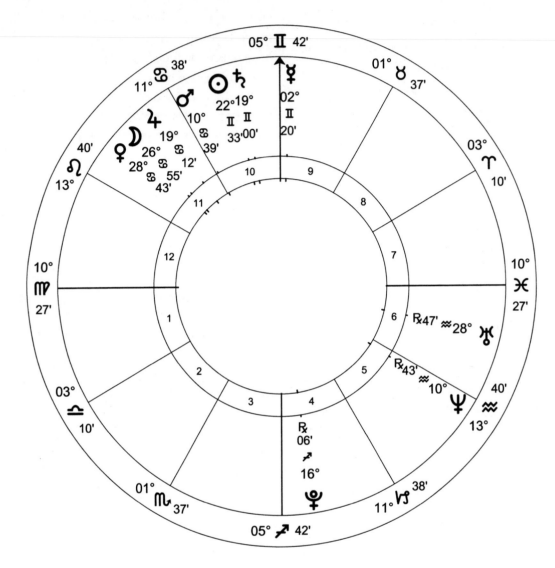

Chart 28: Val

Solar Return / June 13, 2002 / 12:15:48 pm MDT / Helena, Montana / Placidus House

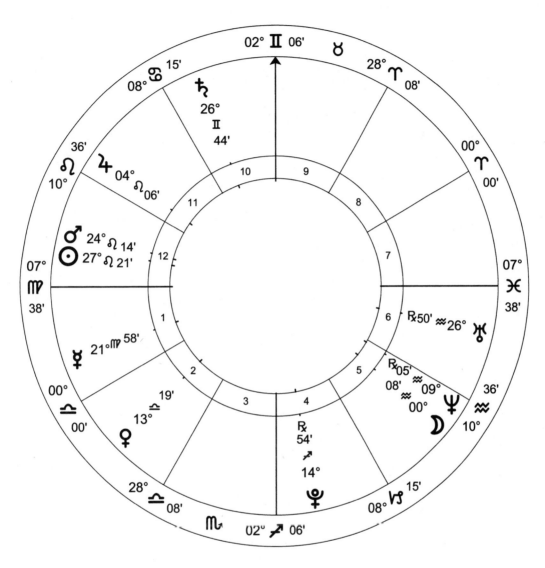

Chart 29: Val

Lunar Return / August 20, 2002 / 7:33:20 am MDT / Helena, Montana / Placidus House

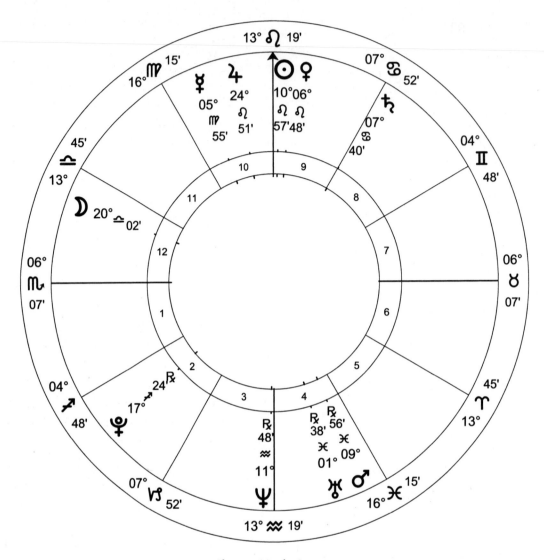

Chart 30: Martha Stewart
Solar Return / August 3, 2003 / 1:11:40 pm EDT / New York, New York / Placidus House

MARTHA STEWART

The solar return in effect during Martha Stewart's trial, sentencing, and time in prison are fascinating and revealing, as are the lunar returns for when she entered and was released from prison. Her natal, progressed, and solar arc charts showed that she would be found guilty and serve a short prison sentence of five months followed by five more months of house arrest.

Martha's 2003 solar return chart (Chart 30) clearly shows what she dealt with that year. There are four planets in succedent houses, indicating completion. Because they are all in some way linked to legal matters and prison, the charts indicate that those events would be concluded. The four planets in angular houses indicate a new endeavor (concluding the legal matters and moving on to prison). But with Mercury in the tenth house in opposition to Uranus and Mars in the fourth, there is also a strong possibility of relocation—in this case, moving to prison. Fixed signs on the angles indicate that she was stuck, with no way out except to comply with the sentence.

The Sun-Venus conjunction in the ninth house (legal matters and courts) is opposition Neptune in the third house. This suggests she thought it was all a bad dream. She was in disbelief with no hope of a successful appeal. (She initially said she would appeal and then changed her mind.) The Sun-Venus-Neptune alignment tells another story. Neptune is the natural ruler of the twelfth house of prisons and Venus rules the solar return twelfth and seventh (attorneys and legal matters). The solar return Moon in the twelfth house rules the ninth house of legal matters.

Martha's 2004 solar return (Chart 31) covers the time she entered prison, served her sentence, and was released to house arrest. Here the Midheaven-IC are fixed signs, and the Ascendant-Descendant are cardinal signs. This is a transition chart. She was getting back to business and beginning her life anew. The same can be seen in the five planets in angular houses, indicative of the new beginning that would occur upon her release.

Solar return Venus, in late degrees of Gemini, rules the fourth house of home, where she was confined under house arrest for five months. With Venus in the fifth house of fun and socializing, she would do little of that because of the house arrest. Notice the twelfth house. It has 29 Sagittarius 44 on the cusp, representing the completion of her time in prison. Jupiter, the twelfth house ruler, is square Midheaven ruler Pluto, so she would have difficulty getting back to her career endeavors. This was true because of the house arrest and business problems. Saturn in the sixth house of work and ruling the Ascendant gives a similar message: restriction (Saturn) in personal (Ascendant) and work matters (sixth house). But her efforts would pay off because Saturn is also trine the Midheaven.

Martha's lunar return chart (Chart 32) for the month she entered prison repeats the completion message, with Mars, the Sun, and Jupiter all in late degrees in the first house. The Sun rules the twelfth, and Mercury, ruler of the Ascendant, is in the twelfth, rising just above the Ascendant. The Moon in the fourth house conjunct Pluto is also in a late degree and square the first house planets, including Jupiter, ruler of the fourth. This is yet another indication of

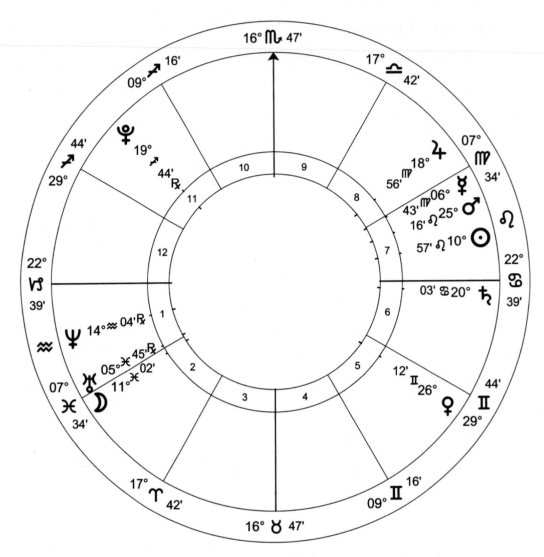

Chart 31: Martha Stewart
Solar Return / August 2, 2004 / 7:05:47 pm EDT / New York, New York / Placidus House

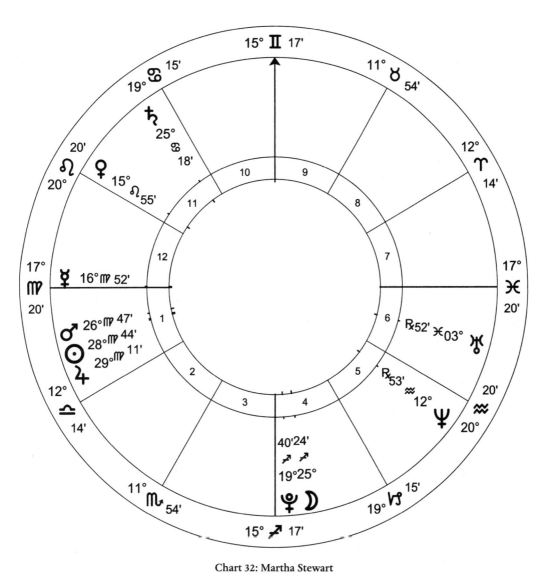

Chart 32: Martha Stewart

Lunar Return / September 21, 2004 / 5:49:43 am EDT / New York, New York / Placidus House

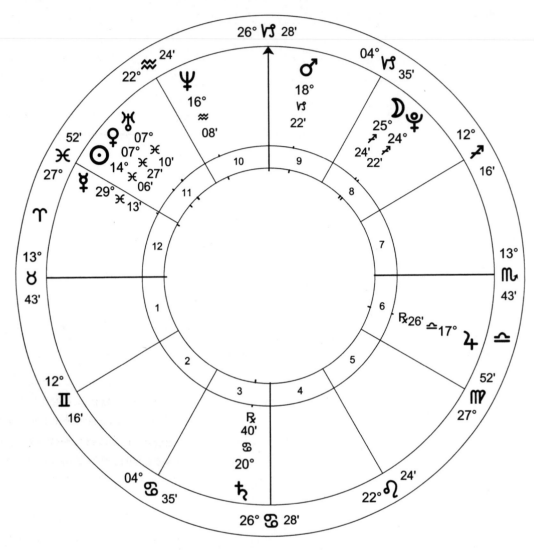

Chart 33: Martha Stewart
Lunar Return / March 4, 2005 / 9:26:43 am EST / Alderson, West Virginia / Placidus House

relocation—and a difficult one—with Pluto in the fourth conjunct the Moon and Pluto opposition the Midheaven; her home life and her career were transformed.

Pluto is trine Venus in the eleventh, so she probably had some congenial relationships while in prison. Some, however, were not so pleasant because Venus is also opposition Neptune. While in prison, Martha was reported to have used her skills to teach crafts classes to some inmates, which is indicated by the Venus-Pluto trine (Pluto rules the third of learning, and Venus rules the ninth of teaching). This probably helped her make the best of it, because Saturn in the eleventh is sextile the first house planets. Nevertheless, it was an intensely emotional time (lunar aspects).

The lunar return for her release (Chart 33), which occurred on the date of her release, is as revealing as the lunar return for when she entered prison. Mercury is in the last degree of Pisces (universal twelfth house ruler) in the twelfth house, where it is sextile/trine the Midheaven-IC. Mars, ruler of Aries (intercepted in the twelfth house) is in the ninth of legal matters and opposition Saturn in the third, with Saturn ruling the ninth. These planets are also square Jupiter in the sixth house, forming a t-square and pointing to strongly emphasized areas of activity: the t-square shows the time restraints to pursue her work (she was allowed to be away from home for a set number of daily hours), the necessity of reporting to her probation officer (Saturn in the third), the obligation to follow the court order (Mars-Saturn), and the inability to expand (Jupiter) her business (sixth house). So, although she was released from prison, she still had legal responsibilities to ful-fill: the house arrest and all its attendant restrictions. The Moon, ruler of the fourth house, is conjunct Pluto in the eighth and square Mercury, so although she was free, she wasn't free to come and go as she pleased.

The change in her life style that occurred upon her release is reflected in the Venus-Uranus conjunction (Venus rules the Ascendant). This aspect also indicates a change in friends (Uranus in and ruling the eleventh), and adds confirmation that she had developed friendly relationships with some fellow inmates while in prison.

PLANETARY RETURNS

The returns of Mercury and Venus often occur near your birthday because the Sun, Venus, and Mercury are always close to together. The timing varies depending upon the retrograde periods. (Mercury is retrograde three to four times each year, and Venus about every eighteen months).

The most unusual phenomenon about planetary returns involves a characteristic specific to the retrograde pattern. It is possible to have two or three planetary returns quite close to one another. If your Mercury is at 16 Aries, for example, and Mercury turns retrograde at 19 Aries, you would have a Mercury return in the first direct period, another in the retrograde period, and a third in the second direct period. This can happen with any planet that has a retrograde period (the Sun and Moon do not).

Which one of these return charts is valid? All of them. Only the final one will be in effect for any amount of time, however. The other two will only be active for a week, or several weeks, in the case of Mercury and Venus, and there could be a month or more between Mars returns. For the other planets, it could be several months or even a year.

Generally, each of the planetary returns in a series will reflect associated events in process, just like any transiting retrograde planet aspects to your natal, progressed, or solar arc planets. If you have one of these, watch the first two charts closely for aspects to them that can trigger an event. All will be related.

Val: Mercury Return Example

The Mercury return chart shows where the focus will be in Mercury-related events. Mercury is associated with communication, mental focus and interests, learning, thought processes, contracts, vehicles, appliances, pets, neighbors, siblings, and agreements. The house placement and aspects of Mercury in the return chart thus reveal where and how any of these Mercury-related events and actions will occur most frequently.

Because Mercury, like every other planet, rules many different situations and life events, it's not only helpful but necessary to first study the other factors influencing the natal chart (progressions, transits, eclipses, etc.). This will help you narrow the focus and area of emphasis. Easy aspects from Mercury in the return chart will show where you can effectively communicate, while hard aspects will reveal where there will be challenges.

Val's chart was previously used as an example of the predictive factors that indicate relocation, and one that was motivated by the desire to join her fiancé.

The obvious choice for relocation and marriage would be a Venus return chart, because Venus is the universal ruler of possessions and

relationships. So why use a Mercury return chart? It's a good example of how you can see other life events in a seemingly non-related return chart. And in this case, Mercury is a strong influence in her life because it rules her natal Sun and Ascendant.

This Mercury return chart (Chart 34) is impressive in the amount of information that can be gleaned from it. First, note that the Ascendant-Descendant is twenty-nine degrees, indicating completion and the end of one chapter in her life in preparation for a new one. She relocated, leaving her current life behind, and she and her fiancé would conclude the dating phase of their relationship when they married. The Moon, ruler of the Ascendant, is in the eleventh house of goals, and trine Neptune in the seventh house. Neptune rules the ninth house of travel and long distances. This aspect also indicates she had great faith in her decision to relocate in order to be with her fiance.

Venus—the universal planet of relationships and possessions—is placed in the second house of possessions and opposition Uranus, planet of change. Venus rules the fourth house of home in the return chart. This aspect thus indicates both relocation and moving her possessions and a change in a relationship.

Mars, ruler of the tenth house of career, is conjunct Jupiter, ruler of the sixth house of daily work. This fortunate contact indicates that she could quickly and easily find a new job in the new location, which she did.

A comparison of Val's chart with the Mercury-return chart shows Saturn in the return chart conjunct her natal Venus-Sun-Mars stellium, an indication of a long-lasting marital relationship. The Venus-Uranus opposition in the

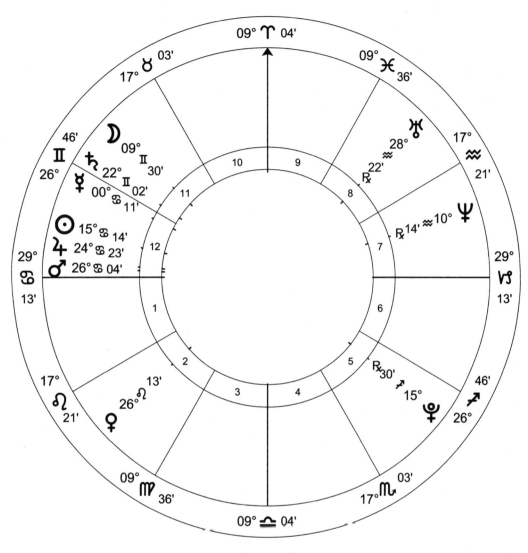

Chart 34: Val

Mercury Return / July 7, 2002 / 7:00:10 am MDT / Helena, Montana / Placidus House

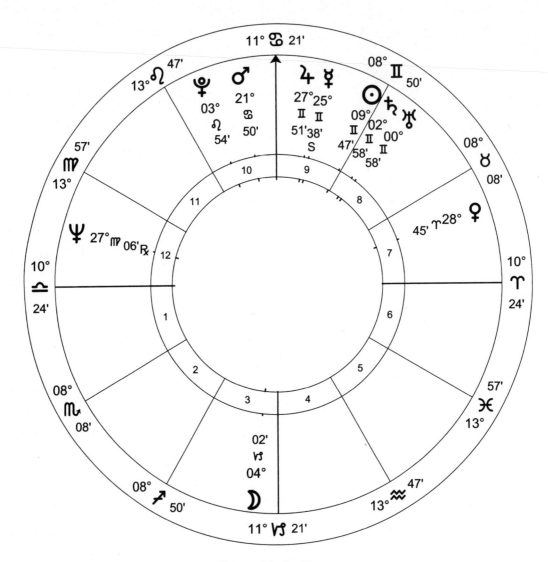

Chart 35: Marilyn Monroe
Venus Return / May 31, 1942 / 2:07:19 pm PST / Los Angeles, California / Placidus House

return chart aligns with natal Jupiter conjunct the IC, activating Jupiter's natal sextile to Mercury conjunct the natal Ascendant (and opposition the Descendant). Return Mercury was also square solar arc Jupiter (natal Descendant ruler) in the fourth house.

Return Mercury in the twelfth house is an interesting placement, considering what she did when this chart was in effect. In the return chart, Mercury rules the third and twelfth houses, and during that year, she began a journal to record her innermost thoughts (Mercury) and feelings (Cancer).

Marilyn Monroe: Venus Return Example

This return chart gives insights into the lighter side of life because Venus rules affection, fun, love, what you attract, socializing, relationships, and popularity. Venus is also a money planet, so it's a good idea to take special notice of any difficult aspects in the return chart. They can show where you might have extra expenses, or where there might be relationship challenges. Venus also rules possessions–the materialistic side of life.

Again, it's important to consider the main themes in your natal, progressed, and solar arc charts as well as transits and eclipses. Used in combination with the Venus return, you can then fine-tune your forecast. The placement of the Venus return Ascendant-Descendant in your natal chart can be particularly revealing because this planet is so closely aligned with relationships.

Marilyn Monroe married Joe Daugherty in 1942, and the couple divorced in 1946. The Venus returns in effect for the two events are a good illustration of how to determine the difference, based on the Venus return charts.

In the 1942 Venus return (Chart 35), Venus is at 28 Aries 45 in the seventh house, with Aries on the cusp. Venus is sextile retrograde Mercury conjunct Jupiter in the ninth house of courts and legal matters, with Gemini, ruled by Mercury, on the house cusp. This can be interpreted as confirmation of the story that she married in order to avoid being returned to an orphanage. Venus in a late degree indicates completion of a relationship, which in this case was a wedding, and Venus rules the first house, representing her. Further confirmation to the story might be the return Sun in the ninth house trine/sextile the Ascendant/Descendant. Mars in the tenth house, representing her husband (Mars rules the seventh) is unaspected because the square to Venus and the sextile to Neptune in the twelfth house are wide. Nevertheless, the sextile might suggest ulterior motives (twelfth house) and a sudden decision (Venus-Mars square) to change her status (tenth house). Deception is also suggested by the Mercury-Jupiter conjunction square Neptune.

Mercury is also retrograde in the Venus return in effect the year of the divorce, and almost at the same degree as it was in the Venus return for 1942. In the 1946 chart (Chart 36), Mercury in Pisces is conjunct the Descendant and square the 1942 Mercury in late degrees of Gemini. Return Sun is opposition Neptune in the first house, reflecting the disillusionment between the two partners (first-seventh house). The Sun is also sextile Uranus (sixth house ruler) in the ninth house of courts. Another story has it that Joe and Marilyn split up because of her blossoming career, which would be confirmed by Mercury in the seventh house ruling the tenth. The Mars-

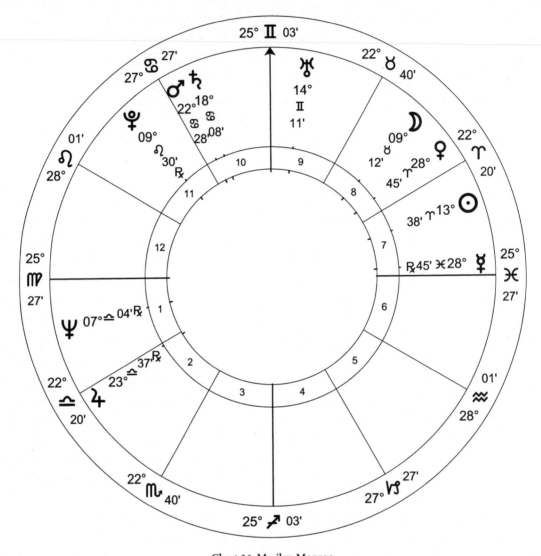

Chart 36: Marilyn Monroe
Venus Return / April 3, 1946 / 4:44:27 pm PST / Los Angeles, California / Placidus House

Saturn conjunction in the tenth indicates that this year was a better one for career efforts and alliances than for personal relationships. Both of these planets are sextile/trine the Ascendant-Descendant (and in a wide trine to Mercury), which suggests she chose her career over her marriage.

Martha Stewart: Mars Return Example

The Mars return, which occurs about every two years, shows where you will invest maximum effort and initiative and the area of life where there will be a high level of action and initiative. This chart can also give insights into new endeavors and how you can achieve goals. But Mars is associated with conflict, accidents, and aggression, so the difficult aspects can identify where these are most likely to occur.

The natal chart, along with the progressions, solar arcs, transits, and other predictive factors is the first step in analyzing the Mars return. Be particularly watchful for difficult aspects to natal, progressed, and solar arc Mars, especially from outer transiting planets. These aspects can show areas where you can achieve maximum success as well as run into difficulties.

Martha Stewart's Mars return (Chart 37), which occurred about seven weeks prior to the guilty verdict, offers further confirmation of her fate. Mars is intercepted in the first house, effectively "trapping" the energy there without an easy outlet. It is trine Pluto in the ninth house of courts, indicating that her legal difficulties would be concluded but also that her freedom (ninth house) would be curtailed (interception). The trine to Pluto (ruler of her natal Ascendant) also indicates that the outcome could be transformative if she chose that path.

Note the three planets in the return chart's twelfth house of institutions (prison). Uranus rules the twelfth, Neptune rules the first, and Venus rules the second (self-worth and possessions, which she was without in prison) and co-rules the seventh, where Libra is intercepted. She was removed from the people she is close to, including business contacts and her elderly mother.

The Moon-Jupiter conjunction in the sixth house is trine the Sun in the eleventh, echoing the message in the solar and lunar return charts that she formed some friendships in prison. Others, however, were not so pleasant because Mars in the first house is square the Sun, which rules the sixth house. The conjunction and trine suggest that she might have been somehow inspired (Jupiter) by the work (sixth) she did in prison. In fact, she used creativity (Moon rules the fifth) in projects with her fellow inmates (Sun in eleventh). Saturn in the fourth indicates a restriction in home life, and Mercury opposition the IC suggests she would be living away from home while focused on her "career."

Jupiter Return

The Jupiter return is in effect for about twelve years, the time it takes for this planet to circle your chart and return to its natal position. This chart is related to material wealth (possessions, income, windfalls), spirituality, education and knowledge, travel, faith and hope in the future, and expansion.

The aspects Jupiter makes in the return chart, and the aspects made by other planets to your natal planets provide insight into the major areas of Jupiter emphasis during the succeeding twelve years. Because this is a return chart, any aspects

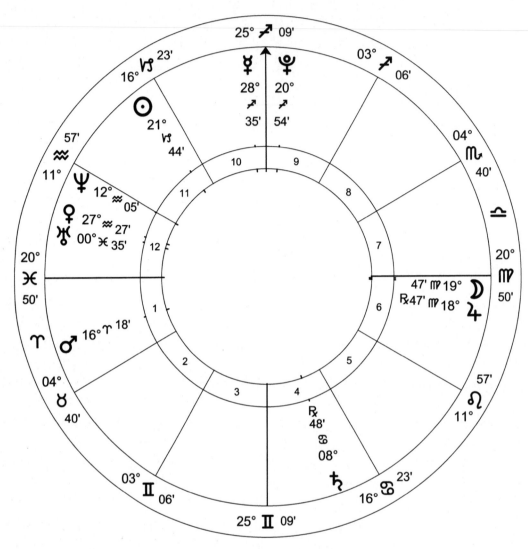

Chart 37: Martha Stewart
Mars Return / January 12, 2004 / 10:09:02 am EST / New York, New York / Placidus House

involving Jupiter in your natal chart will of course also be activated by the return Jupiter. Look for outer transiting planets that will activate these aspects both at the time of the return and during the twelve-year period. They will be particularly important if at the time any outer transiting planets are aspecting the return chart planets and angles.

Carol: Jupiter Return Example

Carol is a high school counselor whose natal energy is strongly Jupiterian. She has Mercury and the Sun in Sagittarius (ruled by Jupiter) and four planets in the ninth house (natural house of Jupiter). She has a strong faith and is highly spiritual, while also being very practical (Saturn rising), and excels at working with teens. She takes a group of teens to Mexico every spring to build houses. Every summer, she and a group of teens from her school join other school groups on a two-week trip trip to another country.

Her Jupiter return (Chart 38) has Jupiter in the seventh house of relationships, which are also influenced by Saturn (in the sixth house of work) conjunct the Descendant. Venus (natural ruler of relationships) in the ninth house rules her tenth of career and fifth of recreation, and is square Pluto in the twelfth. The Jupiter return chart also has Mercury conjunct Mars opposition Neptune. The travel houses in the Jupiter return are ruled by Mercury (Virgo on the ninth house cusp) and Jupiter and Neptune (Pisces on the third house cusp). Mercury rules the return chart seventh house, and Jupiter rules the Ascendant. Travel is definitely indicated in this Jupiter return chart, but not all will go smoothly with all of her traveling companions.

Pluto in the Jupiter return chart rules the return chart eleventh house of groups and is conjunct her natal Mercury, again pointing out the possibility of difficulties with fellow travelers. Jupiter return Moon (co-ruler of the seventh house because Cancer is intercepted) conjunct her natal Mars repeats the message.

Carol and a group of students from her school departed for Greece on June 14, 2010, with much excitement and high hopes for a great trip as the transiting Moon was conjunct her return Jupiter and natal Uranus. She had no reason to think the trip would be anything but fabulous—until the next day. As the transiting Moon joined the Mercury-Mars conjunction in her natal chart, she began to realize that one of the adults from another school group was decidedly uncooperative and controlling. He subsequently tried to regularly change the daily planned itinerary and went off on his own, fully expecting the other adults to chaperone the teens he was responsible for. The biggest tip-off that there would be difficulties with someone on the trip, however, was transiting Saturn in the ninth house of travel square the Jupiter return Ascendant-Descendant. Saturn is often associated with delays, and the rest of the group waited thirty minutes or more every morning for the other school group to arrive at the bus.

Part of the trip was by ship with daily stops at various Greek islands. Carol, who had never before had problems, was seasick. Note transiting Neptune conjunct Uranus in the Jupiter return chart. Uranus rules her natal fourth house, and she spent time "at home" in her cabin, eventually adjusting to the motion. The seasickness was triggered by transiting Mercury

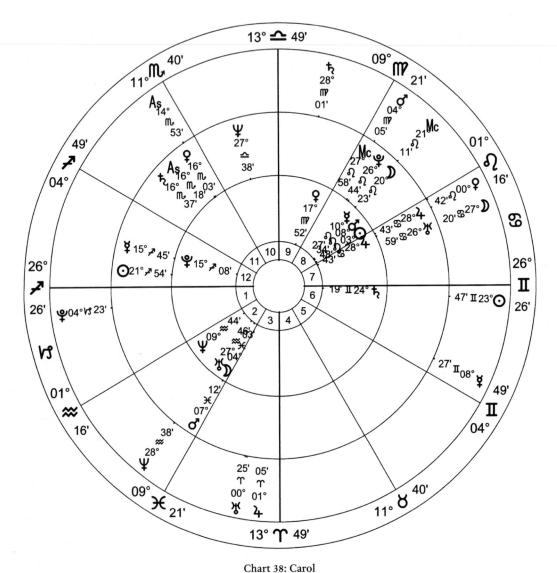

Chart 38: Carol
Inner wheel: Jupiter Return / July 26, 2002 / 5:01:09 pm MST / Phoenix, Arizona
Middle wheel: Birth Chart / December 14, 1954 / 4:28 am CST / Madison, Wisconsin
Outer wheel: Transits / June 14, 2010 / 4:30 pm / Phoenix, Arizona
Placidus House

opposition the Jupiter return Pluto (conjunct natal Mercury) in the Jupiter return twelfth house of solitude and health. It lasted off and on for several days until transiting Venus moved away from the Jupiter return Mercury-Mars-Neptune configuration.

A better choice might have been better to skip or postpone this trip, but, overall, she enjoyed the experience despite the difficult individual and the bout of seasickness.

Saturn Return

A Saturn return occurs every twenty-eight to thirty years. The first is often characterized as a time of maturation, when most people make the transition from fun-loving youth to responsible adult and take career and family matters more seriously. This is when many people begin to fully understand what it means to live life in the real world.

At the second Saturn return (between ages fifty-six and sixty), many people begin to think seriously about when to retire from the work force. They also question life as they've known it, placing more emphasis on what they want to do rather than what they have to do. Life priorities become an important question, and it's much easier to say no to all but the best opportunities and those that really appeal to them. That may not be completely possible, but the shift in thinking nevertheless occurs on some level.

The Saturn return is interpreted like other return charts, but because this one covers such an extended period of time, it is more big-picture than, for example, the Mercury return. Look to outer planet transits to the return chart, as well as progressions, solar arcs, and eclipses that align with the return planets. Most of all, look

to Saturn's cycle—the periods when transiting Saturn forms the first square, the opposition, and the second square to natal (and return) Saturn. These represent turning points, lessons to be learned, and the inevitable reality checks of life. The sextile and trine aspects can also trigger events at times (look for a trigger from a quickly moving planet such as the Sun, Mercury, Venus, or Mars).

With the Saturn return chart, you should be particularly aware of its connection to the natal chart because this will show you the main areas of emphasis for Saturn-related events. The natal and return houses ruled by Saturn and Saturn's placement in the return chart are also important.

Kim: Saturn Return Example

Kim had her first Saturn return in 2004 (Chart 39), several months before her thirtieth birthday. She is self-employed, and at the time was single. Note that Saturn in the return chart is in the sixth house of daily work, reflecting her commitment to her job. Saturn in the sixth house in a Saturn return chart can indicate health issues, and in this chart, Saturn rules the twelfth, another health house, so this is a possibility at some point in the future. But Saturn here can also indicate the desire to be of service to others, which she does in her job in the service industry and on a regular basis as a volunteer. Although Kim had one serious relationship in her mid-twenties, she was still looking for a mate, and in October 2009, met Steve, a man who interested her.

Why do astrologers look at the Saturn return chart for a possible marriage? Because Kim's natal chart has Saturn-ruled Capricorn on the Descendant.

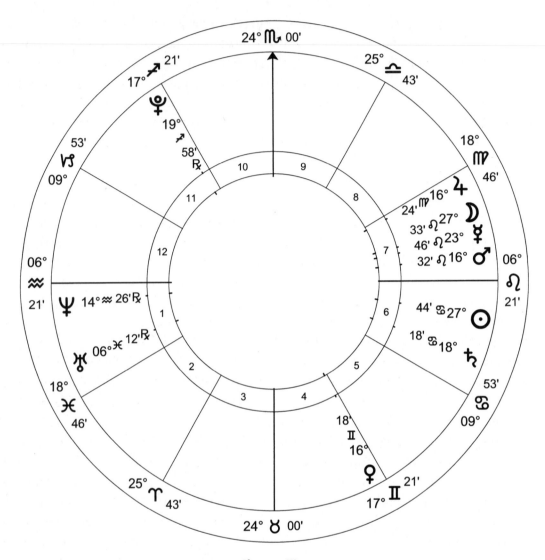

Chart 39: Kim
Saturn Return / July 19, 2004 / 8:00:53 pm MST / Mesa, Arizona / Placidus House

Kim's Saturn return chart has four planets in the seventh house, so it could be said with a great deal of certainty that she would meet someone at some point. Of course, that could be at any time between age thirty and sixty! Not very helpful information in itself, so we look to the planetary contacts to the Saturn return chart for timing.

Kim's Saturn return chart has Aquarius (co-ruled by Saturn) rising. This sign on the Ascendant emphasizes freedom and independence, but it also has a more conservative and serious side because Saturn is co-ruler of Aquarius. Uranus, ruler of Aquarius, is in the first house of the return chart, reinforcing the Aquarius qualities. Its placement in Pisces is another indication of her personal (Ascendant) involvement in charitable causes (Pisces, natural ruler of the twelfth house), as is Neptune in Aquarius.

Neptune is opposition Mars, an aspect that can indicate deception and disillusionment in love, or the ultimate in romance, when placed across the first-seventh house axis. As it turned out, it was both. The opposition is connected with two other planets: Venus in opposition to Pluto. These planets are sextile/trine the Mars-Neptune opposition. With this strong configuration and the other three seventh-house planets, an astrologer has plenty to work with for timing.

Kim's natal chart has a Venus-Neptune conjunction at 8–9 Sagittarius that is sextile/trine the Saturn return Ascendant-Descendant. This natal aspect is associated with idealistic love, and it is easy for people with this influence to fall in love with love.

Mars in the Saturn return chart rules the third house (Kim and Steve attended high school together, but did not know each other because he is several years older). They met through mutual friends when Kim was out socializing with friends from work, which is one way the Venus-Pluto opposition in the return chart played out (Pluto in the eleventh house). The return chart Sun in the sixth house (work) rules the return chart Descendant.

A lunar eclipse in August 2009 at 13 Aquarius 43, across the first-seventh houses of the return chart, and conjunct the Neptune-Mars opposition, set the energy in motion. When they met at the end of October 2009, it was under the influence of the October 18 New Moon at 24 Libra 59, which was sextile the Moon-Mercury conjunction in the return chart seventh house and square the Sun in the same chart.

When they met, transiting Saturn was in the last degrees of Virgo sextile the return chart Sun. Transiting Jupiter had just stationed direct at 17 Aquarius in opposition to return Mars, and would move forward to contact the other three seventh-house planets. Mars was also aspected by transiting Venus at 18 Libra. Transiting Mars was conjunct the return chart Descendant, and transiting Neptune was opposition Mercury in the return chart. Both transiting Sun and Mercury were square the return Ascendant-Descendant. Transiting Uranus provided the element of surprise and the sudden attraction with its exact opposition to return Mercury (Uranus was at 23 Aquarius).

Love and romance bloomed, and the relationship was all Kim had hoped for—or so she and her natal Venus-Neptune conjunction thought. They became engaged the following June and set a September 15 wedding date.

Initially, all went according to plan, and there were many transits to Kim's Saturn return chart on the wedding day:

- Mercury in the seventh house opposition Uranus
- Transiting Venus was in the ninth house square the Ascendant-Descendant
- Transiting Mars was in the ninth house sesquisquare/semisquare Venus opposition Pluto
- A Jupiter-Uranus conjunction in the second house aspected Neptune opposition Mars by semisquare/sesquisquare
- Saturn in the eighth house trine/sextile the Ascendant-Descendant
- Transiting Neptune opposition the Moon. The July 11, 2010 solar eclipse was at 19 Cancer 24, conjunct Kim's natal/return Saturn, ruler of her natal Descendant.

Neptune is everywhere! Great at its best for love and romance. A disaster at its worst.

Within a few weeks, the romance of their dating days began to disappear, and then Kim discovered the second page of the marriage license had not been signed. This had to be done before it could be filed with the county clerk's office, so she gathered all the necessary signatures except for one: Steve refused to sign it, in essence holding the marriage license hostage until Kim resolved some financial issues.

It wasn't long before it became a moot point because the time frame for filing the signed license soon expired, and they would need to apply for another.

Although they weren't legally married and the relationship was not going well, Kim continued to devote considerable energy to it. At her request, they attended counseling sessions, but Kim felt Steve was not putting any effort into the relationship, and eventually she stopped trying. He noticed and suggested they talk. The outcome: Kim moved out in June 2011, much to Steve's disbelief, and no divorce was necessary.

The wedding transits to the Saturn return chart activated the four-planet configuration of Venus opposition Pluto and Mars opposition Neptune, which is a decidedly unfavorable one for marriage in any chart, whether natal, progressed, solar arc, or return. Also of importance are the aspects made by the transiting planets in the second, eighth, and ninth houses of the return chart: her money, his money, and legal matters.

Not all lessons associated with a Saturn return chart are as momentous as this one, but these charts do indicate where lessons are to be learned. In Kim's case, the emphasis is very definitely on relationships, and a reflection of her natal chart with the Venus-Neptune conjunction and Saturn-ruled Capricorn on the Descendant.

CHAPTER EIGHT

INNER PLANETS AND TIMING TRIGGERS

The inner transiting planets have two functions: they spark everyday events such as a compliment, a call from a friend, a moment of frustration, or a minor disagreement, and they act as triggers for long-term trends that signal major events.

In Chapter 9, you will find interpretations of the planetary aspects. Although these mainly focus on minor life events, you can use the information as a guide to interpret major life events. The planetary energy is the same.

The difference between minor and major events is that there are other factors to consider in major events—progressions, solar arcs, outer transiting planets, eclipses, and New and Full Moons. For example, progressed Mercury conjunct the IC suggests major changes on the home front—relocation, remodeling, a family member moving in or out. Transiting Mercury conjunct the IC, however, might prompt you to deal with accumulated paperwork or to touch base with your parents.

In general, the squares, oppositions, conjunctions, semisquares, and sesquisquares create action. Trines and sextiles produce an easy flow of energy that can temper difficult aspects. Conjunctions go either way, depending upon the planets involved. Whether positive or negative, conjunctions intensify the effect of the two planets. Overall, the Sun, Moon, Venus, and Jupiter have a more positive influence than do the other planets.

In general, the transiting Sun represents you and your sphere of activity; it can also represent men. Mercury is communication, short trips, relatives, and younger people. Venus rules money, gifts, love, and relationships; it also symbolizes people and things that attract you. Mars is action, energy, initiative, and men; it usually acts early (use a two degree orb to be safe), and is active when accidents occur. The Moon is connected with emotions and women.

This chapter focuses on inner transiting planets as triggers for progressions and solar arcs.

USING THE EPHEMERIS

An ephemeris is the predictive astrologer's number one tool. This book lists the planets places for every day by sign and degree.

Most astrologers use astrological calculation software to generate charts and some programs will advance the progressions, solar arcs, and transits by minute, hour, day, week, month, and year. These can be useful because you see the static natal chart in the center with the progressed (or solar arc) and transiting planets advancing together in real time.

But there is still no substitute for flipping through an ephemeris in search of transiting planets in specific signs and degrees, and for the New and Full Moons and eclipses. You'll also find an aspectarian in an ephemeris that gives the aspects between the transiting planets for each day. An ephemeris also lists the date and time that each planet turns retrograde and enters a new sign.

There are several different ephemerides available. They cover different lengths of time ranging from one year to 151 years, and the format on the page varies from one to another. Some list the planets places at noon Greenwich Mean Time (GMT), while others list them for midnight GMT. No one ephemeris is better than another. Which you choose depends upon personal preference. The single year ephemerides are handy for quick reference on a daily basis.

An ephemeris is also useful to quickly find any progressed planets that are turning direct or retrograde (see Chapter 2). Find your birthday (month, day, and year) in the ephemeris and count ahead, beginning with your birthday as the first year. This is a quick way to discover at what age any planets in your chart will switch direction. Pay particular attention to these years if this will occur in your chart because they are usually tied to significant events.

On the next page is an example from *AstroAmerica's Daily Ephemeris*, which is available in ten-year and twenty-year editions. All times are for midnight Greenwich Mean Time.

At the top of the page is the month and year, and to the left is data for an eclipse that occurs that month. The upper box has a line for every day in the month. At the left is the date. The second column lists the sidereal time (used for chart calculation), followed by columns for each of the planets. The degrees, minutes (and seconds for the Moon) and signs of the planets are indicated for each date. It is this box that you would scan when looking for a planet in a particular degree and sign.

The lower half of the page includes a box with the lunar phases (New Moon, First Quarter, Full Moon, and Third Quarter) that occur that month. To the right of this box is the date and time when the Moon in each sign forms its last aspect (after which it is void of course) and the date and time the Moon enters the next sign (Ingress). Next to the right is a box that shows the declinations of the planets for each day in the month. (Some astrologers use declinations, which measure the distance of a planet north or south of the ecliptic. The two declination aspects are the parallel, which is similar to

13 06:55 20♍10 ☉ Solar Eclipse (mag 0.788)
28 02:49 04♈40 ✹ Total Lunar Eclipse (mag 1.282)

September 2015

Day	S. T. h m s	☉ ° ' "	☽ ° ' "	☿ ° '	♀ ° '	♂ ° '	♃ ° '	♄ ° '	♅ ° '	♆ ° '	♇ ° '	☊ True ° '
01 Tu	22 39 22	08♍ 15 31	09♈ 39 26	05♎ 05	14♌ R58	14♌ 47	04♍ 27	28♏ 59	19♈R59	08♓R25	13♑R07	01♎D04
02 We	22 43 19	09 13 33	24 29 14	06 10	14 46	15 25	04 40	29 02	19 57	08 23	13 06	01 05
03 Th	22 47 15	10 11 37	09♉ 00 40	07 12	14 37	16 03	04 53	29 05	19 56	08 21	13 06	01 06
04 Fr	22 51 12	11 09 42	23 10 15	08 12	14 30	16 42	05 06	29 08	19 54	08 20	13 05	01 07
05 Sa	22 55 08	12 07 50	06♊ 56 48	09 09	14 25	17 20	05 19	29 11	19 52	08 18	13 04	01 08
06 Su	22 59 05	13 06 00	20 20 54	10 04	14 23	17 58	05 32	29 15	19 51	08 16	13 04	01R 08
07 Mo	23 03 01	14 04 12	03♋ 24 19	10 55	14D 24	18 36	05 45	29 18	19 49	08 15	13 03	01 07
08 Tu	23 06 58	15 02 25	16 09 28	11 43	14 26	19 14	05 58	29 21	19 47	08 13	13 03	01 05
09 We	23 10 55	16 00 41	28 39 04	12 28	14 31	19 52	06 11	29 25	19 45	08 11	13 02	01 04
10 Th	23 14 51	16 58 59	10♌ 55 44	13 10	14 39	20 30	06 24	29 28	19 43	08 10	13 02	01 01
11 Fr	23 18 48	17 57 19	23 02 00	13 47	14 48	21 08	06 37	29 32	19 41	08 08	13 01	01 00
12 Sa	23 22 44	18 55 40	05♍ 00 09	14 20	15 00	21 46	06 50	29 36	19 39	08 07	13 01	00 58
13 Su	23 26 41	19 54 03	16 52 19	14 49	15 13	22 24	07 03	29 39	19 37	08 05	13 01	00 57
14 Mo	23 30 37	20 52 29	28 40 38	15 13	15 29	23 02	07 16	29 43	19 35	08 03	13 00	00D 57
15 Tu	23 34 34	21 50 56	10♎ 27 20	15 32	15 46	23 39	07 29	29 47	19 33	08 02	13 00	00 57
16 We	23 38 30	22 49 24	22 14 53	15 46	16 06	24 17	07 42	29 51	19 31	08 00	13 00	00 58
17 Th	23 42 27	23 47 55	04♏ 06 00	15 53	16 27	24 55	07 54	29 55	19 29	07 59	12 59	00 59
18 Fr	23 46 23	24 46 27	16 03 49	15R 55	16 50	25 33	08 07	30 00	19 27	07 57	12 59	00 59
19 Sa	23 50 20	25 45 01	28 11 52	15 50	17 15	26 11	08 20	00♐ 04	19 25	07 55	12 59	01 00
20 Su	23 54 17	26 43 37	10♐ 33 57	15 39	17 41	26 48	08 33	00 08	19 22	07 54	12 59	01 00
21 Mo	23 58 13	27 42 15	23 14 02	15 20	18 09	27 26	08 45	00 12	19 20	07 52	12 59	01R 00
22 Tu	00 02 10	28 40 54	06♑ 15 51	14 54	18 39	28 04	08 58	00 17	19 18	07 51	12 58	01 00
23 We	00 06 06	29 39 35	19 42 27	14 22	19 10	28 41	09 11	00 22	19 16	07 49	12 58	01D 00
24 Th	00 10 03	00♎ 38 17	03♒ 35 36	13 42	19 43	29 19	09 23	00 26	19 14	07 48	12 58	01 00
25 Fr	00 13 59	01 37 01	17 55 05	12 55	20 17	29 56	09 36	00 31	19 11	07 46	12 58	01 00
26 Sa	00 17 56	02 35 47	02♓ 38 15	12 03	20 52	00♍ 34	09 48	00 36	19 09	07 45	12D 58	01 01
27 Su	00 21 52	03 34 35	17 39 38	11 04	21 28	01 11	10 01	00 40	19 07	07 43	12 58	01 01
28 Mo	00 25 49	04 33 24	02♈ 51 25	10 02	22 06	01 49	10 13	00 45	19 04	07 42	12 58	01 01
29 Tu	00 29 46	05 32 16	18 04 13	08 56	22 45	02 26	10 26	00 50	19 02	07 41	12 59	01R 01
30 We	00 33 42	06 31 09	03♉ 08 23	07 48	23 25	03 04	10 38	00 55	19 00	07 39	12 59	01 00

Data for	09-01-2015
Julian Day	2457266.50
Ayanamsa	24 04 33
SVP	05 ♓ 02 29
☽ ☊ Mean	02 ♎ 04 R

● ◐ PHASES ○ ◑

05	09:55	◑	12♊32
13	06:41	☉	20♍10
21	08:59	◐	28♐04
28	02:51	✹	04♈40

LAST ASPECT Day	h m	☽ INGRESS Day	h m	
01	16:38	02	09:03	♉
04	10:21	04	11:49	♊
05	23:05	06	17:41	♋
09	01:29	09	02:37	♌
11	13:04	11	13:56	♍
14	02:08	14	02:42	♎
16	04:22	16	15:43	♏
18	19:49	19	03:32	♐
21	08:59	21	12:33	♑
22	23:13	23	17:52	♒
25	04:03	25	19:44	♓
26	16:33	27	19:30	♈
29	07:46	29	18:58	♉

DECLINATION

Day	☉	☽	☿	♀	♂	♃	♄	♅	♆	♇
01 Tu	08N28	03N06	03S 46	09N01	17N29	10N42	18S 07	07N12	09S 10	20S 56
02 We	08 07	07 32	04 20	09 11	17 18	10 37	18 08	07 11	09 11	20 56
03 Th	07 45	11 25	04 53	09 20	17 07	10 32	18 09	07 10	09 12	20 56
04 Fr	07 23	14 32	05 25	09 29	16 56	10 27	18 10	07 10	09 12	20 57
05 Sa	07 01	16 43	05 56	09 38	16 44	10 23	18 10	07 09	09 13	20 57
06 Su	06 38	17 55	06 25	09 46	16 33	10 18	18 11	07 08	09 13	20 57
07 Mo	06 16	18 07	06 53	09 54	16 22	10 13	18 12	07 08	09 14	20 57
08 Tu	05 54	17 23	07 20	10 01	16 10	10 09	18 13	07 07	09 15	20 57
09 We	05 31	15 50	07 45	10 08	15 58	10 04	18 14	07 06	09 15	20 58
10 Th	05 08	13 35	08 08	10 15	15 46	09 59	18 15	07 06	09 16	20 58
11 Fr	04 46	10 45	08 30	10 21	15 35	09 54	18 16	07 05	09 16	20 58
12 Sa	04 23	07 31	08 49	10 27	15 23	09 50	18 17	07 04	09 17	20 58
13 Su	04 00	03 59	09 07	10 32	15 11	09 45	18 18	07 03	09 18	20 58
14 Mo	03 37	00 20	09 22	10 36	14 58	09 40	18 19	07 03	09 18	20 58
15 Tu	03 14	03S 20	09 34	10 40	14 46	09 36	18 20	07 02	09 19	20 59
16 We	02 51	06 53	09 44	10 44	14 34	09 31	18 21	07 01	09 19	20 59
17 Th	02 28	10 09	09 50	10 47	14 21	09 26	18 22	07 00	09 20	20 59
18 Fr	02 05	13 02	09 54	10 49	14 09	09 21	18 23	06 59	09 21	20 59
19 Sa	01 41	15 24	09 54	10 51	13 56	09 17	18 24	06 58	09 21	20 59
20 Su	01 18	17 06	09 50	10 52	13 44	09 12	18 26	06 58	09 22	21 00
21 Mo	00 55	18 01	09 42	10 53	13 31	09 07	18 27	06 57	09 22	21 00
22 Tu	00 31	18 01	09 31	10 53	13 18	09 03	18 28	06 56	09 23	21 00
23 We	00 08	17 01	09 15	10 53	13 05	08 58	18 29	06 55	09 24	21 00
24 Th	00S 15	15 00	08 54	10 52	12 53	08 53	18 30	06 54	09 24	21 00
25 Fr	00 39	12 00	08 30	10 50	12 40	08 49	18 31	06 53	09 25	21 00
26 Sa	01 02	08 10	08 01	10 48	12 27	08 44	18 32	06 53	09 25	21 01
27 Su	01 25	03 44	07 28	10 46	12 13	08 40	18 34	06 52	09 26	21 01
28 Mo	01 49	00N59	06 52	10 42	12 00	08 35	18 35	06 51	09 26	21 01
29 Tu	02 12	05 39	06 13	10 38	11 47	08 30	18 36	06 50	09 27	21 01
30 We	02 35	09 55	05 31	10 34	11 34	08 26	18 37	06 49	09 27	21 01

ASPECTARIAN

01 03:40 ☉ ☍ ♆
03:56 ☽ # ☿
05:04 ♀ ☌ ♂
05:33 ☽ □ ♇
08:25 ☽ △ ♀
08:37 ☽ △ ♂
16:38 ☽ ☌ ♅
22:00 ☽ ∥ ♅
23:48 ♀ # ♆
02 03:02 ☽ ∥ ☉
09:41 ☽ # ♆
10:04 ☽ ∥ ♀
17:02 ☽ △ ♃
18:14 ☽ ∥ ♃
22:54 ☽ ✶ ♆
03 02:07 ☽ △ ☉
06:51 ☽ △ ♇
09:20 ☽ □ ♀
12:25 ☽ □ ♂
04 10:21 ☽ ☍ ♄
14:27 ☉ ∥ ♅
21:06 ☽ □ ♃
05 00:17 ☽ ∥ ♂
02:23 ☽ □ ♆
04:12 ☽ △ ☿
13:16 ☽ ✶ ♀
19:28 ☽ ✶ ♂
23:05 ☽ ✶ ♅
23:09 ☉ △ ♇
06 06:15 ☿ # ☉
08:30 ♀ SD
07 04:28 ☽ ✶ ♃
09:02 ☽ △ ♆
12:32 ☿ # ♅
15:02 ☽ □ ☿
18:06 ☽ ☍ ♇
21:42 ☽ ✶ ☉
08 06:54 ☽ □ ♅
14:37 ♀ ∥ ♃
19:53 ♂ △ ♅
22:13 ☽ ∥ ♂
09 01:29 ☽ △ ♄
19:24 ☿ □ ♇
10 04:39 ☽ ✶ ☿
07:25 ☽ ☌ ♀
17:21 ☽ ∧ ♅
20:00 ☽ ☌ ♂
11 03:06 ☽ ∥ ♀
06:45 ☽ ∥ ♃
11:17 ☽ # ♆
13:04 ☽ □ ♄
15:26 ☽ # ☿
12 03:09 ☽ ∥ ♅
03:46 ☽ ☌ ♃
06:15 ☽ ☍ ♆
16:11 ☽ △ ♇
23:58 ☽ ∥ ☉
13 17:50 ☿ ∥ ♆
14 02:08 ☽ ✶ ♄
23:25 ☽ # ☉
15 02:14 ☿ # ♃
05:11 ☽ □ ♇
10:34 ☽ ☌ ☿
11:08 ☽ ✶ ♀
18:28 ☽ ☍ ♅
16 01:01 ☽ # ♅
04:22 ☽ ✶ ♂
17:47 ☽ ∥ ♆
18:42 ☽ # ♃
21:34 ☽ ∥ ☿
17 05:01 ☽ # ♀
06:56 ♃ ☍ ♆
07:48 ☽ △ ♆
07:49 ☽ ✶ ♃
17:51 ☽ ✶ ♇
18:11 ☿ SR
18 01:35 ☽ □ ♀
02:47 ♄ ♐
03:51 ♃ # ♆
09:44 ☽ # ♂
18:46 ☽ ✶ ☉
19:49 ☽ □ ♂
19 03:40 ☽ ☌ ♄
18:53 ☽ □ ♆
20:03 ☽ □ ♃
20 09:29 ☽ ✶ ☿
14:05 ☽ △ ♀
16:42 ☽ △ ♅
21 08:12 ☽ △ ♂
22 02:52 ☽ ✶ ♆
04:58 ☽ △ ♃
11:59 ☿ ∥ ♆
12:04 ☽ ☌ ♇
14:56 ☽ □ ☿
23:13 ☽ □ ♅
23 04:00 ♀ △ ♅
08:21 ☉ ♎
18:35 ☽ △ ☉
18:35 ☽ ✶ ♄
18:37 ☉ ✶ ♄
24 01:11 ☿ # ♃
16:09 ☽ △ ☿
18:58 ☽ # ♂
22:32 ☿ □ ♇
25 02:05 ☽ ✶ ♅
02:19 ♂ ♍
04:03 ☽ ☍ ♀
06:56 ♇ SD
07:53 ☽ # ♀
16:42 ☽ ∥ ♆
20:31 ☽ ☍ ♂
20:40 ☽ # ♃
20:41 ☽ □ ♄
26 01:03 ☽ ∥ ☿
01:13 ♂ □ ♄
07:20 ☽ # ♅
08:12 ☽ ☌ ♆
11:40 ☽ ☍ ♃
16:33 ☽ ✶ ♇
27 10:59 ☽ ∥ ☉
20:40 ☽ △ ♄
28 00:42 ☿ # ♅
04:35 ☽ # ☉
10:33 ☽ ☍ ☿
15:57 ☽ □ ♇
29 01:31 ☽ ☌ ♅
02:37 ☽ # ☿
06:22 ☽ ∥ ♅
07:46 ☽ △ ♀
15:29 ☽ ∥ ♃
21:18 ☽ # ♆
23:52 ☽ △ ♂
30 04:02 ☽ ∥ ♀
07:15 ☽ ✶ ♆
09:57 ☽ ∥ ♂
12:16 ☽ △ ♃
14:39 ☿ ☌ ☉
15:54 ☽ △ ♇

⚷ Chiron

01 Dec. 00 N 19

03	19♓38R
06	19 30
09	19 22
12	19 13
15	19 05
18	18 57
21	18 49
24	18 40
27	18 32
30	18 24

a conjunction, and the contraparallel, which is similar to an opposition.)

The ephemeris page also contains an aspectarian of the transiting planets. It shows all the aspects (including parallels and contraparallels) made by the planets during the month. They are listed by date and time.

TIMING EVENTS

Events rarely happen on the exact date that a progressed, solar arc, or outer transiting planet forms an aspect with a planet or angle. Usually, it's within a week or two, which isn't all that helpful if you're waiting for a job offer, for example. So if one of these exact aspects doesn't indicate the timing of an event, what does?

An inner planet transit.

The transiting Sun, Moon, Mercury, Venus, or Mars (or more than one of these planets) will give you the timing within a day or two. These triggers activate eclipses, progressions, solar arcs, and outer planet transits, setting events in motion. If you're looking for the timing of an event that could occur at any time within several months, begin with the New and Full Moons during that period. One or more of these will generally aspect the appropriate planet(s) in your chart, identifying a four- or two-week period as one with potential.

For example, suppose you're aiming for a promotion and see a solar eclipse in your first house that is square progressed Mercury in your tenth. But nothing happens. Rather than curtail your effort, assuming you've been passed over, this is time to communicate your interest and to take advantage of every opportunity to bring yourself to the attention of decision-makers.

In this case the eclipse activated the potential. But the energy will remain dormant until other transits come into play.

Looking forward, you see transiting Saturn will enter your sixth house in about three months, where it will form a trine to progressed Mercury in the tenth. The nearest New Moon will occur the week after Saturn makes its trine, and like the solar eclipse, it aspects progressed Mercury, this time by opposition from the fourth house. The odds are definitely leaning in your favor.

Then, after looking in the ephemeris for inner planet transits to progressed Mercury during the week of the New Moon, you see that Mars and Venus will do that by opposition within a few days. Transiting Mars and Venus will also, of course, form a sextile to transiting Saturn in the sixth house.

The final transit to look for is the Moon. In this example, it would probably be a sesquisquare to progressed Mercury because the Moon would reach that position a few days after the New Moon. This lunar aspect will thus occur on the same day that transiting Mercury forms an opposition to progressed Mercury, while Mars is still approaching the exact opposition to the same planet. (Remember, Mars often acts early.)

By following this procedure, you will almost always identify the date on which an event will occur.

Timing Example, Amanda

Amanda, the woman who needed to establish a credit history, is a college student with a part-time job in her future career field. She was named employee of the year for 2008, at

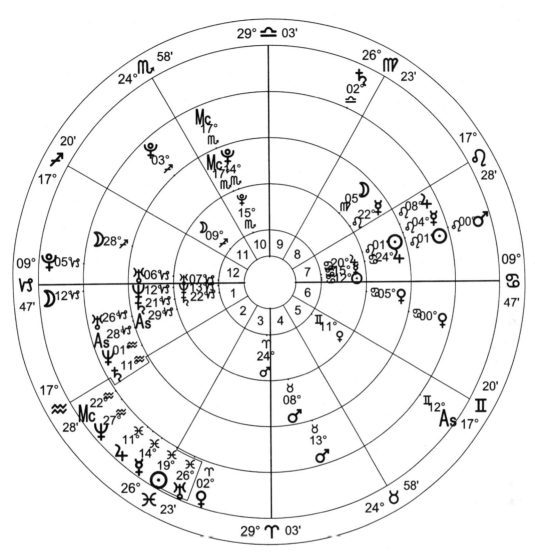

Chart 40: Amanda
Innermost wheel: Birth Chart / July 4, 1990 / 7:25 pm MST / Desert Samaritan Hospital, Phoenix, Arizona
Middle inner wheel: Secondary Progressed / March 9, 2010 / 12:11:40 pm MST / Desert Samaritan Hospital
Middle outer wheel: Directed Solar Arc / March 9, 2010 / 12:11:40 pm MST / Desert Samaritan Hospital
Outermost wheel: Job Layoff Transits / March 9, 2010 / 11:00 am MST / Phoenix, AZ
Placidus House

the start of the widespread economic downturn. Throughout much of 2009, rumors were rampant that the company, whose business was related to housing, might cease operations. A few people were laid off in 2009, but the doors were still open. Amanda and more than one hundred other employees were laid off March 9, 2010, when the company closed its doors.

In Amanda's natal chart (Chart 40), the job/career planets are Mercury (sixth house ruler) and Venus (Midheaven and tenth house ruler). But because her Midheaven is in the last degree of Libra, we should also consider the rulers of Scorpio, Mars and Pluto. The Moon could also be considered as a co-ruler of the sixth house. Note that Jupiter, Saturn, and Mars are in a t-square configuration in cardinal signs (and a grand cross with the Midheaven if a wider orb is used.). When one of these planets is aspected, it very quickly (cardinal signs) activates the energy of all the planets.

The January 15, 2010 solar eclipse at 25 Capricorn was the tip-off that she would need to deal with job/career matters that year. It was square the natal Midheaven and natal Mars, and conjunct/opposition the natal Saturn-Jupiter opposition. (The natal Saturn-Jupiter opposition represents the need to balance restriction and expansion, and with Saturn ruling her Ascendant and in the first house, she would naturally be more cautious. Saturn is also the universal career planet.) The eclipse was also conjunct solar arc Uranus (change), conjunct the solar arc and progressed Ascendants, and opposition progressed Jupiter.

Since career/job matters would be a focus for the following six to twelve months, and with the knowledge that her job could be in jeopardy,

the next task is to look for a time frame when something might occur. The New Moon of February 14 is a possibility, because at 25 Aquarius it was trine the natal Midheaven and sextile the progressed Moon in the twelfth house of hidden matters and secrets. This New Moon was conjunct transiting Neptune (natural ruler of the twelfth house). Both these twelfth house influences suggest there would be something going on of which she was unaware.

The New Moon energy would be active for the succeeding four weeks, so the next influence to study is the following Full Moon (completion), which occurred February 28 at 10 Virgo. It was square the natal Moon-Venus (tenth house ruler) opposition, sesquisquare/semisquare the natal t-square, trine progressed Mars (tenth house co-ruler), trine the natal Ascendant-Uranus-Neptune conjunction, sesquisquare solar arc Uranus (change), and trine solar arc Mars. Solar arc Saturn was trine natal Venus and solar arc Jupiter was trine natal Moon (activating the natal Moon-Venus opposition).

Altogether, the Full Moon indications appear to be more positive than negative, or at least fifty-fifty—until you look more deeply into the aspects involving the activated planets. First, the Full Moon was in the eighth house of other people's (employer's) money, as was the progressed Moon, which was trine natal Uranus, ruler of her second house of income. The progressed Moon was also sesquisquare natal/progressed Saturn, setting off the natal t-square. Activating the Midheaven, a hotspot because of the January solar eclipse, was the progressed Ascendant square that angle.

Remember that the New and Full Moons at this time of year are in approximately the same degrees, which means that the March and April New and Full Moons would aspect the same planets and angles in her chart. This, of course, leaves the question open regarding the timing of the layoff that she thought might be coming.

Before moving on to the inner transiting planets, it's important to check for reinforcing trends represented by the outer transiting planets. Transiting Saturn was semisquare the progressed Midheaven, transiting Uranus was sextile solar arc Uranus, and transiting Jupiter was trine natal Sun and sextile natal/progressed Neptune. All but one of these is a positive aspect, which might lead you to question whether the New and Full Moon timing is on target. What these aspects represent is opportunity (sextile) to make money (Neptune, ruler of the second) through other people (Sun in the seventh) and networking (Uranus).

The next step is to look at the transiting planets during the two week period following the Full Moon in search of a possible date. There were a number of key transits on March 9, the date the layoff occurred. The transiting Sun was trine natal Jupiter (activating the t-square), and transiting Mars was conjunct the progressed/solar arc Sun (eighth house ruler) and opposition solar arc Neptune (third house ruler and second house co-ruler). Transiting Venus was sesquisquare the progressed Midheaven (and opposition transiting Saturn in semisquare to the same angle). Transiting Venus also formed a trine with solar arc Pluto (tenth house co-ruler).

Transiting Mars was particularly key to the timing. It turned direct March 9, the date of the layoff. Matters put on hold during the retrograde period regained momentum.

There were several aspects from transiting Mercury (news and sixth house ruler) in the second house: trine natal Mercury (in the seventh), trine natal/progressed Pluto (in the tenth), semisquare the progressed Ascendant, and sesquisquare the natal Midheaven.

There should also be aspects to natal and/or progressed Venus if March 9 is a valid date for the layoff. Transiting Venus was separating from a square to solar arc Venus and approaching a square to progressed Venus, half way between the two. Look for these kinds of aspects and also those to the midpoint between a natal and progressed planet. These are both often hotspots in the chart.

There were three final triggers that made this date a potential one for a layoff. The first was the transiting Moon conjunct natal/progressed Neptune (third house ruler) and opposition natal Sun (eighth house ruler). This aspect, as do others involving the natal Sun and Mercury in opposition to natal Neptune, reflects the disbelief, disillusionment, and sense of loss that accompanies a layoff.

When she received the news, the transiting Midheaven was opposition progressed Mercury, and the transiting Ascendant was conjunct natal Venus. You will often see the transiting angles function as a final trigger.

This event did ultimately have a positive ending. A nearby business was looking for a part-time employee and the head of that company asked Amanda's previous employer if one of his laid-off employees might be interested in the job.

The March 2010 New Moon was at 25 Pisces at the end of her second house and aspecting the natal Saturn-Jupiter opposition by sextile/trine. It

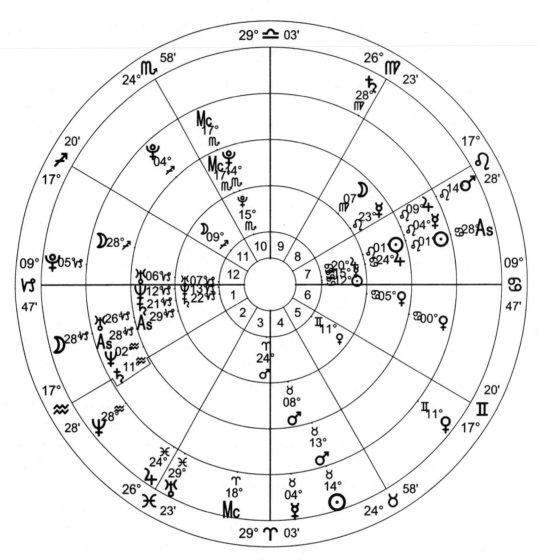

Chart 41: Amanda
Innermost wheel: Birth Chart / July 4, 1990 / 7:25 pm MST / Desert Samaritan Hospital, Phoenix, Arizona
Middle inner wheel: Secondary Progressed / May 4, 2010 / 12:11:40 pm MST / Desert Samaritan Hospital
Middle outer wheel: Directed Solar Arc / May 4, 2010 / 12:11:40 pm MST / Desert Samaritan Hospital
Outermost wheel: New Job Transits / May 4, 2010 / 10:45 am MST / Phoenix, Arizona
Placidus House

was followed by the Full Moon of March 30 at 9 Libra, which was square the natal Ascendant-Descendant and trine natal Venus from the ninth house. Although this New and Full Moon did not produce a job (and you would not expect it to because of the houses of the New and Full Moons), it was at that time that she delivered her resume to the neighboring business.

The next month had plenty of chart activity (Chart 41) related to job/career, beginning with the April 14 New Moon at 24 Aries opposition her natal Midheaven and square the natal Saturn opposition Mercury. The New Moon was followed by a Full Moon at 8 Scorpio in the tenth house trine progressed Venus in the sixth house, opposition progressed Mars in the fourth, sextile progressed Moon in the eighth, and sextile progressed/natal Uranus in the twelfth. It was also trine natal Sun, and square solar arc Saturn. So the potential was there in April for a job offer.

But that did not happen until May 4 (still under the New and Full Moon energy of April). It wasn't until then that the planets lined up to activate the necessary factors in her chart. Note that lucky Jupiter was at the same degree as the March New Moon, under which she had delivered her resume to what would be her new employer. You should always look for planets that activate what was aspected when initial action was taken, or an initial event occurred, that relates to a potential future date. Retrograde planets moving back and forth in aspect to a planet are excellent for pinpointing future timing.

On the date she got the job, transiting Venus was conjunct natal Venus (tenth house ruler); transiting Sun (eighth house ruler) was conjunct solar arc Mars (tenth house co-ruler), sextile natal Mercury (sixth house ruler), and trine natal/progressed Neptune (third house ruler); and transiting Mercury was sextile progressed Venus in the sixth. Transiting Saturn, which was retrograde, had retreated into Virgo and was trine the progressed Ascendant, an aspect that was triggered by the transiting Moon conjunct the progressed Ascendant and square the natal Midheaven.

Here again the transiting Ascendant and Midheaven were excellent timers. The transiting Midheaven was trine natal Jupiter at the time of the job offer, and the transiting Ascendant was square the natal Midheaven and opposition the progressed Ascendant.

Timing Example, Jennifer Aniston

Astrologers are often consulted by people who want to know when an opportunity will arise to begin a significant relationship that could lead to commitment. The key indicator to look for when forecasting and identifying a time frame is the Ascendant-Descendant (relationship axis): natal, progressed, and solar arc. Sometimes only one of them will be aspected, and sometimes two or three of them will be aspected along with the ruler of the seventh house and planets in that house. At times you'll also see aspects to the Midheaven-IC, which represent a change in status and the couple establishing a new home.

The Descendant ruler and Venus (natal, progressed, and/or solar arc) are also usually active when commitment is in the forecast. Be sure to check progressed Venus in the ephemeris. This planet changing direction (retrograde or direct) often indicates major relationship events.

Actors Jennifer Aniston and Brad Pitt were married July 29, 2000. The union lasted just a

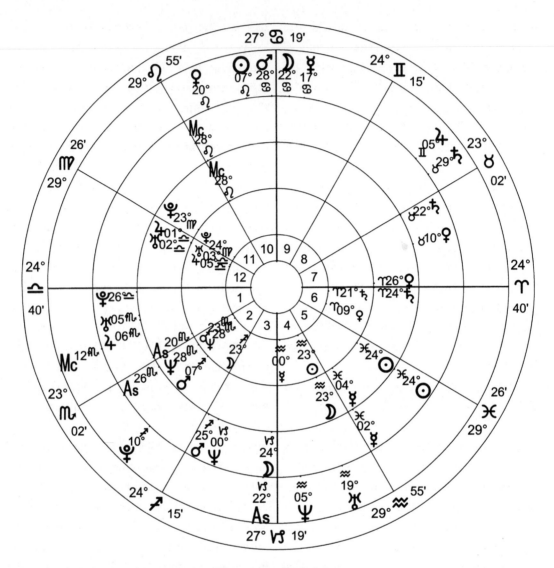

Chart 42: Jennifer Aniston
Innermost wheel: Birth Chart / February 11, 1969 / 10:22 pm PST / Los Angeles, California
Middle inner wheel: Secondary Progressed / July 29, 2000 / 12:11:40 pm PST / Los Angeles, California
Middle outer wheel: Directed Solar Arc / July 29, 2000 / 12:11:40 pm PST / Los Angeles, California
Outermost wheel: Wedding Transits / July 29, 2000 / 7:02 pm PDT / Malibu, California
Placidus House

few months short of five years, although the couple announced the separation January 7, 2005. Divorce papers were filed August 22, 2005, and the divorce was final on October 2 of the same year.

There were many aspects at the time of the marriage (Chart 42) that included several to both the natal and progressed Ascendant-Descendant. The most obvious progressions are progressed Saturn conjunct the natal Descendant, and progressed Venus square the natal Midheaven-IC.

Progressed Saturn, which moves very slowly, was arriving at that point thirty-one years after she was born and would soon cross the Descendant, indicating the possibility of another major relationship event. At the time of the wedding, it was well within orb, only eighteen minutes from the exact conjunction. Saturn rules the fourth house in her chart, adding the interpretation of a change in status (square to the Midheaven) and relocation (square to the IC). As a planet, Saturn rules responsibility and commitment, and can indicate longevity in a relationship when active at the time of a marriage. Conversely, Saturn can make the individual feel trapped and alone, cooling the passions and the commitment, and making it difficult to connect on an emotional level. Some astrologers also interpret this as a karmic connection.

Progressed Venus had crossed the Descendant in 1992, and was approaching a square to the natal Midheaven-IC when the couple married, indicating a change in status. This is a good example for timing because it would be natural to assume she would enter into a significant relationship as progressed Venus crossed the Descendant. But in 1992, that would have been the only such aspect and there was no Ascendant-Descendant involvement. Instead, because Venus rules her Ascendant, she was very involved in attracting the people and making the connections that would launch her career.

Among the outer planet transits, Uranus and Pluto offered yet other possibilities for commitment. Transiting Uranus was square the progressed Ascendant-Descendant, and transiting Pluto was trine natal Venus, in hard aspect (semisquare, sesquisquare) to all four natal angles, and sesquisquare progressed Saturn.

Uranus is frequently active in commitment charts, and can indicate a sudden decision in addition to a change in status. When Uranus is transiting the Ascendant-Descendant, it's important to check whether the planet is stationing, retrograde, or direct, and whether it will make another contact to the same angles. When a second contact is in the near future, the marriage can be short-lived.

The active Pluto in Jennifer's chart is of particular interest. Although the couple may be the only two people who know the true significance of this transit, it indicates power and control issues, especially with the close involvement with progressed Saturn, natal Descendant, and progressed Venus. Transiting Pluto was also trine natal Venus. On a practical level, Pluto, ruler of Jennifer's second house, reflects the extravagant and expensive wedding.

Mars rules Jennifer's Aries Descendant, but there is not a lot of activity with this planet. On the wedding date, the progressed Moon was square natal Mars. Note that her natal chart has a Venus-Mars sesquisquare, so any planet that aspected either of these also activated the other one.

Moving on to the eclipses, there were two during the month of the wedding. The first, a lunar eclipse (Full Moon) was at 24 Capricorn 19, aspecting all four natal angles as well as progressed Venus and Saturn, solar arc Pluto, and the progressed and solar arc Ascendants and Descendants. The second eclipse, a solar eclipse (New Moon) at 8 Leo 12, was trine natal Venus.

On the wedding date, there were five transiting planets at the top of her chart, putting her in the limelight. Transiting Mars (ruler of the seventh house) was trine natal and progressed Neptune, which were conjunct (one minute from exact in an approaching aspect). But here we also see transiting Saturn opposition the Mars-Neptune conjunction, an aspect that would repeat in November 2000 and April 2001. Saturn and Neptune do not mix well. Saturn is reality, and Neptune is fantasy. This is not the best of aspects under which to begin a marriage, and probably about the time of the last aspect in 2001, the romantic illusion had faded. Also on the wedding date, the transiting Sun was trine progressed Mars, and transiting Venus trine natal Saturn.

Rather than stop with the wedding date, it can be enlightening to look beyond the event and study the aspects that will be in effect during the next several years. This can indicate any difficulties and possibly how they can be handled by the couple. In some cases, this can be especially valuable information if an individual is unsure about a possible commitment.

This marriage ended in divorce, and a look at the intervening years reveals a number of planetary factors that indicated that possibility. There is generally a turning point, a date with many aspects, that indicates the ending of a relationship. Before that, however, you will see the trends begin to shift that way and build, with more and more progressions, solar arcs, and outer transiting planets becoming active. This of course reflects what is happening between the two people: a gradual deterioration of the relationship.

Below is the chain of major aspects involving the Ascendant-Descendant, Venus, and Mars in Jennifer's chart between the wedding and the divorce:

- 2000–2001: transiting Saturn opposition natal/progressed Neptune
- 2001: transiting Uranus semisquare natal Venus
- 2001–2002: transiting Saturn opposition progressed Mars
- 2001–2002: transiting Uranus square progressed Ascendant-Descendant
- 2001–2002: transiting Uranus conjunct natal Sun
- 2001–2002: transiting Uranus square natal Mars
- 2002: transiting Saturn opposition solar arc Mars
- 2002: progressed Mercury square progressed Mars
- 2002–2003: transiting Uranus square solar arc Ascendant-Descendant
- 2003: progressed Saturn exactly conjunct the natal Descendant
- 2003: progressed Venus turns retrograde
- 2003–2004: transiting Saturn square natal Venus

- 2004: transiting Saturn sesquisquare natal Mars
- 2004: transiting Saturn square natal Ascendant-Descendant
- 2004: transiting Neptune square solar arc Venus

There are a significant number of Uranus aspects in 2001 and 2002, when the relationship undoubtedly began to undergo stress and strain, possibly because Jennifer was in an independent period with Uranus conjunct her Sun. A shift likely occurred in 2002, when there were difficult aspects involving Mars, but the real turning point was 2003, when progressed Venus turned retrograde and progressed Saturn moved into the seventh house. From there, the relationship deteriorated under all the Saturn aspects, which were further highlighted by the October 14, 2004, solar eclipse at 21 Libra 06 conjunct her natal Ascendant and opposition natal Saturn and progressed Venus, Saturn, and the Moon in the seventh house. A lunar eclipse on October 28, 2004, at 5 Taurus 02 was in her seventh house and square natal Mercury (ruler of the ninth house of legal matters), sesquisquare the natal Moon, opposition solar arc Pluto, and sextile solar arc Mercury.

The separation was announced as transiting Saturn was square Jennifer's Ascendant-Descendant (Chart 43), progressed Saturn, progressed Moon, progressed Venus, and progressed Saturn (the same points contacted by the solar eclipse). Saturn was also trine natal Mars and the progressed Ascendant, and sesquisquare progressed Mars.

Most telling of the aspects was the progressed Ascendant conjunction natal Mars (sev-enth house ruler) and square natal Sun. The seemingly positive progressed Mars trine natal Venus was not at all an easy aspect because it activated the natal Venus opposition Jupiter conjunct Uranus (Venus opposition Uranus is a classic divorce aspect). Natal Venus also was involved in a sesquisquare with the progressed Ascendant, and progressed Mars was semisquare/sesquisquare the natal Ascendant-Descendant.

There is another outer planet aspect that deserves mention in the context of the divorce: transiting Pluto conjunct natal Moon and square natal/progressed Pluto. Jennifer undoubtedly has deep emotions and can be obsessive at times (natal Moon-Pluto square). This aspect also drives her to achieve financial wealth. On another level, however, the second is the house of self-worth, and this event must have devastated her far more than all but those closest to her realized.

Prior to the January 4, 2005, announcement that the couple was splitting up, there was a New Moon on December 12 at 20 Sagittarius 22 conjunct Jennifer's Moon. The December 26 Full Moon was at 5 Cancer 12 square her natal Venus and the natal Jupiter-Uranus conjunction, and opposition solar arc Neptune.

Also in December, Mercury turned direct on the 19th at 10 Sagittarius conjunct her progressed Mars. Transiting Venus was at the same point on December 24, along with the transiting Moon in Gemini, and transiting Mars had advanced to conjunct progressed Mars and trine natal Venus on the date of the announcement.

Can astrology tell us when the decision was made, at least in her mind? She likely came to this conclusion over several days during the week of December 20, with a final decision

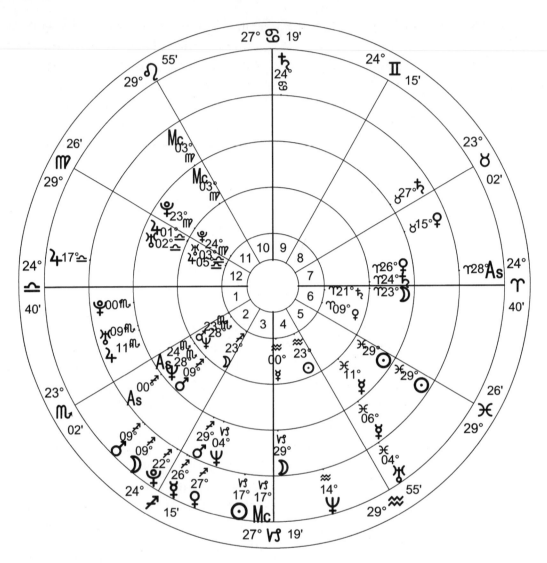

Chart 43: Jennifer Aniston
Innermost wheel: Birth Chart / February 11, 1969 / 10:22 pm PST / Los Angeles, California
Middle inner wheel: Secondary Progressed / January 7, 2005 / 12:11:40 pm PST / Los Angeles, California
Middle outer wheel: Directed Solar Arc / January 7, 2005 / 12:11:40 pm PST / Los Angeles, California
Outermost wheel: End of Relationship Transits / January 7, 2005 / 12:00 pm PST / Los Angeles, California
Placidus House

under the December 26 Full Moon that triggered the natal Venus-Uranus opposition. Just prior to the Full Moon, transiting Mercury and Venus were conjunct her progressed Mercury.

On the date of the announcement, transiting Mercury and Venus were approaching a conjunction to solar arc Mars and a square to progressed/solar arc Sun. The Moon was in Sagittarius, where it triggered the aspects of transiting Mars.

CHECKLIST FOR TIMING EVENTS

1. List the progressed to natal and progressed to progressed planet aspects, along with keywords or comments for each.

2. List the houses the planets occupy and the houses they rule, along with keywords or comments for each.

3. List the solar arc to natal planet aspects, along with keywords or comments for each.

4. List the houses the planets occupy, and the houses the planets rule, along with keywords or comments for each.

5. Identify the prevailing trends, such as money, career, family, or relationships.

6. List any eclipses that activate the progressed or solar arc planet aspects, along with the houses they occupy.

7. List the New and/or Full Moons that aspect the progressed or solar arc planet aspects, along with the houses they occupy. Major hard aspects (conjunction, square, opposition) are usually the most effective.

8. Search for inner transiting planets within the New/Full Moon time frame that aspect the progressed and solar arc aspects. Begin with Mars, the action planet, and move backward to the Sun. Remember, some hard aspects, including the semisquare and sesquisquare, are necessary to trigger an event.

9. Zero in on the dates with the most aspects within a two to three day time frame, and look at the Moon's position. Find the date the Moon forms a hard aspect to the transiting planets in aspect to the progressed and solar arc aspects. This date has the highest potential for an event.

10. Now create two tri-wheel charts, either by drawing the planets in a chart form or by calculating the charts on a computer. The first tri-wheel should have your natal chart in the inner wheel, your progressed chart in the middle wheel, and the transits for your selected date in the outer wheel. The second is the same, with the solar arc chart substituted for the progressed chart. Or use a quad-wheel chart with the solar arcs in the third wheel.

During this process, be sure to take your natal chart into consideration. What appears to be a negative event or outcome could be positive if the same aspect in your natal chart is positive. The reverse is also true; easy aspects involving a difficult natal aspect may not have a positive outcome.

You can also use the above steps to predict the outcome of a specific event when you know the scheduled date for an interview, presentation, first date, travel, etc. When you understand the aspects in effect for that date, you will be more aware of potential difficulties and can often take action to minimize them.

DAILY FORECASTING

Everyday life is full of minor events, most of which go almost unnoticed. Some, however, such as a clash with a coworker or family member, can leave you feeling unsettled. Frustration can put a damper on the day when you stand in a long line at the bank or to pay for groceries, or shop without finding what you want. Some social gatherings are fun and upbeat, while others trigger thoughts of making a quick exit.

All of these events and more can be tracked in the daily planetary positions, both the transiting planets in aspect to each other and in aspect to your natal, progressed, and solar arc planets and angles. By knowing in advance what you might expect, you can take precautions to avoid a difficult coworker, select a good day for shopping, or know when to host a social event.

Much of this depends upon the transiting Moon, which moves through all the houses and signs about every twenty-eight days. As the Moon transits the zodiac, it aspects other planets, activating them. For example, days with the Moon in Libra are generally good for dates and socializing. But not if the Moon will be square Saturn.

The interpretations later in this chapter are guidelines for daily events. Use them as a starting point to spark your thinking rather than view them as self-limiting "musts" and "shoulds." The aspect interpretations can be used for aspects between transiting planets as well as aspects from the transiting planets to your natal, progressed, and solar arc planets and angles.

EVERYDAY EVENTS

Astrology can be an effective guide in knowing the best days for specific activities. You can do this in several ways. Of course, the more information you have the better the potential outcome. But practicality also has a role. Busy people rarely have time to study a series of charts and aspects in order to determine the best day to shop for clothing or host a party. My recommendation is that you use only the transiting planets, taking into consideration the house they're transiting in your natal chart and the rulers of these houses. A thorough study that includes solar and lunar returns and transiting planet aspects to your natal, progressed, and solar arc planets is better reserved for major events such as applying for a loan or mortgage, purchasing a vehicle, or taking a major vacation.

The easiest way to evaluate the astrological influences on a given date is to use the ephemeris. First find the Moon sign, and then look at the aspectarian to determine what major planetary aspects (conjunction, sextile, trine, square, opposition) the Moon will make while it is in that sign. You can also use astrological calculation software, but you need to be careful because it's not always easy at first to see the lunar aspects. With practice, however, using software can be just as effective.

Jacklyn's Shopping Trip

This example using Jacklyn's natal chart (Chart 44) illustrates how to find a good date for a specific activity—shopping for clothing. First look in the ephemeris for the dates when the Moon is in Leo, the sign that rules clothing. In March 2010, the Moon was in Leo on the 25th and 26th. Now, turning to the aspectarian, it lists these transiting planet aspects for the two dates in Mountain Standard Time (subtract seven hours from GMT ephemeris time):

March 25th
Moon sextile Saturn (4:22 a.m.)
Moon conjunct Mars (5:16 a.m.)
Moon trine Sun (10:58 a.m.)

March 26th
Moon trine Mercury (8:07 a.m.)
Moon trine Venus (6:38 p.m.)

March 27th
Moon opposition Neptune (12:05 a.m.)

Overall, these look like good days for shopping just based on the lunar aspects. If the Moon-Mars conjunction had been during normal retail hours, March 25 would not be a good choice because she would tend to buy on impulse. Later that morning, though, there was a Moon-Sun trine, which would be excellent, as would later in the day on the 26th as the Moon approached a trine to Venus.

Before looking at where these planets fall in her chart, it's important to review the concept of approaching and separating aspects. An approaching aspect is one that has not yet become exact as would be the case up until 10:58 a.m. on the 25th, the time the transiting Moon formed an exact trine with the transiting Sun. After that trine, the Moon-Sun contact would be called a separating aspect.

Looking at Jacklyn's chart, when the transiting Moon is in Leo, it is in her ninth and tenth houses. The Moon's movement can be estimated on *average* at about one degree for every

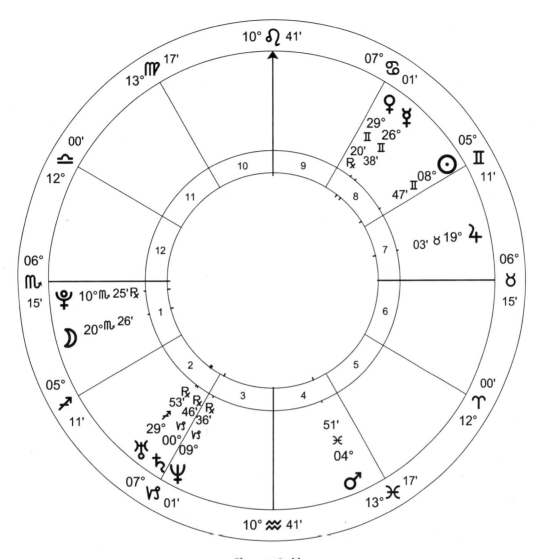

Chart 44: Jacklyn
Birth Chart / May 29, 1988 / 4:50 pm MST / Phoenix, Arizona / Placidus House

two hours of time, so it would move into her tenth house (10 Leo 41 on the cusp) almost twenty-two hours after it entered Leo (2:40 a.m. MST on the 25th, according to the ephemeris), or around midnight. In fact, the Moon entered Leo, and her tenth house, at about 8:30 p.m. on the 25th. Why was it earlier?

Two hours per degree for the Moon's movement is an *average*. Leo is a sign of long ascension, meaning the Moon (and any planet) takes longer to transit this sign. The signs of long ascension are Cancer, Leo, Virgo, Libra, Scorpio, and Sagittarius, and the signs of short ascension are Capricorn, Aquarius, Pisces, Aries, Taurus, and Gemini.

Using the average of two hours per degree, it would take sixty hours for the Moon to transit a sign (2 hours x 30 degrees, or two and one-half days). With a sign of long ascension, it takes the Moon a little more than forty-eight hours to transit a sign, or about two days. But in a sign of short ascension, the Moon transits a sign in a little more than thirty-six hours, or about a day and a half. So, in reality, in order to accurately estimate the Moon's motion, you would need to be aware of this timing.

If Jacklyn wanted to shop online, the Leo Moon in the ninth house (long distance) would probably be a better choice, given that the aspects on both dates were favorable. However, if she wanted to shop in a store, the 26th would be a better choice. With the Moon in the tenth house, she would attract more attention and thus more easily find a clerk to help her.

The second house of your natal chart is also a consideration when looking for good dates to shop. You can approach this in one or both of two ways. Jupiter is the ruler of Jacklyn's second house (Sagittarius on the cusp). A date with favorable lunar transiting aspects to Jupiter would be a good choice, but because Jupiter at the time was in Pisces, the Leo Moon would not form a major aspect to it. In Jacklyn's chart, natal Uranus is in the second house, and this planet would receive a trine from the transiting Leo Moon before changing signs and moving into Virgo to form a trine with natal Saturn, also in the second house. This Moon-Saturn aspect would thus be a good time for her to shop—if it weren't in the middle of the night.

Days on which the transiting Moon forms favorable aspects to transiting Jupiter, ruler of her second house, would be others to consider, as would days when the transiting Moon is in Sagittarius or early Capricorn in her second house.

Most days are a mixture of hard and easy aspects, and it's rare to find any two to three day period when the Moon forms only easy aspects. This is one reason why it's important to pay attention to when aspects become exact. Once they begin to separate, their influence quickly dissipates. Keep this in mind, for example, if a day has a single favorable aspect followed by a string of unfavorable ones. If you shopped on such a day, you might like the item in the store and then change your mind upon returning home.

There is another lunar factor you need to be aware of: the void-of-course Moon. This event occurs at some time during the Moon's transit through each sign. The Moon is void of course between the time it makes its last major exact aspect to another planet and the time it enters the next sign. For example, if the last major aspect a Taurus Moon forms is a square to

Saturn at 24 Aquarius 15, the Moon would be void of course until it entered Gemini, the next sign. In rare instances the Moon can be void of course within a few hours of when the Moon enters or leaves a sign. Usually it's during the last half or third of its transit through a sign.

The classic definition of a void-of-course Moon is "nothing will come of it." If you follow this guideline (an overall good choice), you would not want to shop while the Moon is void of course because you wouldn't find what you were looking for.

Again, you want the greatest number of positive aspects in effect during the time of the activity. Suppose, for example, that on the night of a first date the Libra Moon will trine Venus an hour or so after you meet for dinner, and then thirty minutes later the Moon will square Saturn. Conversation would be congenial as the Moon approached Venus, and there would likely be some level of attraction. But as soon as the Moon began to separate from Venus and approach the square to Saturn, you might find your date boring and have no interest in seeing

---

BEST DAYS FOR VARIOUS ACTIVITIES
UNDER FAVORABLE TRANSITING ASPECTS

Shop for clothes: Moon in Leo, Venus or Sun aspect

Shop for groceries: Moon in Cancer or Virgo

Shop for home decor: Moon or Venus in Cancer, Venus aspect

General shopping: Moon in Taurus is thrifty

Sales and lucky finds: sometimes favorable lunar aspects to retrograde Mercury can trigger deep discounts and significant markdowns on mismarked items

Send out resumes: New Moon in the sixth house, Moon in Virgo

Job interviews: Moon in the sixth or tenth house, Moon in Virgo or Capricorn, Mercury or Saturn aspect

Travel by car: Moon or Mercury in Gemini, Mercury aspect

Travel by air: Moon in Aquarius, Moon in the ninth house, Uranus or Jupiter aspect

General travel: Moon in Gemini or Sagittarius, Mercury or Jupiter aspect

Dates: Moon in Leo or Libra; Moon in the fifth or seventh house, Venus aspect

Repairs: Moon in Virgo, Moon in the sixth house, Mercury aspect

Social event: Moon in Libra, Moon in the fifth, seventh, or eleventh house

Party: Moon in Leo, Moon in the fifth house

Haircut: Moon in Capricorn, Saturn aspects

Hair styling: Moon in Capricorn, Venus aspects

Pets: Moon in Virgo, Moon in the sixth house

Dining out: Moon in the fifth house

him or her again. But if after the Venus aspect, the Moon went on to form a sextile with Uranus, you might see possibilities for friendship in addition to romance.

As should now be apparent, you can make yourself crazy trying to look at everything and find the perfect day for any activity. There is no such thing! This is why I find it best to keep things simple and look only at the transiting planets for everyday activities, and sometimes the natal house that rules the specific activity. With a little experimentation, you can find the signs and planetary aspects that work best for you and your chart for everyday activities.

DIURNAL CHARTS

A diurnal chart is another technique you can use for everyday activities. In essence, the diurnal chart is the daily equivalent of the monthly lunar return and the annual solar return. It is calculated for the current date using the individual's birth time (and time zone in effect at birth) and birth place. (In my experience, charts calculated for the birth place are more accurate than those that are relocated.)

You can read a diurnal chart on its own, but it can be far more effective if you study it in conjunction with the natal chart. The diurnal chart can bring natal chart potential into the forefront of activity on a specific date. For example, one woman who has three planets in the fifth house of speculation, won more than $5,000 playing slot machines during the several days that her natal fifth house planets were trine the diurnal chart Ascendant. So look for dates when natal planets aspect not only the diurnal Ascendant but any diurnal chart angle. These are usually

---

ASPECTS TO THE DIURNAL ASCENDANT

Use these interpretations as a starting point, and be sure to consider matters related to the natal house ruled by the planet. The conjunction is generally favorable with the Moon, Sun, Venus, Mercury, and Jupiter, and challenging with Mars, Saturn, and, sometimes, Pluto.

Sun in easy aspect: Encourages self-confidence and leadership ability, and is favorable for contact with men and children

Sun in hard aspect: Unfavorable for contact with men and people in authority, and can indicate minor difficulties with children

Moon in easy aspect: Good for contact with women and the public, and indicates adaptability and a desire for variety

Moon in hard aspect: Fluctuating emotions and a high level of sensitivity are indicated by this aspect, which is unfavorable for contact with women and the public

Mercury in easy aspect: Good for all forms of communication, contact with siblings and neighbors, and taking tests

Mercury in hard aspect: Restlessness is common with this aspect, which can bring unwelcome news or difficulties with a vehicle or mechanical device as well as neighbors and relatives

---

Venus in easy aspect: Favorable for shopping for clothing and jewelry, social events, dates, massage, and beauty treatments

Venus in hard aspect: Unfavorable for dates and social events, and clothing purchased now may be returned or never worn

Mars in easy aspect: High energy favors physical activities, including sports

Mars in hard aspect: Accidents, anger, and arguments are possible, as is a traffic ticket, and nervous energy is high

Jupiter in easy aspect: Communication with in-laws or someone at a distance is possible, and this placement favors travel

Jupiter in hard aspect: High expectations could fail to materialize, and overoptimism can lead to disappointment; legal matters are unfavorable

Saturn in easy aspect: Favorable for planning, organization, completing projects, and career matters, and there may be communication from an elderly person or someone from the past

Saturn in hard aspect: Avoid new endeavors and energy-draining activities; vitality is lowered; possible dental problems

Uranus in easy aspect: Unexpected yet positive events, communication from friends, and involvement in a group or team effort

Uranus in hard aspect: Potential for unexpected news and mechanical or electrical problems; not the time to purchase electronics

Neptune in easy aspect: Good for romance and creative activities; intuition is strong

Neptune in hard aspect: Potential for deception and disillusionment, confusing communication, sensitivity to medication and alcohol, secrets may be revealed

Pluto in easy aspect: Determination and willpower are strong, and a windfall is possible; excellent for cleaning closets and storage spaces

Pluto in hard aspect: Unfavorable for relationships; high potential for frustration, controlling people, anger, and financial difficulties

the most active days from a diurnal chart perspective. If the interpretation is unclear or you want additional information, look to the natal house that contains the diurnal Ascendant. The area of life governed by this house is sometimes relevant.

It's important to remember, however, that the Moon's degree (and sign and house) shown in the chart is for your birth time; that is, if you were born at 8:00 a.m., the chart will show the Moon at its 8:00 a.m. position on the date of the diurnal. This means it could advance a considerable distance throughout the day if the birth time was in the early morning, or be at the end of its transit for a night birth.

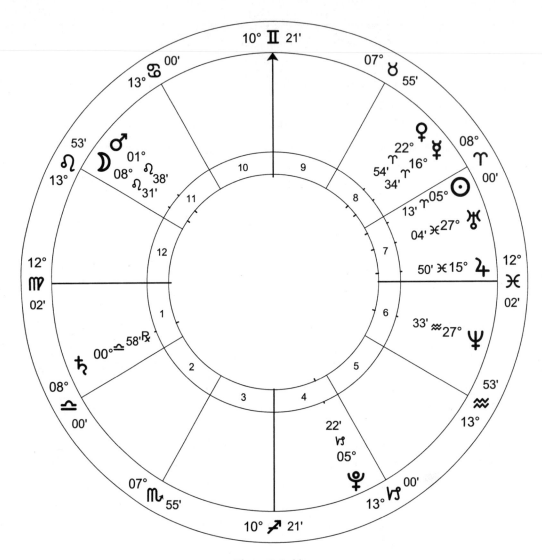

Chart 45: Jacklyn
Diurnal Chart / March 25, 2010 / 4:50 pm MST / Phoenix, Arizona / Placidus House

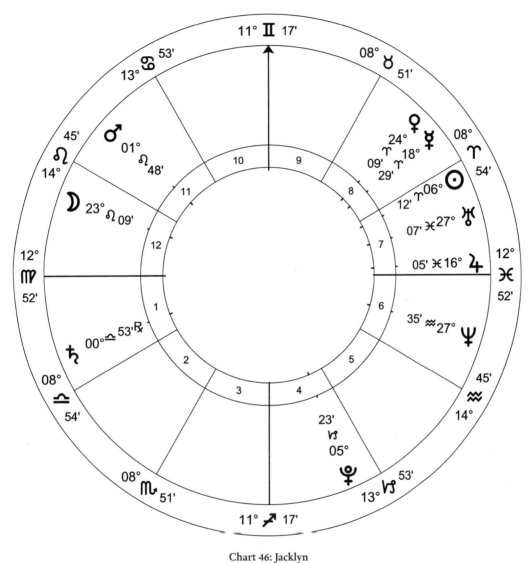

Chart 46: Jacklyn

Diurnal Chart / March 26, 2010 / 4:50 pm MST / Phoenix, Arizona / Placidus House

There is often another benefit from using the natal and dirunal charts together. By merging the information in both you can see how to maximize the day's transits and activities. Jacklyn's chart is a good example of this.

Jacklyn: Diurnal Example

After two days that offer favorable shopping times for Jacklyn were identified, the task now becomes to determine which day is best. The diurnal charts for the two dates are helpful in answering that question, or more correctly, giving her two options.

The first diurnal chart (Chart 45) has the transiting Moon in the eleventh house, making March 25 a good choice if she wants to shop and spend the day with friends. In the March 26 diurnal chart (Chart 46), the Moon is in the twelfth house (better for going solo), where it forms a trine with first Mercury and then Venus in the eighth house of other people's money. These aspects could lead her to sale items. Note also that Venus in the eighth house rules the second house of the diurnal chart, increasing the possibility for saving money. Mercury rules the diurnal chart Virgo Ascendant (Jacklyn), and with Mercury also ruling the diurnal Midheaven (an influence similar to the transiting Moon in her tenth house on the 26th), a helpful clerk could notice her and help her find what she wants on sale.

Anthony's Driver Test: Diurnal Example

Gaining a driver's license is a teenage right of passage. Nearly every young person looks forward to the event that parents approach with at least some level of trepidation. Having acquired a learner's permit, possibly attended driving school, and practiced for hours, teens fully expect to pass the driving test on their first try. Some pass, some don't.

Although fully prepared with many hours of practice behind him, Anthony failed his first attempt at the driving test because of parallel parking. The examiner told him to park within a set of four pylons, but Anthony instead managed to squash two of them with the car's tires. He later said he didn't understand the word "pylons," and that he would have passed if the examiner had used the word "cones." Anthony's mother was amused, as was the examiner. About two weeks later, Anthony passed the driving test and did quite well on the parallel parking segment.

A look at the diurnal charts for the two dates shows why they had different results. Each of the charts has the diurnal chart on the inside wheel and Anthony's natal chart on the outside wheel. On both dates he took the test in the afternoon, around 3:00 p.m.

Anthony failed the driver's test on March 19, 2010 (Chart 47). This chart has 27 Taurus 06 on the Ascendant. His natal Mars-Pluto conjunction was conjunct the diurnal chart Descendant and opposition the Ascendant. This is the first red flag. Mars is associated with haste, Pluto with control. Together, the placement of these planets conjunct the Descendant in the seventh house represent another person, which in this case is the examiner. But because these planets are favorably aspected to the Sun-Uranus conjunction in the diurnal eleventh house (goals), the driver's test infraction would not be a serious one, such as an accident.

The diurnal chart Moon is at 12 Taurus 41. By the time he took the test, however, the Moon

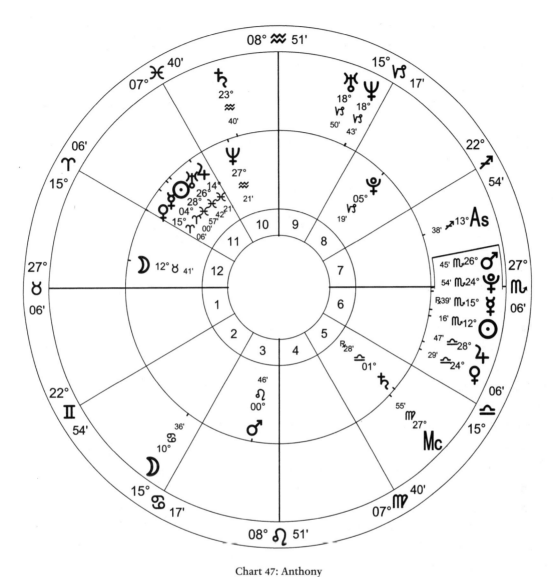

Chart 47: Anthony
Inner wheel: Diurnal Chart / March 19, 2010 / 9:25 am MST / Phoenix, Arizona
Outer wheel: Birth Chart / November 4, 1993 / 9:25 am MST / Phoenix, Arizona
Placidus House

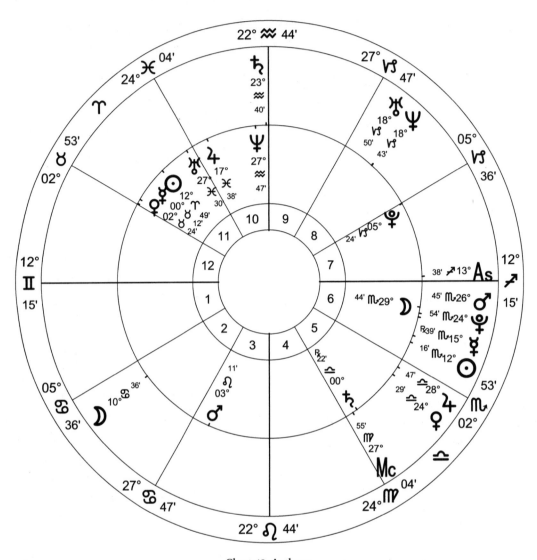

Chart 48: Anthony
Inner wheel: Diurnal Chart / April 2, 2010 / 9:25 am MST / Phoenix, Arizona
Outer wheel: Birth Chart / November 4, 1993 / 9:25 am MST / Phoenix, Arizona
Placidus House

had advanced about three degrees, where it was opposition his natal Mercury, the planet that rules tests and vehicles. The Moon is also relevant to the test because it rules the third house (vehicles, tests) of the diurnal chart. Mars in the diurnal third is sesquisquare diurnal Jupiter, which compounds the haste of natal Mars opposition the diurnal Ascendant.

So March 19 was not an auspicious date for Anthony's driving test. On April 2, however, he had no problems with the driving test and passed with a high score.

The first positive indicator in the April 2 diurnal chart (Chart 48) is Gemini (vehicles, tests) rising. Anthony's natal Ascendant was on the Descendant of the diurnal chart, forming a connection between him (Ascendant) and the examiner (Descendant). Also helpful was the diurnal Sun at 12 Aries 49 sextile/trine the Ascendant-Descendant.

With Cancer still on the diurnal third house cusp, the diurnal Moon remains an important factor in whether he would pass or fail. By the time he took the test, the diurnal Moon at 29 Scorpio 44 had changed signs, moving into Sagittarius, where it was trine diurnal Mars in the third house.

As in the case of Anthony's driver's test, diurnal charts can be helpful in selecting the best date for everyday activities. These charts can also show when there might be developments concerning major trends in your chart. Look for the dates when the diurnal chart angles are in aspect to a progressed, solar arc, or outer planet transit configuration.

TRANSITING RETROGRADE INNER PLANETS

Anyone who knows a little about astrology, as well as a sizeable number of other people, are aware of Mercury's retrograde periods, which occur three or four times a year. The general public is less aware of the retrograde periods of Venus and Mars, possibly because they are less frequent. Venus is retrograde about every eighteen months, and Mars is retrograde about every two years.

The value of these retrograde periods tends to get lost in all the doom-and-gloom forecasts about miscommunication and mechanical breakdowns (Mercury), relationship difficulties (Venus); and a lack of action (Mars). These characteristics are valid, albeit at times overemphasized, or used as an excuse. More to the point, retrograde periods are a time to pause, reflect, and prepare for moving forward when the planet turns direct. If you're a highly active person, for example, retrograde Mars can be very frustrating. But that is all the more reason why you can benefit from the retrograde period and a brief time out to catch up with life and yourself.

When action related to the retrograde planet is taken, the event or activity resurfaces during the next retrograde period. For example, if you purchase a washing machine when Mercury is retrograde, it could have a mechanical problem during the next retrograde period. Gifts purchased under a retrograde planet are often returned or exchanged. Software companies seem somehow to be aware of Mercury retrograde periods because you'll see updates issued during that time. Makes sense. Of course they want to profit from additional upgrades in the future.

There is one caveat when the inner planets are retrograde. If one of these planets is retrograde in your natal chart, transiting retrograde periods can actually work out well for you.

In general, when Mercury is retrograde, it's unwise to sign documents; make major and possibly life-changing decisions; or purchase a phone, appliance, vehicle, or anything mechanical. Batteries often die when Mercury is retrograde, and sometimes the need for a major repair will come to your attention. In the case of the latter, hold off until Mercury turns direct if you can. If not, get a second opinion and estimate. The best option, of course, and part of Mercury's message, is to maintain mechanical devices. If you ignore problems when they arise, retrograde Mercury will often bring you a reality check in the form of an expensive repair.

The cardinal astrological rule with retrograde Venus is never marry or commit during this time. Sometimes the relationship is "undone" at the next (or any succeeding) Venus retrograde period. Sometimes it's not, but why take the chance? Venus is also a money planet, so these matters require caution during retrograde periods. Postpone major purchases and especially household decor and furnishings, clothing, jewelry, luxury items, and gifts. This is not the time to seek a loan or mortgage, but you could use retrograde Venus to review your credit report and deal with any errors.

Retrograde Mars can be particularly frustrating, both personally and in the world at large. During these periods it seems as though all action and initiative grinds to halt. Nothing happens. Decisions are postponed. It's the classic "hurry up and wait" scenario. And no matter how hard you try to gain momentum, nothing moves. It's as though the entire world decides to go on vacation at the same time. The purpose? To learn patience, of course.

Retrogrades are an invaluable tool in predictive astrology. The reason is simple: when a planet turns retrograde, it retraces its steps, again contacting planets it aspected as it approached its retrograde station. (A planet stations, or appears to stop, when it turns retrograde or direct.) The same thing happens after the planet stations direct. Here, again, the ephemeris is handy because you can quickly and easily see the degrees the retrograde planet will contact.

Suppose, for example, you have natal Venus at 15 Gemini conjunct natal Sun at 19 Gemini in the sixth house. You want to search for a new job and see that Mercury will station retrograde conjunct your natal Sun. If you submitted applications as Mercury, approaching its retrograde station, was conjunct Venus, you could then be called for an interview when Mercury, after stationing retrograde conjunct your Sun, returned to Venus about ten days later. Unless you have planets in degrees earlier than Venus at 15 Gemini, you might hear nothing more until Mercury, after stationing direct, again forms a conjunction with Venus four to five weeks later. At that point you could attend a second interview and be offered the job a few days later when Mercury is conjunct your Sun.

You'll also see things like this happen: a man mailed a package on October 14, 2006, when Mercury, which was direct, was at 16 Scorpio. Mercury subsequently turned retrograde on October 28 at 25 Scorpio, and then stationed direct at 9 Scorpio on November 28. The package was finally delivered November 28, when Mercury returned to 16 Scorpio, the degree under which the package was mailed.

LUNAR DIARY

A lunar diary is one the best ways to gain practical forecasting skills and to learn how your chart reacts to various transits. After doing this for a month or two, you'll begin to see patterns emerge that can be helpful when forecasting major events.

Make notes for a full month as the transiting Moon moves through each house in your chart and forms aspects to your natal planets. You can look for the aspects ahead of time, but a better option is to make notes in a mobile device as minor events occur during each day. Then compare your notes to the house position and transiting aspects that were in effect at the time. Most astrological software can generate a "hit list" of aspects to your chart for any time frame.

Something else to note is what happens as the Moon aspects the planets in your chart by degree, from the lowest degree to the highest (from zero through twenty-nine degrees). You should see a pattern emerge here also, with a similar chain of reaction to any event, such as communication, followed by aggravation, followed by an upbeat mood, followed by praise, etc. Keep track of how these chains unfold depending upon whether the aspects are hard or soft. You will quickly see how closely events and your reaction to them are tied to your natal planetary placements and configurations. This knowledge can help you learn to better manage situations because you'll know what in your chart triggers which response.

If you're really ambitious after keeping a diary for a couple of months, you can expand the lunar diary project to include aspects to progressed and solar arc planets.

INNER PLANET TRANSITS

Sun

Sun in the Houses

Sun in Aries/First House: The time is ripe for new endeavors, especially personal ones, because you're interested in fulfilling your own needs and desires. Confidence and motivation are high at this time, but take care not to lapse into a self-centered or self-absorbed mind set. Consider and include others when making plans, and listen to alternate viewpoints.

Sun in Taurus/Second House: Reassess your values, both material and personal, during this transit. This can be an excellent time to clean and organize closets and storage spaces, but you'll have a tendency to hang onto more than you should. You might also have a desire to update your look, which you can do on a budget. This lunar influence is great for finding bargains.

Sun in Gemini/Third House: The daily pace picks up, and if it feels like you're on the go from morning 'til night it's probably not much of an exaggeration. You'll also need to manage calls and mail; otherwise, both could eat up your time. Force yourself to set aside thirty minutes a day for yourself, and try to take a day or weekend trip, both of which can be restful and relaxing.

Sun in Leo/Fifth House: Your focus is on fun with the Sun here. So make plans to socialize, see a sporting event, and romance a love interest. This is also a great time to learn or spend time with creative projects and hobbies. If you're a parent, this transit accents more involvement with your children. This time can be favorable for investments if other factors are in agreement.

Sun in Virgo / Sixth House: This is a great time for a lifestyle change because your focus now is more on health and wellness, including beginning an exercise program and gradually shifting to a more nutritious diet. Both can help maximize productivity at work, where demands can be high at this time. You also could acquire a pet, and get involved in a volunteer activity.

Sun in Libra / Seventh House: Relationships and cooperative efforts are in focus with the Sun here. Use this time to connect with people, spend extra hours with your mate, and function as a mediator when necessary, encouraging compromise. This transit can also be beneficial for consultations with experts such as an attorney or accountant. The New Moon in the seventh house can trigger an engagement.

Sun in Scorpio / Eighth House: Your focus is on money matters, especially joint resources, including insurance, partner's income, and credit and creditors (check your credit reports). If other factors are in agreement, this can be a favorable time to apply for a loan or mortgage. The Sun here can also be helpful for getting rid of unwanted items because you're more willing to part with them.

Sun in Sagittarius / Ninth House: This influence encourages you to expand your horizons and knowledge through travel, learning, reading, or talking with people. The Sun here is favorable for taking a quick class for fun or to enhance a job skill. You're also likely to have contact with people at a distance as well as in-laws and former schoolmates. Spirituality is also emphasized at this time.

Sun in Capricorn / Tenth House: You're in high focus now, so it's important to be a leader and let decision-makers see the best you have to offer. Career gains, including a promotion, are possible, especially if the New Moon makes favorable contacts to your chart. Your ambitions also come alive under this influence, so get energized and go after what you want.

Sun in Aquarius / Eleventh House: After all the recent career activity, it's time to take a break to get together and socialize with friends and coworkers. Take advantage of networking opportunities, which can enhance and reinforce your goals. You might also get involved in a team project at work or another organization where you can connect with like-minded people.

Sun in Pisces / Twelfth House: Consider this time a gift from the universe when you can retreat from your busy life through daily meditation or solitude. Your sixth sense is active now, but you're also susceptible to those who might have less than your best interests at heart. Also take precautions to protect your health as this transit can trigger a cold or virus.

Sun Hard Aspects

Sun-Sun: You can be at the center of the universe now, or experience frustration when events don't go according to plan. The outcome of this aspect has much to do with your ego. Keep it in check and the world is more likely to grant your wishes simply because you'll have all the determination necessary. But don't drive yourself too hard. Be kind to your mind and body.

Sun-Moon: Your emotional needs drive you to succeed now, but difficulties can arise if your ego and feelings clash, pulling you in two directions. Try to put a little distance between yourself and current events so you can get a fresh perspective. That will help you to balance the two influences. Your reactions now could be tied to subconscious desires and unresolved issues.

Sun-Mercury: Errands, calls, meetings, and mail can consume much of your time, so try to plan ahead. Throughout it all your brain works overtime, which can make it tough to fall asleep. Unwind before bedtime. It's also important to be receptive to other viewpoints because under this aspect you have a higher than usual ego investment in your own ideas.

Sun-Venus: Relationships are either at their best or somewhat strained. Much depends upon your willingness to compromise and to work in tandem for mutual gain. This aspect can put you in touch with new people, and trigger a romantic rendezvous. But it's not the best for shopping because you'll either walk away empty-handed or indulge in expensive luxuries.

Sun-Mars: New endeavors do well if you plan before you act as this is not the time for impulsive moves. Your energy and drive are high now, which can be positive if you carefully direct it into productive outlets. But slow the pace in order to limit the chance of an accident on the road, at home, and at work. Also do your best to avoid difficult people and step away at the first sign of conflict.

Sun-Jupiter: Optimism can get the best of you now simply because you want to do it all. If you take on only what you can complete and then deliver as promised you'll reap the good fortune this aspect can trigger. Solid effort and a practical approach are the way to make your own luck. This aspect also favors learning if knowledge is your motivation.

Sun-Saturn: This aspect can reflect lowered vitality as well as delays and stumbling blocks that lead to frustration. But it also encourages you to persevere and can be a real asset for planning and organization. You'll be more productive if you can work on your own rather than as a team member. Conflict with a supervisor or another authority figure is possible.

Sun-Uranus: An independent streak takes hold when this aspect is in effect, prompting restlessness and a desire to be free of all restriction. That works if you're on vacation, but it's not the best if work demands attention. Do the next best thing: take a break, go for a walk. Change and the unexpected can occur, requiring you to adapt. You could clash with a friend or group.

Sun-Neptune: Daydreams and a desire to escape the daily grind accompany this aspect. Avoid alcohol and be cautious with medication. Used positively, this aspect can enhance your creativity and your intuition, and meditation is a good outlet to activate both. With the right words, you can charm most anyone now, but beware because others can do the same to you.

Sun-Pluto: Power issues come to the forefront now even if it's tough to define why the ego clash even occurred. Analyze your motives if you're the source of the issue, which could be rooted in self-esteem, and steer clear of controlling people. Also use your common sense and stay away from locations and potential situations where you could be subject to physical harm.

Sun-Ascendant: Because your focus is on you now, take care not to alienate others as you pursue your own interests. View people instead as a mirror image of yourself, reflecting what you both like and dislike about yourself. Chances are, you'll learn more than a few things about life and relationships, compromise and cooperation, and how to maximize your strengths.

Sun-Midheaven: Under this aspect you can connect with important people who could help advance your ambitions. But resist the urge to broadcast your accomplishments. Be subtle instead. It will get you further. At home, put family needs on an equal footing with your own, or better yet, be the one who compromises. Spend quality time with those you love.

Sun Easy Aspects

Sun-Sun: Most everything goes smoothly under this positive influence, which is also great for social events because you feel confident and at one with yourself. Sports and hobbies are positive ego-satisfying outlets, and you can more easily connect with and enjoy time with children. If other factors are favorable, you could do well with an investment.

Sun-Moon: You feel and look good, and your friendly aura attracts people under this aspect. Relationships with women can be especially favorable now, and it's a good time to host a small get-together for friends or enjoy leisurely hours with family. If you work with the public, people will be receptive to your ideas and assistance, and possibly offer praise for your efforts.

Sun-Mercury: Curiosity enhances your communication skills, which are an asset in everything from routine talks to meetings and interviews. Sign contracts, shop for and repair mechanical devices, and handle personal paperwork.

Sun-Venus: This aspect signals an upbeat mood along with popularity and an affectionate nature. Do dinner with your mate, or a date and friends. Finances and business negotiations benefit from this influence, but be sure to look at the downside as well as the upside, because you can easily gloss over the details. It's also a good time to shop and get a makeover or new hairstyle.

Sun-Mars: Everything fresh and new appeals to you now, and you can easily zip through most anything you tackle, thanks to high energy, initiative, and confidence. Slow down enough, though, to be sure you've covered all the details, and resist the urge to scatter your efforts by beginning several new projects. Exercise and sports are particularly refreshing.

Sun-Jupiter: A lucky streak is a winning combination with your enthusiastic optimism, and chances are, you'll be in the right place at the right time to take advantage of a moment of good fortune. This aspect is good for travel if other factors are in agreement, as well as upbeat news from a distance or regarding education. Put your faith in the future and back it up with solid planning.

Sun-Saturn: A strong work ethic equates to high productivity and potential career gains now or in the future. This is a favorable time to apply for a job or promotion. The same is true of real estate deals, home improvements, and property purchases or rentals if other aspects are in agreement. Contact with elderly people is positive, even uplifting, because your patience is enhanced.

Sun-Uranus: Most of all, this aspect encourages you to embrace the freedom to be yourself in group activities and when socializing with friends. Change is appealing and variety negates boredom, as does being with people who are in some way unique. This time frame is positive for electronics purchases, but keep your budget in mind because gadgets hold a special appeal.

Sun-Neptune: Let intuition be your guide in sensing what others think and feel, and offer a helping hand to those who need it. But don't let others take advantage of the sympathies this aspect can activate as it encourages you to see only what you want to see. This is a great time for romance and creativity, both of which are complimented by music.

Sun-Pluto: Willpower is your prime resource while this aspect is in force, and it can help you accomplish whatever you focus on. Use it wisely and profitably for positive, constructive change, including tossing out or organizing distracting clutter. People sense the power within you now, and you can attract the attention of movers and shakers, especially by leading by example.

Sun-Ascendant: You can build relationships, both personal and professional, through social and business gatherings. Doing this comes naturally now because people respond to your energy. Take care, though, with the conjunction, which can make you self-absorbed. Personal tasks are favored now, and you can successfully launch new endeavors if other factors are in agreement.

Sun-Midheaven: This is the time to stretch yourself and expand your ambitions while setting new goals for achievement. Although career advancement is possible, this aspect is more likely to bring you to the attention of decision-makers. Family time adds depth to your life now if you invest the time and energy into strengthening these relationships.

Moon
Moon in the Signs and Houses

Moon in Aries/First House: Your emotional responses are quick and up front now, and everyone knows exactly where you're coming from. This is positive if you're sensitive and tactful. Then others are likely to respond with mutual caring and kindness. If you come on too strong, though, you could drive away the very support you need at this time.

Moon in Taurus/Second House: This influence is helpful for budgeting, and can help you find thrifty bargains, but if you're feeling low, resist the tendency to shop or eat to lift your spirits. Do something constructive instead. Bolster self-esteem by treating yourself well with healthy food. Gardening, even with potted plants, can settle your soul. Drop a few coins in a piggy bank.

Moon in Gemini/Third House: It's tough to separate thoughts from feelings under this influence because you think how you feel and feel how you think. If you can separate the two, this is a good time to invest your heart and soul in a challenging project because you'll have the incentive to satisfy your emotional needs. You could also be in touch with siblings or neighbors.

Moon in Cancer/Fourth House: You feel comfortable and secure at home, so try to spend more time there the next few days. Cook for fun, entertain friends, enjoy quality time with family, or get started on a small home improvement project. People in general may respond more emotionally now, and you're more inclined to reach out to those closest to you.

Moon in Leo/Fifth House: Give voice to your love, whether for a friend, partner, or child. They'll especially like the extra attention, as will you when you hear the positive response. Play brings joy to your life now, and the Moon here brings out your generosity. Create something heartfelt for your home or a family member. Take care with investment decisions, however, which can be emotionally driven.

Moon in Virgo/Sixth House: On a practical level, domestic chores are tiring but satisfying and you'll be delighted with the end result. Avoid the inclination to criticize those closest to you, or to suffer in silence if someone hurts your feelings. Pets can touch your heart and trigger an emotional moment, as can involvement in a charitable cause. Female coworkers could be helpful.

Moon in Libra/Seventh House: You share an affectionate rapport with others, especially your partner and loved ones. If conflict arises, however, try to mask your emotions because people will more easily sense this weak spot now. You can successfully encourage cooperation and facilitate compromise both at home and at work. This is a good time for professional consultations.

Moon in Scorpio/Eighth House: Emotional connections are intense, and you're possessive of people and things. This can be detrimental to a close relationship, driving a wedge between you and the other person. Remind yourself that security comes from within. A positive use of this influence is to free yourself from unneeded and unwanted possessions.

Moon in Sagittarius/Ninth House: This is a time to smile, laugh, and be happy and free-spirited. See a comedy, spend time with light-hearted friends, or explore the wonders of nature. Expanding your knowledge base is also a key theme here, something you can do by talking with people, reading, or the Internet. You could reconnect with childhood or school friends, or hear from in-laws.

Moon in Capricorn/Tenth House: This is a position of high visibility, and one that fuels your ambitions. So it's easy to take a serious approach that says you're "all business." Lighten the mood as you interact with others, especially those who could further your aims. Practical activities such as planning and organization fit well with the Moon here, as do property matters.

Moon in Aquarius/Eleventh House: This influence emphasizes friendship and group activities, so the Moon here favors teamwork and networking, as well as social events. You can more easily maintain a healthy distance with people, making this a time when emotions will have a lesser role in relationships. Gadgets and electronics attract your interest.

Moon in Pisces/Twelfth House: Listen to your intuition. It can be a helpful guide in everyday activities. Be cautious, though, about sharing secrets, even with those you see as trustworthy. Solitude is appealing now because you're more sensitive to your environment. Loud noises and voices can be particularly unsettling, while quiet music is soothing.

Moon Hard Aspects

Moon-Moon: This aspect can trigger moodiness and deep feelings even if it's not apparent to others. You're more sensitive now, and even minor slights can unsettle or upset you. Interaction with females can be positive or negative, depending upon other factors, but in any case you should be cautious if an important discussion cannot be postponed.

Moon-Mercury: Keep this in mind: thoughts are more emotionally based now, with your heart guiding your head. This is not the time for important discussions or decisions, which are likely to change when your feelings shift in a new direction. If other factors are positive, however, this time can be favorable for well-rehearsed presentations that focus on facts.

Moon-Venus: This aspect is good for window shopping, but not spending, and social events as long as you don't overindulge. Moderation in all things is the best choice. A minor upset is possible with someone close to you, possibly because he or she feels neglected. Extra attention can minimize the possibility if your mind is focused on giving rather than getting.

Moon-Mars: Your actions are based on emotion now, meaning you can be impulsive. Try to ignore petty annoyances and frustrations that are realistically of no consequence in the big scheme of things. Consider the source, think calm thoughts, and move on. Otherwise, it's possible that a minor event could escalate into a major one. Be cautious with tools and on the road.

Moon-Jupiter: Optimism and a desire for freedom motivate you to move forward with confidence. Just be sure your direction is anchored in reality rather than based on faith alone. When channeled into a constructive endeavor, this energy can yield great results, although you'll

need to be open to new ideas and viewpoints rather than be locked into your own.

Moon-Saturn: This aspect can have you feeling down in the dumps, with low energy and a general aura of pessimism. The weight of responsibility, whether real or perceived, can cause you to characterize this time as an uphill battle. With support from others lacking, you can feel lonely. But this aspect can also trigger ambition. Find joy in something simple.

Moon-Uranus: You're restless and impulsive now and your emotions and mood can fluctuate from one extreme to another. You crave excitement and change, and it's tough to focus on the task at hand. Mental stimulation can help minimize your short attention span. Try using a new approach for routine tasks, take a walk, do a puzzle, or learn a quick time-saving technique.

Moon-Neptune: You're sensitive to people and your environment, and the briefest comment or action can trigger an upset because your emotions are so near the surface. Resist the urge to jump to conclusions because it's easy to misinterpret what someone says or does. This aspect can enhance your sixth sense, and daydreams are a good escape for this sentimental phase.

Moon-Pluto: When this aspect is active, intense feelings can prompt jealousy and possessiveness, as well as an emotional power struggle. The reason for it can be valid or only your perception, but it's difficult to know what is reality and what is imagination. Remove yourself, even if only mentally, to gain a fresh perspective. Calm thoughts can give you strength.

Moon-Ascendant: This aspect encourages you to communicate your feelings to those close to you, and to offer them your assistance, care, and concern. This can help fulfill your current need for emotional contact while building mutual support. But it's also possible to use an overly emotional approach with relationships, which can result in your efforts being rebuffed.

Moon-Midheaven: You're pulled in two directions: career and family. Pressures in both these areas can be difficult to manage, but this is all the more reason to consider your priorities and to realign them as necessary. Fortunately, you easily sense what others want and need, which has the side benefit of being an asset if you have a presentation or interview during this time.

Moon Easy Aspects

Moon-Moon: From public life to private life, you're in touch with your feelings as well as the people who surround you. Family life can be especially meaningful now, and comfort food enjoyed at home with loved ones is more than usually satisfying. This is also a good time to toss around home improvement ideas and to purchase furnishings or decor to enhance your space.

Moon-Mercury: Communication is your main focus under this aspect and you easily connect with almost anyone you try to reach. This is a good time to make calls, send e-mail, and post messages on social networking sites. Females are especially receptive to requests now and can be helpful in answering questions and providing needed information.

Moon-Venus: This aspect favors social events, dates, and romantic dinners. Equally appealing is time at home with those you love, because family members (or roommates) are on the same wavelength and in a congenial mood. You can also use this planetary energy to rearrange furniture, plant a garden, plan or host a party, or shop for decor.

Moon-Mars: Share your upbeat energy and high confidence wherever you go. It will quickly and easily rub off on others, making this a great time to take the lead in a small project or brainstorming session. This aspect also favors physical activity such as a workout at the gym, and is good for sporting events. Ease up on the gas, however, because you'll want to speed.

Moon-Jupiter: Your happy, easygoing mood is infectious, bringing smiles, laughter, and good cheer to those you touch. This aspect is also good for broadening your knowledge on a specific subject or the world at large. It can trigger positive news from afar or in legal or educational matters if other influences are in agreement. Favors are granted if you ask.

Moon-Saturn: You feel secure, although reserved, and patience is helpful in dealing with minor challenges and unimaginative people. This aspect is better for quiet activities and talks than for big or lively events. It also favors high productivity and a satisfying sense of accomplishment. Take advantage of any opportunity to brighten an older person's day.

Moon-Uranus: Organizational meetings, group activities, and friends give you a lift and possibly a pleasant surprise. Grab the opportunity to introduce yourself to new people and to network because one of them could provide an unexpected link to someone who could in some way open a door for you. Also use your imagination to trigger innovative ideas and approaches.

Moon-Neptune: Sentimental and sensitive now, you have a soft spot for loved ones, close friends, and those in need. Take care, though, to offer support without taking on their baggage. Daydreams are a delightful diversion, and night dreams can be insightful. This aspect also adds to your charm, making it a favorable time to convince others to see things your way.

Moon-Pluto: Depth of emotion allows you to get in touch with your feelings, not in an upsetting way but in an uplifting one. On a practical level, this aspect is good for tending to domestic repairs and generally restoring order at home and at work. Clean closets and drawers to satisfy the urge for change. You can easily let go of what you no longer want or need.

Moon-Ascendant: Congenial relations with everyone from coworkers to partners make life pleasant. Smile, spread cheer, and offer assistance to encourage and reinforce mutual support. Most of all, you feel good about yourself, ready to meet life head-on and succeed at whatever you do under this aspect. This time also favors loving moments with your mate.

Moon-Midheaven: Job visibility and success give you satisfaction and could bring praise from higher-ups. You can enhance the effect by being seen and heard, by bringing yourself to the attention of decision-makers. Also be there for your family, and share your feelings and love. They won't know how you feel unless you tell them, and this can brighten their day as well as yours.

Mercury

Mercury in the Signs and Houses

Mercury in Aries/First House: Speak up. Express yourself, your ideas, and viewpoints. Doing this is effective because you're clearheaded and think quickly, as long as you pause and really listen to feedback from others. Resist the urge to make snap decisions and sharp retorts. This influence can also trigger restlessness, which can be calmed with a walk or workout.

Mercury in Taurus/Second House: The emphasis is on money matters and this influence encourages you to think and plan before you spend. Look for coupons and special discounts, and then comparison shop. Also seek and read information on current financial trends. On another level, Mercury challenges you to examine your values, particularly those related to money and possessions.

Mercury in Gemini/Third House: Errands, calls, e-mail, meetings, and appointments occupy more of your time now, so plan ahead to accommodate a busy schedule with high demands on your time. Needed information is readily available, and this is also good timing if you want to take a quick class. Expect increased contact with siblings and neighbors.

Mercury in Cancer/Fourth House: This aspect encourages time with family during which long talks can strengthen ties. It's also favorable for entertaining friends and relatives, and for family reunions and researching your roots. Hands-on domestic projects can be rewarding, especially if you first make a detailed plan and then learn or improve do-it-yourself skills.

Mercury in Leo/Fifth House: This is a good time to socialize, read for pleasure, see plays or movies, learn a new hobby, and create something with your hands or mind. Sporting events, games, and outings with children are entertaining. This is also the house of speculation so you can put Mercury to good use now by learning more about investments and how to profit from them.

Mercury in Virgo/Sixth House: Details command your attention at work, where you're more productive than usual. But this influence can also prompt you to miss the big picture, so take time to review work from a wider perspective. If other factors are favorable, a job search could be successful. Exercise, rest, and nutritious food help counteract the effect of nervous tension.

Mercury in Libra/Seventh House: Contracts and negotiations benefit from this transit, which emphasizes compromise. Open communication can strengthen any close relationship, but you may also need to deal with competitors, so it's wise not to reveal all you know. You can develop a good rapport in professional consultations, but be sure to check references.

Mercury in Scorpio/Eighth House: This influence generally favors financial discussions and joint decisions made with a partner. If other factors agree, the timing is favorable for loan, mortgage, and other credit applications. Also check your credit report. There is a hidden side to this transit that encourages you to probe your subconscious in private moments.

Mercury in Sagittarius/Ninth House: Expand your knowledge during this transit by taking a class or learning on your own, through travel, or by sharing and trading information with others. People at a distance can be an excellent source of information, and you may communicate with in-laws and former school friends. Legal matters can come up for discussion, or you could be called for jury duty.

Mercury in Capricorn/Tenth House: Your career can benefit from this transit, which presents a good opportunity to attract attention from decision-makers. Get better acquainted with the boss, be the first to accept an extra assignment, and offer to take the lead in a project. Any of these can help to advance your aims as can presentations. A job search could yield results.

Mercury in Aquarius/Eleventh House: Teamwork is your best avenue to success under this transit, and networking runs a close second. See friends, attend social events, and get involved in a group activity at work or in your free time. Also review and update personal and job goals, or establish them, along with a how-to plan and time line to achieve them.

Mercury in Pisces/Twelfth House: You may hear secrets during this transit, but stop short of sharing your own because they're likely to be revealed, possibly by someone you erroneously consider to be trustworthy. On a personal level, this is a good time for solitude and a slower pace that includes plenty of sleep. Think, read, and meditate to access your subconscious and your inner voice.

Mercury Hard Aspects

Mercury-Mercury: Life is hectic as people, communication, and errands consume your time and energy. Try to stay focused amid all the distractions so you can capitalize on your especially active mind. But resist a tendency to dwell on even mildly upsetting events and issues. Deal with problems head-on, and move on. Ask for advice, but make your own decisions.

Mercury-Venus: Take the initiative to resolve a minor disagreement so it doesn't fester and mushroom into something more. With a little effort, peace is easily achieved. Social events are a pleasant diversion now, and offer the opportunity to meet people and network. You'll be instantly attracted to some people, but dislike others who appear to be on a completely different wavelength.

Mercury-Mars: Little things, minor irritations and frustrations, will get to you under this transit. Any one of them can spark your temper, so make the effort to accept that life doesn't always go as planned and think calm thoughts when the moment arises. Slow down and be cautious when driving, and don't put yourself in a position that could trigger an accident.

Mercury-Jupiter: Your thinking is focused on the big picture, but don't forget the details, which are equally important under this aspect. Also be realistic about what you can complete in an allotted time frame because you tend to be overly optimistic now. It might also be tempting to brag about accomplishments, but that won't sit well with other people even if you do deserve praise.

Mercury-Uranus: This aspect can trigger innovative ideas. Unfortunately, it also encourages impulsive decisions and comments. Think carefully before you speak or write, and counsel yourself to go with the flow even though action is your preference. Unexpected news and developments could require a change of plans. Be sure to back up all computer files and beware of viruses.

Mercury-Neptune: Cover your bases. Confusion and misunderstandings are likely, and your thoughts are hazy even if you think all is crystal clear. Also keep secrets and rumors to yourself rather than risk the chance of someone using the information against you. The advantage with this aspect, however, is that you can almost effortlessly avoid prying questions, partly through intuition.

Mercury-Pluto: The difference between intensity and obsession is a fine line when this aspect is in effect. If you can avoid the latter, you can capitalize on this energy for any task that requires concentration, study, or research. Do your best to maintain distance from those who have power and control issues so you don't end up on the receiving end. Keep opinions to yourself.

Mercury-Ascendant: Take time from your busy schedule to talk with your partner or best friend. This will satisfy your need for mental stimulation and the exchange of ideas will strengthen ties. You may have to remind yourself, however, to keep an open mind even if your initial reaction is to dismiss other ideas. It's possible you will learn something about life and yourself.

Mercury-Midheaven: You can excel at presentations and public speaking now, provided you do your homework rather than talk off the top of your head. The same guideline applies to workplace meetings, where you have an opportunity to both teach and learn from others. Career or family news could accompany this transit, which also encourages you to include loved ones in domestic planning.

Mercury Easy Aspects

Mercury-Mercury: Meetings, appointments, news, all forms of communication, and errands fill much of your time under this aspect. You also can learn as you go, picking up useful bits of trivia just about anywhere. If other influences are favorable, this is a good time to sign a contract or negotiate an agreement. Consult a sibling or another relative if you need advice.

Mercury-Venus: Life feels lighter under this aspect. Your friendly attitude attracts interest from others, including the possibility of a new relationship. Set aside a little time for a hobby, time with friends, or shopping, or see a concert. On the job, you can win support for your ideas and plans, and this planetary influence can be positive for interviews.

Mercury-Mars: You think quickly and can instantly grasp the facts in any situation. That's a plus if your job involves customer service, or you want to sell yourself and your ideas in a meeting. There's also a chance you could become impatient with those who take a bit longer to grasp what you're saying. Take the time to explain the thoughts behind your ideas, which you can do well now.

Mercury-Jupiter: This transit is good for planning, teaching, learning, travel, and business and legal matters. It can also trigger good news that reinforces your positive, upbeat mindset. With only a little effort, you can see both the big picture and the details, which will give you a decided advantage in most any situation. Most of all, this aspect encourages you to broaden your knowledge with alternative viewpoints.

Mercury-Saturn: The strong points of this transit are planning and organization, along with the ability to concentrate and make knowledgeable decisions. Career gains are also possible if other factors are in agreement. In any case, what you do now can reinforce your position and lead to future advancement. A serious discussion can be surprisingly heartwarming and insightful.

Mercury-Uranus: Be spontaneous, and trust your intuition when imagination triggers innovative solutions. Teamwork can garner support for your ideas, as can brainstorming with you in the lead. Friendship and networking are also

featured under this aspect, so be sure to connect with people in your personal life who are mentally stimulating or in some way unique or unusual.

Mercury-Neptune: Go beyond facts and ignore common sense if you can safely do that. The combination will help unleash your creative thinking, which is strong now. But postpone important life decisions because you may not have all the facts or unconsciously choose to see only what you want to see. Most of all, enjoy the moment. See a movie or get lost in a novel.

Mercury-Pluto: You see beyond the obvious now and can easily research solutions to puzzling problems. Study is productive as long as you don't get so wrapped up in the task at hand that you lose sight of all else. You also have a commanding presence now in the sense that people listen when you speak and then seriously consider your thoughts and ideas.

Mercury-Ascendant: Learning is at the forefront under this aspect that triggers your curiosity. Enroll in a quick class, join in a community effort, or organize a get-together for neighbors. Also plan ahead because time management is a must in order to handle increased calls, paperwork, and personal errands. Above all, set aside time to talk with your partner or a close relative.

Mercury-Midheaven: Be sure to make the most of this visible phase by communicating with higher-ups. Make a presentation if you have the opportunity, or try to schedule a meeting for this time slot. This aspect is also good for interviews if other influences are positive because you will come across as knowledgeable. Home life benefits from open communication.

Venus

Venus in the Signs and Houses

Venus in Aries/First House: This is a sociable time that's even more fun because of your popularity. Your powers of attraction are strong, and can bring you almost anything you wish for. Meet and get acquainted with people. Among them could be a new love interest. However, treat your body with kindness, and resist the urge to overindulge in sweets and high-calorie foods.

Venus in Taurus/Second House: This transit is mostly about money and possessions, both of which can come your way. Gifts and a salary increase are possible. But you also have an increased desire to spend, which can make it tough to balance your budget. Save first and spend later. Set aside a few weekend hours to clean out closets, and profit with a yard sale or through a consignment shop.

Venus in Gemini/Third House: Venus here can lend you extra charm and tact, which can be an advantage on the job and in your personal life. It will also be easier to sell yourself and your ideas in an interview or meeting. If other factors are in agreement, sibling relationships are at their best, and you also can connect with people in your neighborhood or through community activities.

Venus in Cancer/Fourth House: Domestic life and the comforts of home are more appealing now, and this time is favorable for entertaining friends and family. Take advantage of this transit to begin a home improvement project or to beautify your space with plants, pillows, or artwork. To maximize success, ask your partner or a close friend for decor ideas.

Venus in Leo/Fifth House: This transit is designed for parties, dates, play, fun, and romance, and you could attract someone new. Time with children will delight you, as will creative hobbies, and you might enjoy seeing a sporting event or concert. Investments can be profitable now if other influences are in agreement, but don't gamble with funds just to satisfy your ego.

Venus in Virgo/Sixth House: Your work life is satisfying, partly because of congenial relationships with coworkers. Make the most of this mutually supportive atmosphere to trade favors and work with others to generate quality output. Be cautious, though, about initiating a romantic relationship with a coworker, which could be short-lived. Pets can bring you a lot of love now.

Venus in Libra/Seventh House: This is a good time to strengthen ties with those close to you, and to resolve relationship difficulties. Even though you may not agree on everything, negotiation can lead to a workable compromise. You can establish a good rapport if you consult a professional such as an accountant. This transit could bring an engagement if other factors are in agreement.

Venus in Scorpio/Eighth House: You can successfully apply for a loan or mortgage if other influences are positive, and the same holds true with investments, insurance matters, and major purchases. Your partner could receive a small windfall or salary increase, or you could receive news of a rebate. Make saving and debt reduction your first priorities.

Venus in Sagittarius/Ninth House: This transit favors travel, especially a romantic trip, and is also good for a reunion or getaway with friends.

Also make a point to expand your knowledge base through online learning, reading, and talking and sharing ideas with people. What you learn now will soon become invaluable and lead to new opportunities in the future.

Venus in Capricorn/Tenth House: Take advantage of every opportunity to shine during this period when you can gain favor with the boss. This transit could bring a promotion if other influences are in agreement, and a job search launched now can have a positive outcome. However, status symbols are more important at this time, which could encourage you to spend outside of your means.

Venus in Aquarius/Eleventh House: Friends and socializing are near the top of your agenda under this influence, bringing opportunities to network and possibly meet a new love interest or career contact. You could be recognized for your contributions to a group endeavor or get involved with an organization that can further your personal or career goals.

Venus in Pisces/Twelfth House: Leisurely, quiet hours with your mate are appealing now, as is time alone to read and create. Volunteer activities are particularly rewarding at this time, and you might visit a close friend or relative who is hospitalized. This transit also activates your sixth sense, especially regarding people, some of whom will share secrets. Listen, but don't tell your own.

Venus Hard Aspects

Venus-Venus: This aspect is generally positive, with its main challenge being the potential for laziness and overindulgence in spending, eating, and sweets. Pleasurable activities attract you, as does socializing with friends or romance with your mate or a love interest. Minor relationship tension can occur, however, when desires clash. Compromise is the solution to restore calm.

Venus-Mars: This aspect is designed for romance and socializing if you choose to direct the Martian energy that way. It can also, however, trigger conflict with a partner or someone close to you, possibly involving financial matters. Don't make snap decisions regarding a relationship, especially a new one, and postpone shopping until another time because you're impulsive now.

Venus-Jupiter: An upbeat mood enhances relationships, and you also could receive a small windfall. But this aspect can trigger excess in everything from spending to rich food. It also tends toward overoptimism, encouraging you to take on more than you can reasonably afford or do. Be especially cautious if someone guarantees a fast return on an investment.

Venus-Saturn: It's tough to connect with people under this aspect, and you feel isolated even if you're unable to define exactly why. Take advantage of this time to get in touch with your feelings about the relationships in your life. If other planetary influences are in agreement, this could be the trigger that prompts you to cut ties with someone. It can also bring regrets about someone from the past.

Venus-Uranus: Relationships are up or down now, positive or negative, but definitely not status quo. Love at first sight is as likely as a sudden ending. Don't be too hasty to satisfy your current desire for independence, freedom, and excitement. Unless major planetary aspects indicate the same, these feelings will pass as quickly as they arise. Resist the urge to spend on a whim.

Venus-Neptune: Romance can capture your heart now, and it's okay to idealize love as long as you're aware that perfection is an illusion. A partner or someone close to you could also bring disappointment and disillusionment. Steer clear of anything other than routine money matters, and avoid major decisions until this aspect passes, because clear thinking can be difficult under this transit. Do the same with loans and investments.

Venus-Pluto: Love and other relationships can be colored by jealousy and possessiveness, either by you or someone close to you. Ease up and view things realistically, or walk away from anyone who attempts to manipulate you. You also could be drawn into a power play by someone with a controlling personality. Be alert for this tendency in others and in yourself, even if it would be out of character.

Venus-Ascendant: Time with friends and loved ones can be especially enjoyable now, as can meeting new people. This is a good period for entertaining at home and attending social events. Treat yourself to a small, inexpensive gift and do the same for someone you love. Or, beautify your home with new artwork, a plant, or family photos.

Venus-Midheaven: Your workplace popularity rises under this aspect, but family relations require more effort because those you love could feel neglected now. Although this influence alone is unlikely to bring you a raise or promotion, it could help to secure a step up in the future when stronger planetary influences are in effect. Host a get-together for colleagues and family.

Venus Easy Aspects

Venus-Venus: Relationships, finances, and your love life can all benefit from this transit, which is also good for seeing a concert or play, and for crafts projects. You could receive what will become a treasured gift, or make a lucky find. If you have a thrifty mindset, first look for coupons and sales, especially on designer items, and then shop with your budget in mind.

Venus-Mars: Introduce yourself if you feel the spark of attraction while socializing with friends. Or invite your mate or current romantic interest to a social or sporting event, or host one of your own. This influence elevates your popularity and attracts supporters, so now might be a good time to ask someone for a favor. There is, however, danger of buying on impulse if you shop.

Venus-Jupiter: Luck is with you in love and money, but it's still wise to hang onto your common sense despite your current optimism. Wishes often come true, but sometimes they don't. Social events are appealing, although you'll need to restrain yourself now because it's easy to overindulge. This is not the time to buy on credit or to apply for a new account because you're likely to spend too much.

Venus-Saturn: If other factors are in agreement, this can be a good time to make conservative, long-term investments and to purchase or rent property. You can also earn praise for career-related efforts that can pay off in the future. Solid relationships benefit from this influence, and you might reconnect with someone from the past. Do-it-yourself domestic projects to beautify your home can be rewarding.

Venus-Uranus: Make yourself available for love during this transit. It could arrive in the most unexpected way. Someone close to you could surprise you with a gift, new friendships click, and you can be a star player in any group activity that requires teamwork. A small windfall is possible, or you might stumble on a lucky find. Most of all, expect a few surprises while this aspect is in effect.

Venus-Neptune: Romance, soft music, daydreams, and fantasy are the ultimate under this planetary influence. Experience them with someone you love. You also can bring joy to many people now, simply by offering kind words or a hug. If you're single, socialize with friends in order to take advantage of the charming aura this aspect often triggers.

Venus-Pluto: Your subtle yet powerful charisma attracts people, and you can experience a rare depth of love as relationship passion intensifies. But be a little cautious if you fall under the spell of someone new who might or might not be what you assume. This aspect also emphasizes financial matters. If other factors agree, you could profit from an investment or gift.

Venus-Ascendant: You're as pleasant as the people you meet under this influence that emphasizes easygoing relationships. Trade favors and compliments, have fun, relax, and socialize. But try to limit sweets and fat calories, both of which are especially tempting now. This aspect also favors meetings, appointments, and professional consultations.

Venus-Midheaven: You can almost effortlessly impress the boss or a prospective employer when this aspect is active. But be aware that you might tend to rely on charm too much when facts and effort could yield even better results. Add a touch of beauty to your home, such as a flowering plant, pillows, or artwork, and consider hosting a party for friends and family.

Mars

Mars in the Signs and Houses

Mars in Aries/First House: High energy equates to a high level of activity under this aspect. That's great for productivity as long as you get enough sleep, which can be a challenge now. Calm yourself before bedtime. Accidents are possible, so don't push your limits or the envelope to the max. You can be successful in a leadership role as long as you curb impatience.

Mars in Taurus/Second House: Mars in Taurus equates to maximum determination, but also the same level of stubbornness. Rather than let the latter take hold, use this transit for constructive activities, such as cleaning out clutter and closets, and committing to a realistic budget that will keep your finances in the black and boost savings. You attract bargains now.

Mars in Gemini/Third House: Think before you speak or send an e-mail or text. It's all too easy now to react prematurely, which can lead to repercussions or an argument. Daily life is fast-paced, but ease up on the gas pedal, because this period has accident potential. Focus instead on learning and motivating others through your words. Stretch your mind to explore and learn a new subject.

Mars in Cancer/Fourth House: Energy and initiative complement each other, making this a good period to work around the house and handle minor repairs. With Mars involved, though, it's always wise to take safety precautions with tools and ladders. Family conflict is possible if discussions turn from fact-based to emotional. Focus on maximum patience and understanding.

Mars in Leo/Fifth House: This transit encourages you to put a lot of energy into fun and pleasure, including sports, time with children, socializing, and hobbies. It's a much better period for vacation time than for work. You can easily use Mars in a different way on the job. Direct this high-powered energy into finding creative solutions. Take care if you exercise as strains and sprains are possible.

Mars in Virgo/Sixth House: Hard work satisfies you, partly because you're motivated to achieve short-term goals. Even so, remind yourself to share the load when necessary. There's no need to do everything yourself. Healthy food, moderate exercise, and sleep are important to restore energy, so take time for yourself. Pets could need extra attention, or snap up any opportunity to escape in order to explore the wider world.

Mars in Libra/Seventh House: Although this transit can stir passions, relationships can also suffer if you're impatient and come on too strong. Emphasize compromise and cooperation, which are the lesson of this transit. Accomplish this and you can avoid conflict and get the best from the partnership. There could, however, be challenges concerning advice from a professional, such as an attorney.

Mars in Scorpio/Eighth House: Avoid spur-of-the-moment purchases and credit decisions, no matter how good a deal they appear to be. This is instead a better time to aim for increased earnings and to join your mate to reassess financial strategy, review insurance coverage, and to discuss how best to pay off debt and reduce expenses. A raise or small windfall is possible.

Mars in Sagittarius/Ninth House: Mars here encourages you to be open to new insights, viewpoints, and knowledge, and then to share that with others. Learn all you can during this period of quick mental activity that also benefits from an open mind. If other factors are in agreement, legal matters could require your attention. Be calm and patient with in-laws.

Mars in Capricorn/Tenth House: Now is the time to go all-out to advance your status and career. But you'll need to do it with finesse in order to avoid stepping on toes. Anything else could negate potential gains. Take advantage of this transit to polish your leadership skills by working with and guiding others despite a strong desire to go it alone and do everything yourself.

Mars in Aquarius/Eleventh House: Contribute your knowledge and energy to group projects at work or in an organization or leisure-time sports team. You can excel at all of these as a leader and spark plug. Tread carefully, though, especially with friends, as an ego clash could limit progress or cause you to part ways. Also take care to protect valuables when socializing at a public venue.

Mars in Pisces/Twelfth House: Although you receive little public recognition for your efforts under this transit, continue to forge ahead. The best choice is to work solo, if possible, and to catch up on any backlog of tasks at home and on the job. Do be cautious about what you share with others. This is not the time to reveal secrets or to let confidential information slip as it could soon become public knowledge.

Mars Hard Aspects

Mars-Mars: The high energy represented by this aspect requires a physical outlet, but don't push yourself too hard. Accidents are possible now, so take care on the road, in the kitchen, and when working with tools or equipment. Also try to curb impatience, which can trigger a tempestuous outburst. New endeavors are favorable if they're based on well thought out plans.

Mars-Jupiter: Strong drive and increased incentive to achieve put you in high gear. But it's easy to scatter your resources now, so be sure to direct energy into finite activities and projects while avoiding the pitfall of overconfidence. Risk-taking has a certain appeal now, but that can lead to an accident or financial loss. Moderation is the best option.

Mars-Saturn: Frustration, impatience, irritation, and anger can steer you off course. You can help to deflect all of these feelings by releasing the energy through precise work that requires high concentration and little or no contact with others. Say as little as possible if you must deal with someone in authority, be cautious when driving, and call an expert if you need a domestic repair.

Mars-Uranus: Impulsive actions can result in accidents, so slow down both on and off the road, and find a positive outlet for your rebellious mood. Moderate exercise with proper precautions can be a good stress reliever, as can challenging, mentally stimulating games. This aspect can also trigger computer problems. Back up files as you go, and beware of viruses. Be cautious with electricity.

Mars-Neptune: It's difficult to focus now, partly because your energy is low and for no clearly definable reason. Postpone new endeavors to another day, and see a movie or read a fantasy novel. Believe little you hear today, even if it sounds like the truth. Chances are, it won't be. People will stretch the truth, omit pertinent facts, and spread gossip. Keep personal information to yourself.

Mars-Pluto: Used constructively, your drive and ambition can be prime assets now that can lead to significant gains. But you could just as easily undermine your efforts by pushing others too hard or coming on strong to the boss. And that can result in a power struggle with you in the middle. Despite what you might be thinking, smile and let others see an easygoing attitude.

Mars-Ascendant: You're edgy now with much bottled-up tension. Release it through moderate physical activity, which can help minimize the chance for conflict. Conversely, you could be someone else's target, so be prepared to keep your composure and to walk away, if necessary. Also be careful with knives and tools, and on the road, because this is an accident-prone aspect.

Mars-Midheaven: Involve others in your activities even though you believe it's easier to do things yourself. This is not the time to risk alienating a coworker, the boss, your partner, or a friend. Despite your best efforts, though, a family member or your mate could go on the offensive, possibly because your career interferes with domestic life. Be quick to make amends.

Mars Easy Aspects

Mars-Mars: High energy equals high output, and new ventures can get off to a great start now if you don't scatter your efforts. Be a leader and make the most of your self-confidence by encouraging others to excel and live up to expectations. Limit caffeine and activity in the evening. You might have a tough time settling in for a good night's sleep.

Mars-Jupiter: This planetary influence encourages you to initiate or follow up on new opportunities with growth potential. Also seek avenues for tactful self-promotion, which can be beneficial if you tone down your enthusiastic optimism just a little and resist the urge to push others to take action. If other factors are in agreement, you could gain through insurance or inheritance.

Mars-Saturn: The time is right to set realistic goals, establish a plan, and then move forward with patience and persistence. You'll gain a satisfying sense of achievement and possibly earn well-deserved recognition. This aspect also favors do-it-yourself domestic projects and repairs, as well as hobbies that yield something practical, such as gardening and woodworking.

Mars-Uranus: Restlessness prompts you to seek variety and change. That's great as long as you find constructive outlets, which you can easily choose to do. Volunteer for a leadership position in a team effort at work or in your neighborhood, enhance your computer skills, or challenge your brain with a strategy game. Despite this being an easy aspect, accidents are still possible.

Mars-Neptune: Take action to make your dreams come true if they are realistic but seem to be unattainable. It's all in your perception and motivation. When your feelings are on track, and with the help of visualization, you can achieve what you wish. This aspect is also a plus for romance, dancing, and music, or a project that taps your creativity and imagination.

Mars-Pluto: You're self-directed and motivated as your inner drive comes alive. All you need do is act on it, which might be the biggest challenge of all. Also look inward, and possibly read a self-help book, because this aspect can activate your subconscious and your sixth sense. Upon reflection, you can learn more about yourself and why you act and react as you do.

Mars-Ascendant: This transit is excellent for physical work, sports, and exercise as long as you don't push your limits. Do that and an accident could be the result. Other personal activities can be equally successful if you let motivation take hold. Remind yourself, though, to listen to other viewpoints with an open mind rather than just express your own. You might learn something.

Mars-Midheaven: Now is the time to go after exactly what you want career-wise. You can make progress toward fulfilling your ambitions if you first set goals and then design your actions to achieve them. Take a similar path on the domestic front by dealing with repairs, beginning renovations, or searching for a new home. Take your time, though. Haste and impulsiveness can have undesirable results.

PUTTING IT ALL TOGETHER

So far you've learned about the wide variety of predictive techniques used by astrologers. As you gain experience, you'll develop favorites, the ones that work best for you. Some astrologers use two or three regularly and others when they need confirmation or want to delve more deeply into an anticipated situation or event. Almost every astrologer begins with the progressions and/or solar arcs and the transits. These are the nuts and bolts of predictive astrology. Solar returns are also very popular tools.

In this chapter, we'll look at how all of the techniques were valid for one person's chart. You will see how the energy gained momentum over a period of about a year until it culminated with a major career change. Remember that the planets are in constant motion, and people rarely, if ever, make major life changes in an instant. There is always a period of planetary, and real life, influences that build up to the point where a decision is made and the event happens.

Dave had a successful retail career as an executive with a major department store chain. In his position as an area sales manager, he had responsibility for a number of stores and was recognized by management as a master troubleshooter. During the year when he was considering a career change, another major department store chain was courting him, hoping to recruit him with the promise of a higher position and a twenty percent raise. But Dave had other ideas. He wanted to open his own metaphysical store.

With a fixed sign Sun, Moon, and Ascendant, change does not come easily to him. And with Scorpio rising and a Venus-Mars conjunction in Cancer in the eighth house, financial security is high on his life priority list. The thought of giving up a steady paycheck and benefits, including a nice 401K plan, was a major struggle for him.

So it is no surprise that he began slowly, hanging on to his day job while beginning to buy inventory. For about six months, he opened his store on his days off and went to work on the other days. Dave said he knew intuitively that he would eventually take the plunge, quit his job, and go full-time with the new store. But he wasn't ready to do that before testing the waters and considerably raising his comfort level with the idea.

January 9, 2001, brought a lunar eclipse at 19 Cancer 39 in Dave's eighth house that was sextile the progressed Sun and semisquare progressed Mercury and the natal Midheaven.

It was not until the end of February, however, when prompted by the New Moon in opposition to his natal Midheaven that Dave began shopping and ordering stock. That New Moon (in addition to the eclipse) was the trigger that set an important progression in action.

Progressed Mercury (Chart 49) was approaching a conjunction with his natal Midheaven. This was not only a once-in-a-lifetime aspect but it was his Midheaven ruler that was forming the aspect and waving a banner with the words "career change" on it.

Also in February, his progressed Sun in the tenth house was square his progressed Ascendant, which was another indicator for a potential change. He (Ascendant and Sun) wanted something new in his career life (Sun in the tenth). Another career influence was the progressed Moon approaching a square to the natal Midheaven and a trine to progressed Venus, as the progressed Sun was semisquare progressed Venus. Venus rules his seventh house of relationships, and his partner Ray was urging him to make the change.

The transits were equally revealing, and also reflect the stress he was under, being pulled in two directions between safety and security and an entrepreneurial venture. Transiting Uranus was approaching a square to his Ascendant (personal change) and would perfect that aspect when it stationed retrograde there at the end of May. Jupiter was approaching a square to the natal Midheaven, close enough with the added energy of the February New Moon to push him to take the chance to begin buying stock for the store (Jupiter rules his second house). Ray's influence can also be seen in transiting Saturn in the seventh house forming a conjunction with progressed Jupiter, and a sesquisquare with the progressed Midheaven.

Mercury was also active in the solar arc chart, with transiting Pluto sextile solar arc Mercury, and solar arc Moon was in his tenth house, just separating from a conjunction to the Midheaven (he'd been thinking about this idea for quite a while). Solar arc Jupiter, ruler of the second house and in the ninth, was semisquare natal Sun in the ninth (he had to handle the various legal matters associated with establishing a business). Ray's encouragement was also active in Dave's solar arc chart, with solar arc Saturn semisquare/sesquisquare to natal Descendant/Jupiter (conjunction)-Ascendant, and transiting Neptune opposition solar arc Venus. He knew Ray was right, but it was difficult to have that much faith in the potential success of such a major new endeavor.

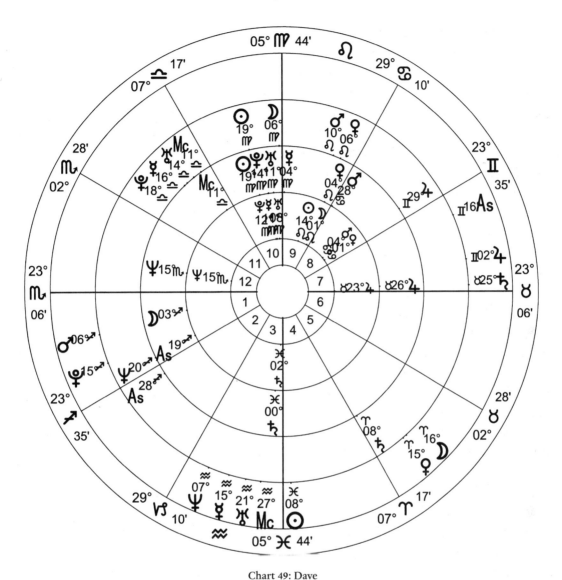

Chart 49: Dave
Innermost wheel: Birth Chart / August 6, 1964 / 1:56 pm MST / Salt Lake City, Utah
Middle inner wheel: Secondary Progressed Naibod in Long / February 26, 2001 / 12:11:40 pm MST / Salt Lake City, Utah
Middle outer wheel: Directed Solar Arc / February 26, 2001 / 12:11:40 pm MST / Salt Lake City, Utah
Outermost wheel: New Endeavor / February 26, 2001 / 12:00 pm MST / Phoenix, Arizona
Placidus House

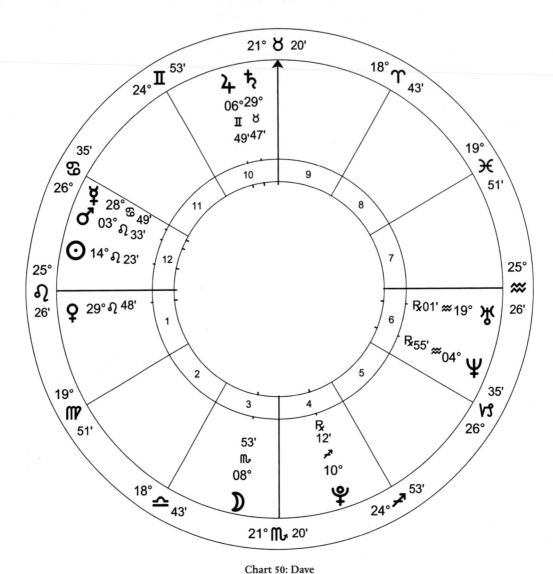

Chart 50: Dave

Solar Return / August 6, 2000 / 6:42:19 am MST / Phoenix, Arizona / Placidus House

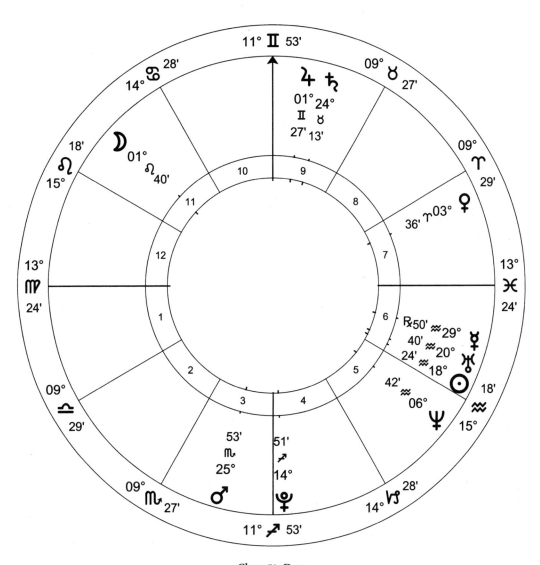

Chart 51: Dave
Lunar Return / February 6, 2001 / 8:00:34 pm MST / Phoenix, Arizona / Placidus House

The solar return chart (Chart 50) in effect from August 6, 2000 to August 5, 2001, is blatant in its message of a job/career change. Venus, ruler of the solar return Midheaven, was at 29 Leo 48 square Saturn (sixth house ruler) in the tenth house at 29 Taurus 47. The twenty-ninth is a degree of completion. Uranus in the sixth house was square the Midheaven, and Neptune, also in the sixth was trine Jupiter in the tenth (faith and optimism). The potential for change is also seen in Uranus in the sixth opposition the Sun in the twelfth (set me free from this day job!).

February's lunar return (Chart 51) has the same message regarding job/career with three planets in the sixth house, including Sun conjunct Uranus (change, and ruler of the sixth house) and Mercury, ruler of the Midheaven. Interestingly, Mercury in this chart is at 29 Aquarius 50 (completion) and retrograde, so he wasn't quite ready to make that job change. However, Pluto opposition the Midheaven was urging him to do just that, and in a big way, as was Mars square the sixth house planets.

Ray's influence is also apparent in the lunar return with the Moon sextile Jupiter (co-ruler of the seventh house) and trine Venus in the seventh house and opposition Neptune (ruler of the seventh house), which was sextile Venus. Even if Dave was unsure about the new endeavor, his partner wasn't, as can be interpreted from this multi-planet configuration.

Dave's desire to move on can even be seen in the Mars return (Chart 52), which occurred about six months prior to February. In this chart, the Sun (Ascendant ruler) is conjunct Mars (Midheaven ruler), and Venus. The twelfth house position can be interpreted as the germi-nation of the idea, especially because Mercury was also in the twelfth. Note that Mercury is also retrograde in this chart, just as it was in the lunar return chart (Chart 51). The Ascendant, ruled by the Sun, is in the first degree, representing the new direction he was consider-ing. Saturn, ruler of the sixth house, is in the tenth conjunct Jupiter in the eleventh of goals. He was optimistic that there was a better career avenue for him.

The Jupiter return (Chart 53) emphasizes completion with its 27 Scorpio 09 Ascendant. Here, too, the sixth and seventh house are high-lighted, with a Jupiter-Saturn conjunction in the sixth, and four planets in the seventh, three of which are square the Midheaven. Ray was a supporter even at this point (the previous June), encouraging Dave to follow his dream, as indi-cated by the trines from the seventh house plan-ets to Uranus and Neptune in the third. But Ray also had his work cut out for him, because Pluto (ruler of the first house, and in that house, Dave) was opposition three of the seventh house planets and, of course, square the Mid-heaven.

Months passed, and Dave's stress level con-tinued to rise, both because he wanted out of his job and because he was trying to manage his job and the new endeavor. Two eclipses in 2001, one in June and one in July, helped move him closer to quitting his job. The June 21 solar eclipse at 00 Cancer 10 was conjunct his natal Venus-Mars conjunction in the eighth house and trine natal and progressed Saturn, which are opposition the natal Midheaven. This was followed by a lunar eclipse on July 5 at 13 Cap-ricorn 39 in the second house trine natal Ura-nus conjunct Mercury and Pluto in the tenth

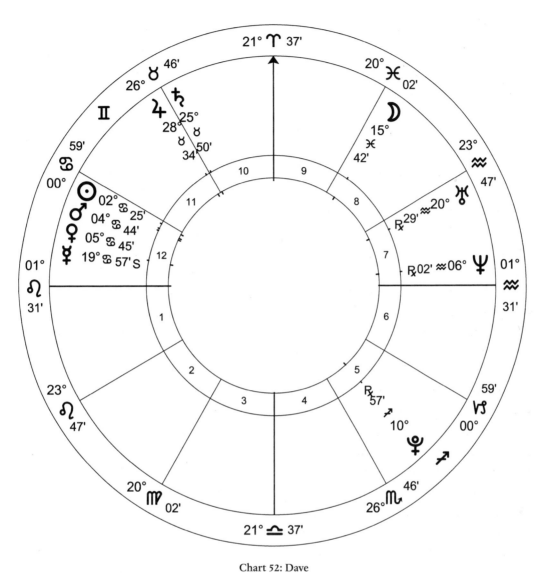

Chart 52: Dave

Mars Return / June 23, 2000 / 7:39:57 am MST / Phoenix, Arizona / Placidus House

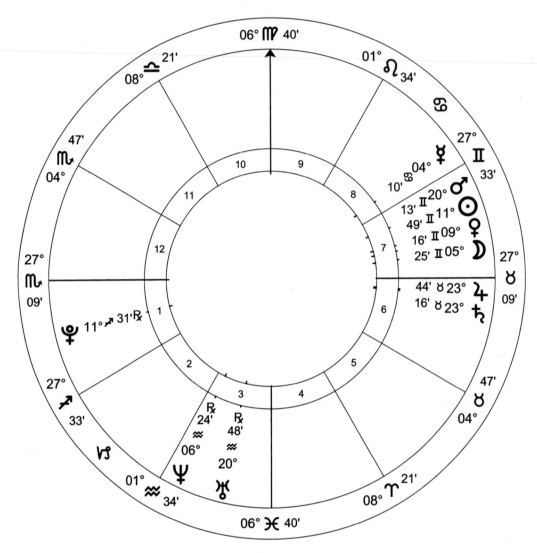

Chart 53: Dave
Jupiter Return / June 1, 2000 / 6:18:38 pm MST / Phoenix, Arizona / Placidus House

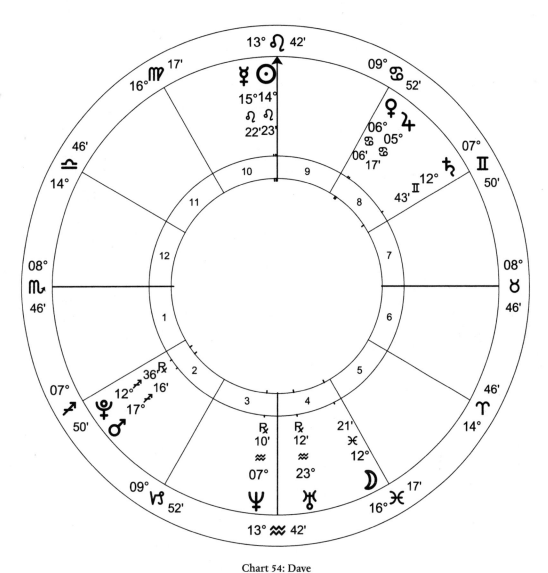

Chart 54: Dave
Solar Return / August 6, 2001 / 12:31:24 pm MST / Phoenix, Arizona / Placidus House

house and sextile natal and progressed Neptune in the twelfth (lingering doubts about the career change). And of course progressed Mercury continued to move closer to his natal Midheaven.

August 2001 brought three return charts—solar, Mercury, and Venus—plus the lunar return. As would be expected, all of them delivered the same message.

The August 6 solar return chart (Chart 54) has the Sun and Mercury conjunct the Midheaven and trine a Mars-Pluto conjunction in the second house of money (Sun rules the solar return Midheaven, Mercury rules the natal Midheaven, Mars rules the solar return sixth house, and Pluto rules the solar return Ascendant). Saturn in the eighth house is sextile the Midheaven, and there is also a fortunate Venus-Jupiter conjunction in the eighth house. This chart is very promising for a successful and lucrative new business, but with the Moon square Saturn, he was still worrying about money.

The August 20 Mercury return chart (Chart 55) has late degrees on the Ascendant and Midheaven, with the Sun also in a late degree sextile the Midheaven, indicating completion (remember that Mercury rules his natal Midheaven and his natal Sun is in Leo). Uranus is trine the Midheaven (positive career change), and benefics Venus and Jupiter are in the tenth house, adding their blessing to a career change. Mercury is sextile Jupiter, and the Moon is sextile Venus. But this chart also shows worry with the Moon and Mercury square Saturn.

The financial concern is clearly seen in the August 2 Venus return chart (Chart 56), which is especially fitting because Venus is a natural money planet. The Sun-Mercury conjunction in the second house is opposition Neptune in the eighth (fear that he would lose it all). But this chart also has a balancing and encouraging factor: a Venus-Jupiter conjunction in the twelfth house, which is a protective influence (Jupiter rules the sixth and co-rules the tenth). The Moon in the seventh sextile the Midheaven represents Ray's encouragement. The Mars-Pluto conjunction in the sixth with Mars square the Midheaven says it all about his job: enough is enough, I'm out of here!

The August 17 lunar return chart (Chart 57) for this period has Neptune square the Midheaven, so Dave was still questioning whether quitting the job was the right move. This Neptune aspect also represents his career vision, which he certainly could achieve as indicated by the positive aspects in this chart: Jupiter in the eleventh house of goals sextile the Midheaven, Mercury in the first house trine the Midheaven, and Saturn (sixth house ruler) in the eleventh sextile the Ascendant. This is an important lunar return chart for another reason: the lunar return Ascendant is the same as his natal Ascendant.

By September 2001, Dave had had enough, and despite his financial security fears, decided it was time to make the break. The Full Moon of September 2 at 10 Pisces 28 opposition his natal tenth house stellium was the turning point.

He resigned on September 11 (Chart 58), with a transiting Saturn-Pluto opposition square the tenth house planets and trine/sextile his progressed Midheaven. This is not the sort of aspect one would consider favorable for a career/job change, which is why it's important to look at the entire chart and all the influences in effect. Consider this: he has lived his entire life with

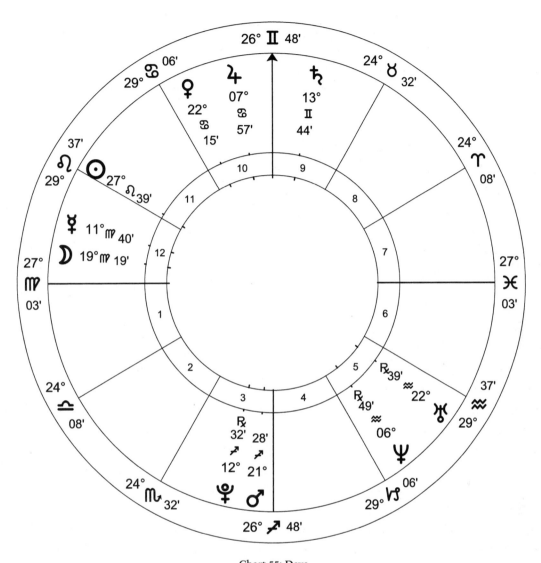

Chart 55: Dave
Mercury Return / August 20, 2001 / 8:18:18 am MST / Phoenix, Arizona / Placidus House

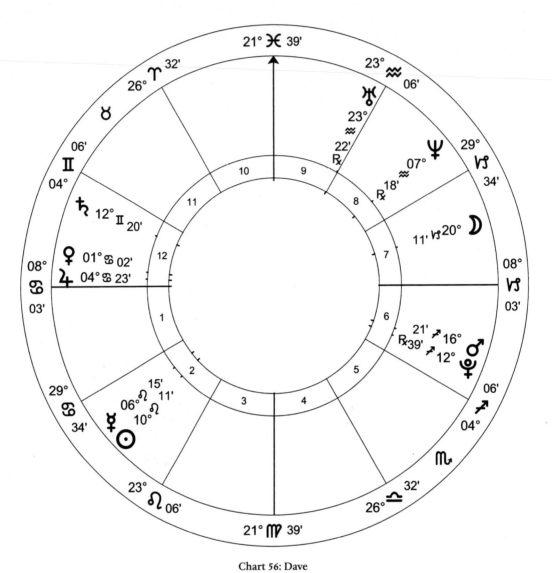

Chart 56: Dave

Venus Return / August 2, 2001 / 3:13:19 am MST / Phoenix, Arizona / Placidus House

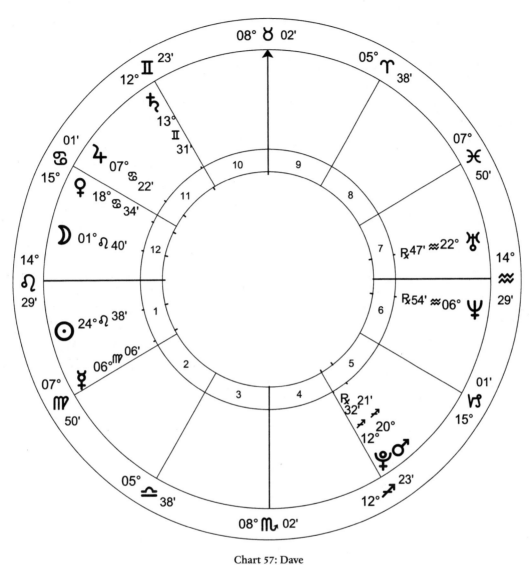

08° ♉ 02'

05° ♈ 38'

12° ♊ 23'

♄ 13° ♊ 31'

07° ♋ 22' ♃

01'

♅ 15° ♋

♀ 18° ♋ 34'

07° ♓ 50'

10   9

11   8

12   7   ℞ 47' ♒ 22' ♅

14° ♌ 29'

14° ♒ 29'

1   6   ℞ 54' ♒ 06' ♆

☉ 24° ♌ 38'

06° ♍ 06'

2   5

☿ 07° ♍ 50'

3   4

01'

15° ♑

℞ 32' 21' ♐

20° ♐ 12°

♇ ♂

05° ♎ 38'

12° ♐ 23'

08° ♏ 02'

☽ 01° ♌ 40'

Chart 57: Dave

Lunar Return / August 17, 2001 / 5:07:14 am MST / Phoenix, Arizona / Placidus House

the ambitious Saturn-Midheaven-Uranus alignment, and Pluto is part of the tenth house stellium, so this was familiar energy to him. Only because he was finally pushed to his limits, and with adequate time to get somewhat comfortable with the idea, did he put his fixed sign planets in the background as a trade-off for further career achievement. This is reinforced by the progressed Moon (feelings) trine progressed Uranus and natal Mercury in the tenth, and progressed/solar arc Sun in the tenth square his progressed Ascendant.

Of particular interest on the resignation date is that transiting Uranus was at the same degree as it had been in February. In between, it was square his Ascendant-Descendant, so Ray certainly promoted the idea of change. Transiting Jupiter was semisquare natal Jupiter in the seventh house, indicating both Ray's support and the good terms under which he left his job (he was told he could return to the company at any time).

In the September 11 solar arc chart (Chart 58), transiting Jupiter is square the Midheaven, and the transiting Saturn-Pluto opposition is trine/sextile the same angle. The Jupiter aspect indicates that he was still somewhat relying on faith, as does transiting Neptune opposition solar arc Venus.

The September 11 diurnal chart (Chart 59) is stunning, even to an astrologer, with a Mercury-Midheaven conjunction that is trine to Saturn in the sixth. Definitely a favorable day to announce a resignation. This chart also has the Sun square the diurnal Ascendant, which is conjunct his progressed Ascendant. Venus is trine Pluto, with both sextile the Midheaven, ruled by Venus.

These charts have a unified message: career/job change, partner's support, and stress and concern about financial security. The positives far outweighed the negatives, and this was proven true. Dave's store is tremendously successful and profitable. After a few years the store was doing so well that Ray was able to resign his day job and the store was moved to a larger and more upscale location.

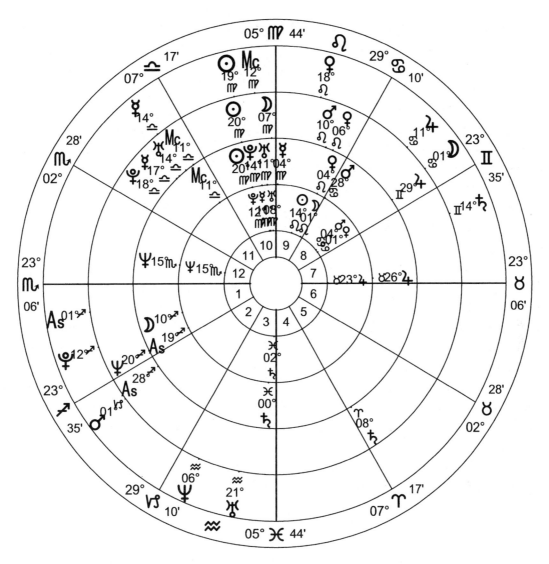

Chart 58: Dave

Innermost wheel: Birth Chart / August 6, 1964 / 1:56 pm MST / Salt Lake City, Utah
Middle inner wheel: Secondary Progressed Naibod in Long / September 11, 2001 / 1:21:44 pm MST / Salt Lake City, Utah
Middle outer wheel: Directed Solar Arc / September 11, 2001 / 1:21:44 pm MST / Salt Lake City, Utah
Outermost wheel: Resigned Job / September 11, 2001 / 12:00 pm MST / Phoenix, Arizona

Placidus House

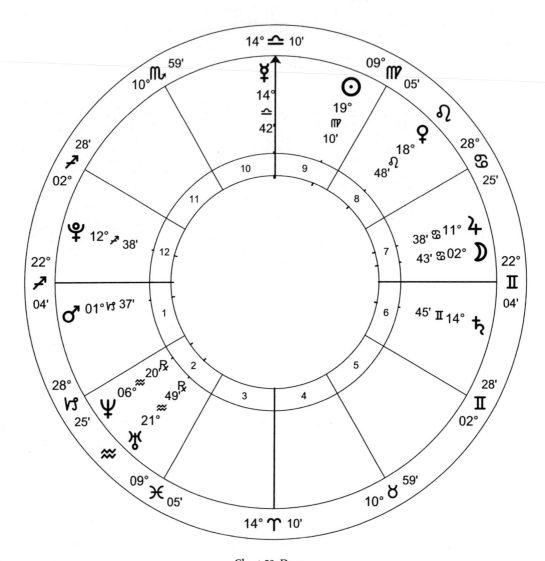

Chart 59: Dave

Diurnal Chart / September 11, 2001 / 1:56 pm MST / Salt Lake City, Utah / Placidus House

CHAPTER ELEVEN

QUICK AND EASY HORARY

Despite the title of this chapter, there is no such thing as "quick and easy horary." Only with years of study and practice can an astrologer hope to master this complex branch of astrology. The extensive rules used to interpret horary charts were developed during several millennia, and all of them must be considered in order to accurately read the chart. There are few horary experts, but those that do invest the time and effort in learning this branch of astrology are exceptionally qualified.

Horary charts fall into two basic categories: yes and no questions, and questions that relate to missing items or the outcome of a situation or event. This quick and easy method is limited to yes and no questions, and should not be used for the more complex questions that require extensive interpretation of the chart using ancient techniques.

This method, which I've used extensively, tends to give either a clear answer or none. When the answer isn't apparent, it generally means the chart requires the use of many, or most, of the vast horary rules and is beyond the scope of this method. Be cautious about using quick and easy horary for major life decisions. It is better suited to everyday life and questions such as, "Will I hear from her today?" or "Should I order a pair of pants?"

When traditional horary methods are used, it's possible to ask a question about anyone. The quick and easy method, however, is generally viable only with first person questions—those asked by you about yourself and situations or conditions in your life. You can do the same with questions asked by other people. What does not work well with this method is questions asked about

231

another individual. These questions require interpretation according to the full breadth of traditional horary rules.

In order to calculate a correct horary chart, you need the exact time you asked the question, as well as the exact wording of the question. This is especially important if you're unable to calculate the chart at the exact moment you ask the question. (You can use astrological software to do this, or go to one of the online sites where you can calculate the chart.) Calculate the chart for the location (city and state or province) where you asked the question.

There are a few basic rules you need to learn in order to answer yes and no questions:

1. Any chart that has three or fewer degrees or twenty-seven or more degrees rising (Ascendant degree) cannot be answered. If three or fewer degrees are rising, the situation has not developed enough for the horary chart to yield an answer. In the second case, with twenty-seven or more degrees on the Ascendant, the matter has already been settled or nothing will come of it.

2. Locate the Moon and note all of the major aspects (conjunction, sextile, trine, square, opposition) it makes before becoming void of course.

3. If the Moon's last aspect is positive (sextile or trine, or conjunction to Mercury, Venus, or Jupiter), the answer is yes.

4. If the Moon's last aspect is negative (square or opposition, or conjunction to Mars, Saturn, Uranus, or Pluto) the answer is no.

5. If the Moon's last aspect is to Neptune, the answer is unclear and the question cannot be answered.

6. The horary chart needs to be in some way relevant to the question. There are several ways to determine this when using this quick and easy horary method: the house where the Moon is located or the planet it last aspects is relevant to the question; the rising sign (Ascendant) rules the question; or the first rising planet (planet closest to the Ascendant, beginning with the first house, then the second, the third, etc.) pertains to the question. For example, the sixth house should be involved if the question concerns a job, or the eleventh if it involves a friend.

WILL I MAKE MONEY ON THE STOCK?

This chart (Chart 60) has a clear yes answer, because the Moon's last aspect is a trine to Jupiter, and doubly so because Jupiter is the planet of abundance. Note that Jupiter is in the eighth house of money, so this is confirmation that the answer is valid.

The Moon makes many aspects before the final one, and these give additional information about the question. Taking them in order, the Moon first forms a square to retrograde Mercury, which could indicate initial regret about the stock purchase. It then moves on to square Venus and the Sun, so the stock would probably drop in price before eventually rising. This is confirmed by the sextile to Mars, which

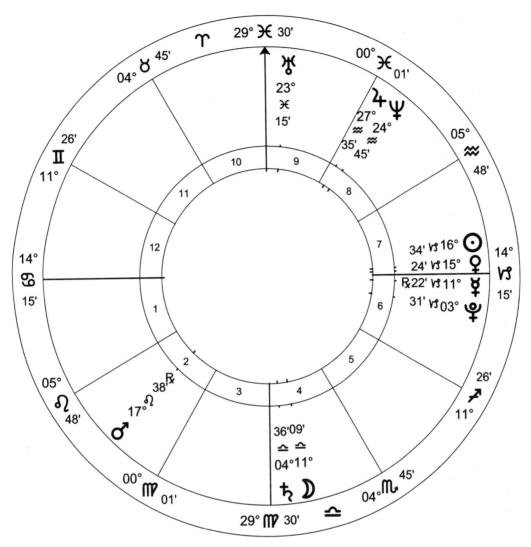

Chart 60: Will I make money on the stock?

Horary chart / January 6, 2010 / 5:19:43 pm MST / Chandler, Arizona / Placidus House

is also retrograde and its placement in the second house of money. Mars is also co-ruler of the fifth house of speculation. So at this point it looks like a bad investment. But with the trine to Jupiter and much patience because of the retrogrades, the stock should eventually net a nice return on the initial investment.

WILL MY HOUSE BE SOLD TO THE INTERESTED PARTY?

The answer to this question (Chart 61) is unclear because the last major aspect formed by the Moon before it leaves Aquarius is a conjunction to Neptune. You can see the initial optimism of the seller from the conjunction to Jupiter, which is the first aspect of the Moon and in the first house. Jupiter is retrograde, however, which could be interpreted as false optimism. That Neptune is retrograde and the ruler of the second house of money might indicate that the prospective buyer will reconsider purchasing the house at some time in the future.

There is even more doubt about the house being sold to the interested party because the Moon forms no major aspects to Venus or the Sun. Venus rules the fourth house of the seller's home, and the Sun rules the seventh house, representing the prospective buyer.

WILL I FIND THE ENVELOPE?

According to this chart (Chart 62), the envelope would be found, which it was about thirty minutes later. The Moon's last aspect while in Virgo is a trine to Mercury, which is valid because that planet rules envelopes. There are two aspects

before the Moon-Mercury trine: a conjunction to Saturn and an opposition to Uranus. Saturn aspects usually indicate a delay, and Uranus is associated with change and the unexpected. As the search continued, a friend (eleventh house ruler Saturn, and Uranus, natural ruler of friends) suggested using the chart directions to locate the envelope.

In order to read a horary chart for direction, you need to consider the chart from the position you were in at the time the question is asked. Think of yourself as standing in the center of the chart. These are the directions represented in charts:

North—IC
South—Midheaven
East—Ascendant
West—Descendant

To make it easier to see the directions, it is helpful to turn the chart upside-down so that the Midheaven is at the bottom of the chart.

Looking at the chart position of Mercury in this horary chart, it is southeast of where the question was asked. Saturn, ruler of Capricorn (Mercury's sign) is associated with earth and wood. This suggests the envelope might be on the floor near a wooden object. In fact, the envelope was found to the southeast and underneath a wooden desk.

WILL I ENJOY MY DATE WITH MELISSA?

An astrologer friend asked this question, wording it like he did rather than asking this question: "Will Melissa like me?" Remember, this quick and easy horary method is generally useful only

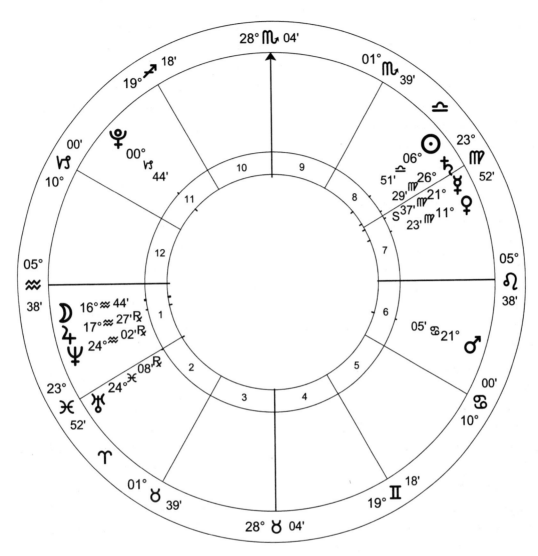

Chart 61: Will my house be sold to the interested party?

Horary Chart / September 29, 2009 / 3:58:55 pm CDT / Chicago, Illinois / Placidus House

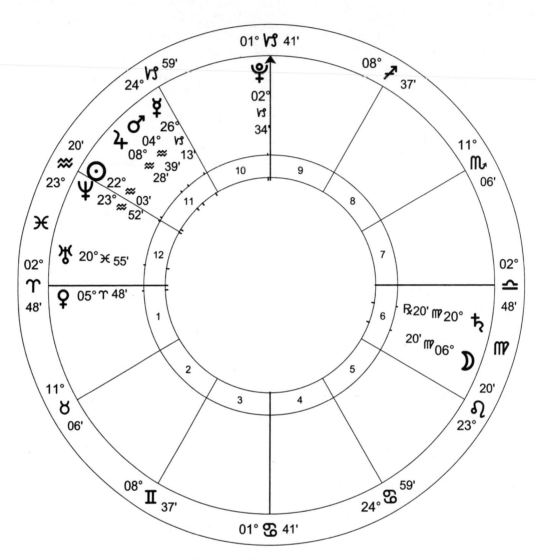

Chart 62: Will I find the envelope?
Horary Chart / February 10, 2009 / 9:11:15 pm MST / Chandler, Arizona / Placidus House

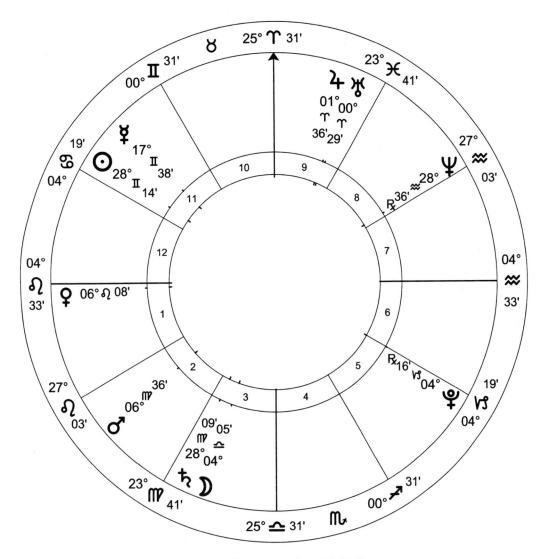

Chart 63: Will I enjoy my date with Melissa?

Horary Chart / June 19, 2010 / 8:12 am MST / Phoenix, Arizona / Placidus House

with first-person questions. However, the alternate question could be answered by using all the traditional horary rules.

This horary chart (Chart 63) has Venus (love) rising in Leo (romance), and the Moon is in Libra (partnership), so it is a valid chart for the question. In fact, with Venus rising and the Moon approaching a sextile to this planet, it would be easy to assume the answer would be yes. But there is more involved in this chart.

Regarding romance, this chart actually has more of a negative connotation. The Moon's last aspect is an opposition to Jupiter, ruler of the fifth house. Jupiter in the ninth house of travel and the Moon in the third house of communication reflects the scheduling of the date, which was delayed because she was out of town.

The Moon's first aspect is a square to Pluto in the fifth house of romance, so conversation (Moon in the third house) would be initially difficult. This would improve, as indicated by the Moon's next aspects, a sextile to Venus and a trine to Mercury.

This chart is an example of why it's important to check the movement of the planets. The last lunar aspect is a trine to Neptune, not the Sun, because the Sun would move into Cancer while the Moon was still in Libra. So the answer is unclear (Neptune). The date evolved as the horary indicated, but they did not have a second one. He was basically ambivalent (Neptune) about Melissa, whose job required travel (Neptune ruling the ninth house), making it difficult to mesh their schedules even if he had wanted to pursue a relationship.

WHERE IS THE SILVER?

From the outset, this question breaks one of the quick and easy horary rules: it asks where an object is located rather than whether it would be found. It's also a good example of the failings of the quick and easy method, as I eventually discovered (Chart 64).

Even though this question asks for the location, my underlying interest was whether it would be found. This is an easy one. The last aspect of the Moon is a trine to the Sun, so the answer is a yes. And indeed it was.

Impatient to find the silver, I took note of some factors in the chart before beginning to search. (Had I just gone about my routine, I would have found it anyway!) Notice that the Moon is in Virgo, the sign that rules boxes. From this I determined that it was in a box. It was. The Sun is in Taurus, the sign that rules silver, and further confirmation that it would be found.

The search took place in a large two-story house with a basement, and many closets and several attic spaces. So there were plenty of potential places to look. I attempted to narrow the search by making the following rulership list:

- Moon: water, basement, silver
- Saturn: dark corner, low place, tools
- Taurus: basement, closet, storeroom, tile
- Sun: recreation room, furnace
- Libra: Attic, high places
- Moon in the eleventh house: SSE
- Sun in the eighth house: WSW

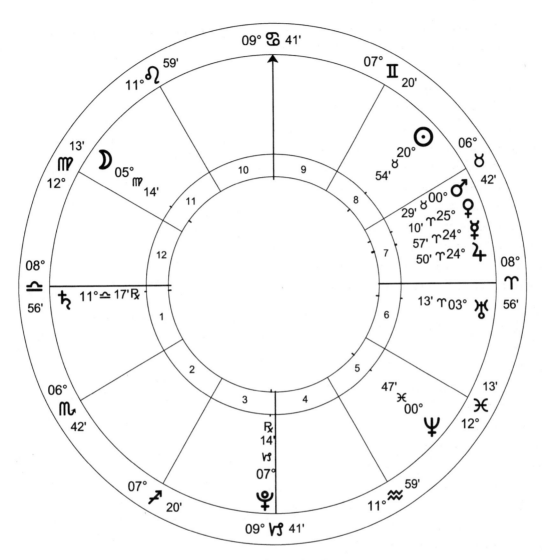

Chart 64: Where is the silver?
Horary Chart / May 11, 2011 / 3:52:02 pm WST / Chandler Arizona / Placidus House

The directions for the Moon and Sun were used because they had a relationship with silver (Moon and Taurus).

Based on the above list, and using the most often repeated factors, I concluded that the silver was in a box on the floor in the basement recreation room, which has a tile floor and nearby areas with tools and the furnace. This room is on the west side of the house, with tools in the WSW location.

Wrong! And it could not have been more so—except for the box.

The silver was found on the first floor in a bedroom on the south side of the house. It was in a closet in the WSW part of the room on a high shelf.

Beware of attempting to do too much with the quick and easy horary method!

These examples barely scratch the surface of horary astrology, but they are a starting point and a brief introduction to this complex subject. There are a number of excellent books on horary astrology (see Recommended Reading list) that explain the many rules and include numerous examples.

PREDICTIVE TIPS

This chapter includes a variety of tips to help you in forecasting. Some of them are common knowledge among astrologers, and others come from experience. As with all else in predictive astrology, try them for yourself to see what works best for you.

Each of the influences listed increases the potential for the event, but is not a guarantee. Remember, there must be at least three indicators for an event to occur. Minor, everyday events are usually associated with inner planet transits and the New or Full Moon, while major events require progressions, solar arcs, and/or outer planet transits, and often involve an eclipse. Return charts offer confirmation of other major transits.

MARRIAGE / COMMITMENT

- The natal, progressed, and/or solar arc Ascendant will always be active

- Progressed Venus changing direction often indicates this event

- Progressed or solar arc conjunctions between the Sun and Venus are often active

- An aspect involving natal, progressed, or solar arc Mars is sometimes present

- Any outer planet crossing the Descendant increases the potential for a committed relationship

- A progressed or solar arc aspect involving the natal, progressed, or solar arc ruler of the seventh house is often active

DIVORCE

- Progressed and/or solar arc aspects involving Venus and Uranus are common
- Transiting Uranus in hard aspect to the Ascendant or Descendant can trigger the end of a relationship
- Transiting Pluto is sometimes active in a divorce if it contacts the Descendant, Venus, or Descendant ruler

ACCIDENTS

A hard Mars-Uranus aspect elevates accident potential. If the aspect involves transiting Uranus or a progressed or solar arc planet, the potential is in effect for a much longer period of time, although it must be activated by an inner transiting planet. However, if transiting Mars is direct and aspecting natal, progressed, or solar arc Uranus, the potential is limited to a few days, provided there are no trends that indicate a longer time frame.

Caution is advisable when transiting Mars is within orb of a conjunction to the natal Ascendant. This transit can trigger cuts, falls, and other accidents.

MONEY

Money matters are ruled by the second and eighth houses. The second governs personal income and debt; the eighth governs your partner's income and debt, debtors in general (bank, credit card company, etc.), inheritance, and insurance (proceeds and premiums). Look for progressed and solar arc aspects involving the second and/or eighth houses, planets in these houses, and the house rulers. The distinction between the two polar opposite houses blurs at times, so you should not limit your study of the chart to just one house or the other. Consider them both because they often work as a unit.

For gambling, including the lottery, there must be aspects that connect the eighth house (the casino's money) and the fifth house (speculation). Any combination of the following (using transits, progressions, and solar arcs) can trigger a win:

- Aspects to natal planets in the fifth and/or eighth houses
- Aspects to natal rulers of the fifth and/or eighth houses
- Transits of the rulers of the fifth and/or eighth houses to other planets in your chart

Don't automatically discount planets such as Mars and Saturn, which are traditionally considered difficult. If these planets fit according to the above guidelines, they can produce a win. A word about Jupiter: this planet, which rightfully deserves its billing as the luckiest of all, does not always have a role in gambling wins, so don't fall into the trap of looking only for Jupiter aspects.

Another gambling technique you might find effective is the transiting Ascendant and Midheaven. This is simply the position of the two angles where they would be if you calculated for a given moment on a given date. They move forward through the zodiac at about one degree for every four minutes. This technique is best used if you have astrological software because you can then generate a hit list of the exact times that the transiting angles aspect your planets. If you do this, set the software selection to generate aspects to the planets according to the guidelines above. This does work, but is best used on days when there are other planetary aspects that activate your gambling planets.

If you're looking for a time frame when you might receive a raise, begin with the New and Full Moons, either of which should aspect your second and/or eighth house according to the guidelines. This is of course easier to identify if your company has an annual review procedure. Once you fully understand how your chart responds to transits, which comes with practice, you can probably determine whether you'll receive a raise that will please or disappoint you, depending upon the aspects.

If you work for a company where you must ask for a raise, also begin with the New and Full Moons. Then find the date that has the most favorable transits involving the second and eighth houses. Of course, if you can manage to acquire your boss's birth data, you can also look at his or her chart!

When applying for a car loan, mortgage, or home equity loan, focus on the eighth house but also consider the second. Favorable aspects involving the eighth house improve the odds that you will receive the loan. But it's very important to also consider the overall trends in your chart that are active at that time. Also look forward. If you see potentially restrictive financial conditions in the near future, such as Saturn transiting the second or eighth house, it might be wise to re-think the idea or to opt for borrowing less. Caution also applies if Jupiter is transiting your eighth house. This is one of

the best, if not the best, influences for attracting money. Just remember that it only lasts a year, and what is affordable now may not be in the long term.

Difficult aspects from transiting Pluto can indicate bankruptcy, an unfortunate and unavoidable reality for some people. These aspects usually involve planets in or ruling the eighth house, but this can also occur with aspects involving the second house. Stress and strain in the financial houses is obviously usually evident prior to the Pluto transit.

CAREER/JOB

When studying a chart for career/job influences, always look at transiting Saturn, the natural ruler of the tenth house. Transiting Saturn's house position in your chart is often a strong indicator of where you are in the career cycle. It's wise to maintain the status quo while Saturn transits your first house (and goes through the first three houses); this is not the time for new endeavors. The next milestone is Saturn conjunct the IC, where it is opposition the Midheaven. This can be a good time to pursue a new opportunity, but its potential is unlikely to develop as quickly as you wish and should therefore be considered a stepping stone.

Saturn transiting the sixth house can make you feel like a slave: lots of work and little or no recognition. When Saturn crosses the Descendant, you suddenly (almost magically) garner more attention and recognition. From this position, Saturn's potentially positive career influence begins to gain momentum, culminating with its transit of the tenth house. You reap

Saturn's benefits as it transits the eleventh and twelfth houses.

Ideally, you should plan ahead so that you can reach a career pinnacle when transiting Saturn crosses the Midheaven and moves through the tenth house for about the next two and a half years. You can gain from Saturn's transit of this house without doing that, but the greatest rewards come if you begin the climb as Saturn crosses the IC.

Of course there is no guarantee that Saturn transiting the tenth house will elevate your status. The level of achievement (or non-achievement) depends much upon whether and how much effort you've expended on the way up to this point. As is always true with Saturn, you get what you deserve. (A transiting Saturn-Sun conjunction is especially noted for this.) The often cited classic example of Saturn in the tenth house is the late former president Richard Nixon, who resigned from office under this transit.

The best times to apply for a job are between the New Moon and Full Moon, when the New Moon is in the second, sixth, or tenth house (Trinity of Wealth houses, see glossary). This is not always practical, however, because these New Moons occur four months apart. You can get much the same effect from a New Moon in another house in favorable aspect to natal, progressed, or solar arc planets in these houses or in aspect to the rulers of these houses.

The reason for using the period between the New and Full Moon is because the Moon is growing in light, which equates to new beginnings. After the Full Moon, the Moon decreases in light; this is a period of completion. If you don't have the luxury of time, however, take advantage of any Full Moon that favorably aspects your chart. There is some logic to this: after all, the goal is to complete a period of unemployment. Although the energy isn't as strong as that of a New or Full Moon, you could also apply for jobs on dates when the inner transiting planets form positive aspects to your natal, progressed, and/or solar arc planets.

To further put the odds in your favor after you've applied for jobs, look through the ephemeris for dates when the inner transiting planets activate your chart. These dates have potential for interviews. Then identify a few hours during the day when the transiting chart looks the most favorable so you can select the best interview time if you're given that option.

Unfortunately, all of these efforts will not be as helpful if the chart trends show a longer term period of unemployment. Even this can be positive, however, because you'll realize the importance of taking a lesser position, if possible, while continuing to search for a job in your field.

In general, transiting outer planets in hard aspect to the Midheaven indicate a potential period for career changes and developments. Whether these will be positive or negative depends upon other transits and the progressions and solar arcs. A Uranus square to the Midheaven, for example, can bring an unwelcome change or an unexpected opportunity for gain.

HEALTH

This is an area best avoided by most astrologers. Only those who have medical training should consider forecasting in this area. If you see difficult slow-moving aspects (outer planet transits, progressions, and solar arcs) involving the twelfth house (and sometimes the sixth) along with relevant eclipses, the best information you can give is to suggest a consultation with a medical professional. Do not speculate! Without specialized training in the medical field and medical astrology, it is unethical and illegal to offer any insights.

You can, however, use your chart to be proactive regarding common viruses. The potential is often signaled by a difficult New or Full Moon and inner planet transits involving the sixth house, and sometimes the twelfth. If you see one of these periods coming (study your chart for the last time you had a cold), take extra precautions and you just might avoid it.

There is another medical-related activity that can benefit from astrology: starting a reducing diet. This is often more successful if you begin at the Full Moon, based on the theory that as the Moon decreases in light, so does your weight.

PROPERTY AND RELOCATION

Relocation is most often indicated by outer transiting planets, progressions, and/or solar arcs crossing, squaring, or in opposition to the IC. There can be multiple moves within a short period of time when an outer planet retrogrades back and forth, making three contacts to the IC.

If you want to purchase a house, look forward a few years. Check the outer planet transits, progressions, solar arcs, and eclipses that will be effect, looking for any downward financial trend that could indicate difficulty in the market as a whole or in paying your mortgage.

Be alert for the possibility of flooding if you see transiting Neptune approaching your IC (or contacting a planet in or ruling the fourth house). This would be a time to consider flood insurance even if you don't live in an area prone to flooding, hurricanes, or severe weather.

Pluto crossing the IC or in hard aspect to a planet associated with the fourth house sometimes indicates termites. This transit also makes it advisable to be sure your property and possessions are well covered by insurance.

DERIVATIVE HOUSES

The concept of derivative houses makes it possible to use your chart to forecast events for people close to you, such as mate, children, parents, friends, and siblings. Although this is not a replacement for reading the specific individual's chart, you can often glean information by using this technique.

In order to read derivative houses in your chart, you first need to identify the house that rules the person you're inquiring about. For example, you would select the seventh house for a mate, and the fifth for a child. Parents as a couple are represented by the fourth house. Some astrologers use the fourth house for the mother, and the tenth house for the father. Others (myself included) use the tenth house for the mother, and the fourth for the father.

Once you know the house that represents the person, turn the chart so that the appropriate house is on the Ascendant. The seventh house (mate) in your chart would then be the first house of your mate, using derivative houses. If you want information about your mate's career, count forward ten houses (for the tenth house of career), beginning with the first house (the seventh in your chart). Your mate's derivative tenth house would thus be your fourth house.

MUNDANE ASTROLOGY

Mundane is the branch of astrology used to forecast events and general conditions of specific locations, usually countries, cities, and states and provinces. The predictive techniques are the same as those used in natal astrology, with some variations. For example, the second house represents a nation's economy rather than an individual's income.

There are two ways to approach mundane astrology: the natal chart of a country, city, or state/province, and ingress and lunation charts. Whether used separately or together, they generally reveal the same indications. The chart of a country, state/province, or city also can be progressed just like the birth chart of an individual and then interpreted using both progressions and transits. (See Recommended Reading list for books that contain this data.)

Ingress and lunation charts can be used to interpret general conditions affecting a particular location during the time frame they are active. An ingress occurs four times a year, when the Sun enters the cardinal signs: Aries, Cancer, Libra, and Capricorn. These mark the beginning of the seasons—spring, summer, autumn, and winter—and each is in effect for about three months. Some astrologers use the Aries ingress as representative of the entire year, while others use all four ingresses. I find the latter method to be more effective.

Lunations are the New and Full Moons that occur every month. New Moons are generally in effect for four weeks, and Full Moons for two. To interpret the effects on a country or state/province, the chart is calculated for the country's capital.

Ingress and lunation charts are sensitive to transits and progressions, just like birth charts. An aspect in an ingress chart, for example, can perfect (become exact) as the progressed planets advance (or retreat in the case of a retrograde planet), and transiting planets can trigger an event when they contact a planet in the ingress or lunation chart.

In general, the signs signify the nature of the event and its duration, the planets signify the specific type of event or the people or things affected by the event, and the houses represent how or in what arena the event will occur. Aspects are interpreted in the same way as they are in other predictive techniques.

PLANETS

- Sun—the ruler, president, prime minister, dictator, head of the government, people in power or authority
- Moon—the people, food, clothing, and shelter
- Mercury—communication, travel, education, transportation, media
- Venus—the arts, money, favorable conditions
- Mars—strife, war, police, military
- Jupiter—religion, legal matters, education, laws, foreign relations
- Saturn—restriction, ambition, goals, property, structure, conservative influences
- Uranus—change, progressive influences, revolution, riots, rebellion, Internet
- Neptune—ideals, fuel, water, confusion
- Pluto—mass change, transformation/renewal, power struggles

HOUSES

- First—the people
- Second—the economy, money, values, banks and other financial institutions
- Third—communication, postal service, media, transportation, education, neighboring countries
- Fourth—property, real estate, homes, agriculture, mining, security
- Fifth—stock market, entertainment venues, gambling, children
- Sixth—workers, workplaces, civil service, military, health
- Seventh—diplomacy, treaties, war, open enemies
- Eighth—debt, insurance, taxes, death, government financial assistance
- Ninth—justice system, education, international relations, religion and religious institutions, travel
- Tenth—the ruler, president, prime minister, head of government, those in authority
- Eleventh—legislative branch of government, groups, labor unions
- Twelfth—hidden enemies, institutions (hospitals, prisons, jails), welfare, unemployment

SIGNS

- Aries—war, battle, conflict, initiative, action
- Taurus—comfort, money, values
- Gemini—communication, education, transportation

- Cancer—food, real estate, property
- Leo—children, leisure-time activities, stock market, gambling
- Virgo—workers, workplaces, health, pets, service
- Libra—open enemies, allies
- Scorpio—debt, death, destruction, insurance
- Sagittarius—international relations, education, travel, justice system, religion
- Capricorn—government, corporations, head of government
- Aquarius—Internet, groups
- Pisces—institutions, unemployment, welfare

SIGNS AND DURATION OF INFLUENCE

- Cardinal Signs (Aries, Cancer, Libra, Capricorn)—matters occur quickly and are of short duration
- Fixed Signs (Taurus, Leo, Scorpio, Aquarius)—matters are ongoing and of long duration
- Mutable Signs (Gemini, Virgo, Sagittarius, Pisces)—matters are indeterminate in duration

COMPARISON OF EVENTS: TWO INGRESSES AND TWO LUNATIONS

January 2011 was an eventful month in the United States and Egypt. United States Represen-
tative Gabrielle Giffords was shot at a January 8 event in Tucson, Arizona, and in Egypt, the citizens revolted against President Mubarak. These two very different events can be seen in the January 4 New Moon chart, but only the Egyptian event is apparent in the Capricorn (previous) ingress.

The winter (Capricorn) ingress chart for Cairo (Chart 65) has the Moon (people) in the ninth house opposition a stellium of the Sun (Mubarak, the president), Pluto (change through force, power struggle), and Mars (war, violence) in the third. All these planets are in a wide square to Saturn (government, structure) in the twelfth. The Moon, which rules the tenth house of the president, is also trine Venus, ruler of the first house and placed in the first house of the people.

Egyptian citizens began their protest January 25, organizing their efforts through the Internet and social media sites (third and ninth houses). In addition to rebelling against Mubarak, whom they termed a dictator, and his government, the citizens were protesting the high price of food (Moon square Saturn), a lack of justice (ninth house), and rampant, high unemployment.

Because five of the planets involved are in cardinal signs, it could be expected that this uprising would be short-lived. Indeed it was, as Mubarak resigned February 17, about three weeks after the initial protest. This ingress chart also shows that the citizens would prevail because the Moon (the people) is trine Venus (ruler of the first house) in the first house (the people). With Venus in Scorpio, a fixed sign, there is every reason for optimism that the end result will be a positive, long-lived one.

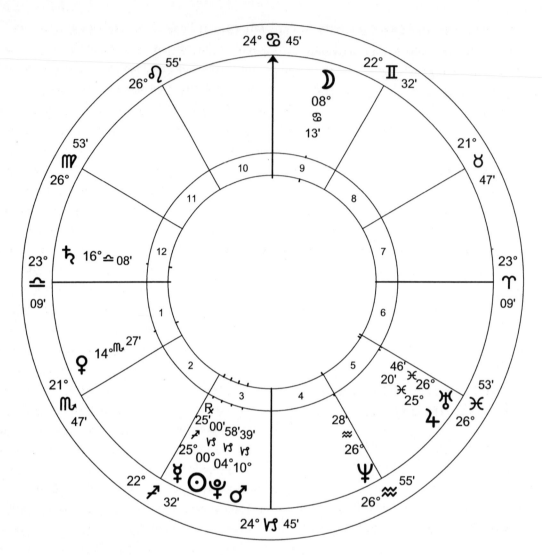

Chart 65: Winter Ingress

Event Chart / December 22, 2010 / 1:40 am EET / Cairo, Egypt / Placidus House

On January 25, the date the protest began, transiting Mercury was square ingress Saturn, and transiting Saturn was stationing retrograde within a degree of ingress Saturn. Transiting Jupiter was square ingress Sun. By the time Mubarak resigned on February 11, transiting Jupiter was square ingress Pluto, and transiting Venus was opposition ingress Moon. The people prevailed.

The rebellion and ultimate resignation of the president are also apparent in the natal and progressed chart of Egypt. On the day the protest began, transiting Mercury (cell phone communication) was conjunct progressed Moon (the people) in Capricorn (government), and transiting Jupiter (justice) in the third house (communication) was opposition progressed Saturn (government) in the ninth house (justice, Internet). Jupiter also rules the first house of the people. The most telling aspect configuration, however, was transiting Venus (ruler of the tenth house of the president) conjunct progressed Mars in the twelfth house and opposition the progressed Sun (president), which was only a few minutes from crossing the Descendant into the seventh house. Venus would cross the Ascendant into the house of the people within a day, where it would form an exact opposition to the progressed Sun (president). A simple interpretation: The hidden enemies (twelfth house) of the government quickly became the open enemies (seventh house) of the government.

As an astrologer looking at this chart, you would immediately look for an indication for if and when Mubarak would resign. He did that as transiting Jupiter, ruler of the first house of the people, crossed the fourth house cusp and opposed the tenth house cusp of the president.

Now look at the winter ingress chart for Washington, DC (Chart 66), the capital of the United States. The planets are in the same signs and degrees, but in different houses because of the time zone. Finding an indication in this chart of the shooting of Gabrielle Giffords is a stretch at best. The Moon in the twelfth house of institutions (hospital) is opposition the Capricorn planets in the sixth house of health. The Moon is also trine Venus, which rules the eleventh house of legislators. Had I looked at this chart in advance, I would have interpreted it as more concerns about unemployment and housing (square to Saturn in the fourth) with eventual improvement during the season in both because of the Moon-Venus trine. Never would I have considered the shooting that did occur. There is a simple explanation for this: the shooting, although a black day for the country, in no way impacted the legislative process or the business of the government.

Now let's look at the January New Moon charts for both of these events. The Egyptian event is obvious (Chart 67). The first house of the people is ruled by Mars, which is in the tenth house conjunct the New Moon and square Saturn in the seventh. Saturn rules the tenth house. Mubarak and his government were clearly at risk because of a war started by the people.

How could we know which side would prevail? Mars, ruler of the first house, was approaching a sextile to the lucky Jupiter-Uranus conjunction in the twelfth house (positive change). Transiting Mars would perfect this sextile before the Sun (the president), which was square Saturn (the president) in the

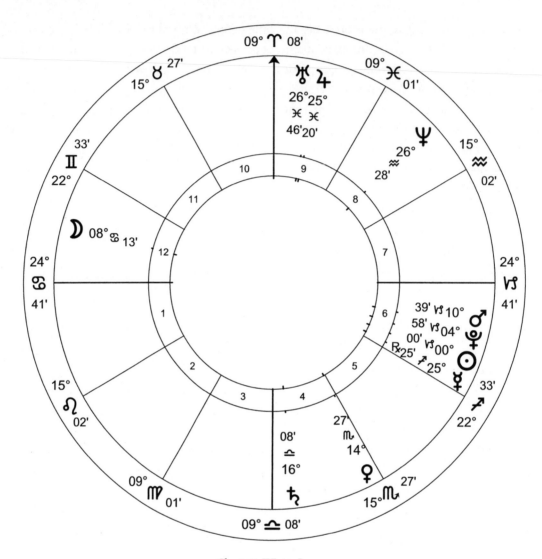

Chart 66: Winter Ingress
Event Chart / December 21, 2010 / 6:40 pm EST / Washington DC / Placidus House

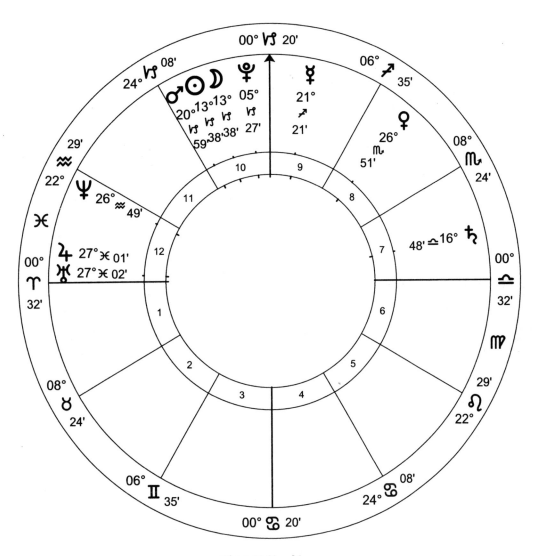

Chart 67: New Moon

Event Chart / January 4, 2011 / 11:02 am EET / Cairo, Egypt/ Placidus House

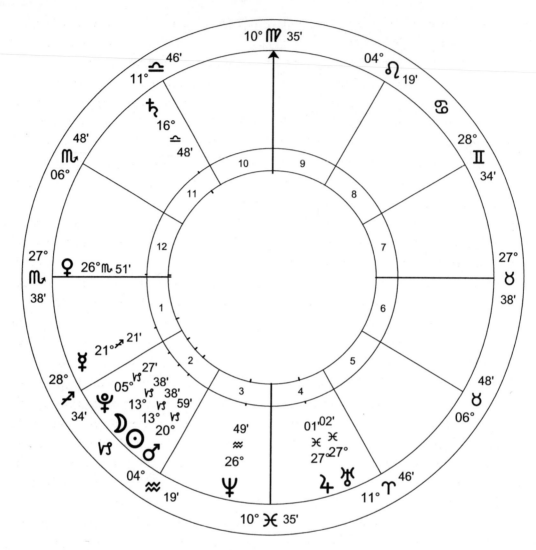

Chart 68: New Moon

Event Chart / January 4, 2011 / 4:02 am EST / Washington DC / Placidus House

seventh house (war), would form the same sextile. As the Moon (the people) transited Capricorn, it would, of course, sextile Jupiter-Uranus long before either Mars or the Sun. In this chart, Venus (ruler of the seventh house and open enemies—protestors) is trine the Jupiter-Uranus conjunction, bringing luck and success to the protestors (open enemies).

The January New Moon chart for Washington, DC (Chart 68), unlike the Capricorn ingress, suggests an event involving a legislator. Here, the three Capricorn planets are in the second house of values and square Saturn in the eleventh house of legislators. With Mars active in this chart, violence involving the legislative branch or a legislator is a strong possibility.

Venus in this chart offers interesting clues (which are far easier to see in retrospect) to the alleged shooter. Venus, which rules the seventh (open enemy) and eleventh (legislator) houses, is in the twelfth (hidden enemies). The twelfth is also significant because it was suggested that the alleged shooter suffers from mental illness. Mars, which is square Saturn, co-rules the twelfth house and rules the fifth house of children. A child was killed in the shooting. With Venus ruling the seventh, the hidden enemy would become an open enemy of a legislator. The trine from Venus to Jupiter-Uranus indicates that justice would be served and also that the nation would experience a spiritually uplifting time in the aftermath of the event.

CUBAN MISSILE CRISIS

The Cold War between the former USSR (Union of Soviet Socialist Republics) and the United States was a dominant global influence from 1947 to 1991. Both countries were superpowers and each had nuclear weapons aimed at the other. The threat of a nuclear blast was never far from American minds. School children participated in drills so they would know what to do in the event of an attack, and many people constructed underground shelters to protect themselves from both a nuclear blast and the ensuing radiation.

A crisis point in the Cold War occurred in October 1962, when a United States Air Force U-2 spy plane photographed Soviet missiles in Cuba, a communist ally of the USSR. The United States immediately demanded of the USSR that all missiles in Cuba be removed and that all missile bases be destroyed. The USSR publicly refused, but an agreement was reached through the United Nations: the missiles would be removed in exchange for the United States. agreeing never to invade Cuba, and the removal of certain U.S. missiles from Europe and Turkey. The hotline—a direct communication link between the White House and the Kremlin—was also established as a result of the confrontation.

The solar ingress chart (Chart 69) in effect at the time of the Cuban Missile Crisis is a good example of how transits affect these charts and activate events. Notice first that Mars, planet of war, is in the ninth house of international relations and square Mercury, ruler of the same house (Gemini on the ninth house cusp), in the first house of the people. The Moon (the people) in and ruling the tenth house of the president is opposition Saturn, ruler of and in the fourth house of home and security. American citizens perceived the event as a very

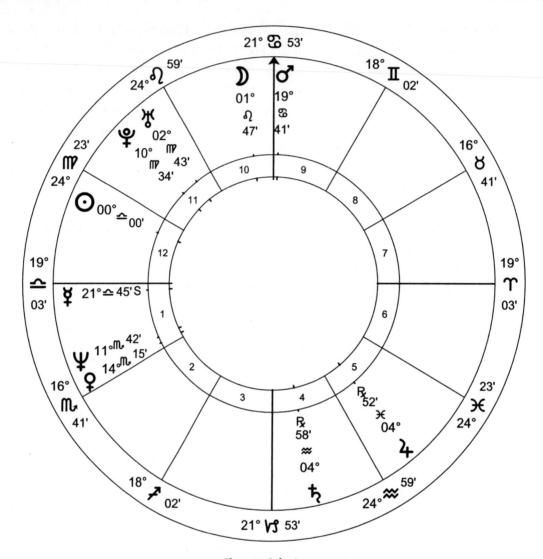

Chart 69: Solar Ingress

Event Chart / September 23, 1962 / 8:35:12 am EDT / Washington DC/ Placidus House

real threat, but were unsure if President John F. Kennedy could handle the situation. Mars is also trine the Venus-Neptune conjunction in the first house (the people), with Venus ruling the same house.

The outcome would be quickly determined because of the cardinal signs on the angles. But what would the outcome be? Based on the chart and its combination of aspects, it could have gone either way. However, the strong presence of Mercury conjunct the Ascendant suggests that communication and negotiation could result in an agreement, which it did.

Also of interest in this chart is the Sun in the twelfth house trine Saturn in the fourth. This indicates the potential for a threat to the homeland (Saturn) by a hidden enemy (twelfth house). The Moon in the tenth is sextile the Sun, and because Saturn is the natural ruler of the tenth house (president), the Sun-Moon-Saturn configuration also reflects the secret and public negotiations that occurred.

The missiles were photographed by the U-2 on October 14, 1962, the date the transiting Sun emerged from the ingress chart twelfth house and crossed the Ascendant while forming a square to Mars in the ninth. On the same date, the transiting Moon was in the seventh house of open enemies, and transiting Mars was conjunct the ingress Moon in the tenth house. Transiting Mercury, which had turned retrograde September 24 (the day after the ingress), was in Libra in the twelfth house. It turned direct on October 15 at 6 Libra, forming a trine with the ingress Saturn in the fourth house.

As all of these transits contacted planets in the ingress chart on October 14, they brought what was previously hidden into the open and made a U.S.-USSR confrontation and nuclear war very real possibilities. The final trigger was the Full Moon of October 13 at 19 Aries 41 opposition-conjunction the ingress chart Ascendant (the people)-Descendant (open enemy), and square the ingress Midheaven (president)-IC (home and security).

In the two weeks between October 14 and 28, when the agreement was reached, the Sun advanced in the twelfth house, indicating the secret talks. It was conjunct the ingress Ascendant and square Mars on the 28th. Here, too, a lunation had a role. The New Moon (Sun-Moon conjunction) of October 28 at 4 Scorpio 28 was square ingress chart Saturn, concluding the matter (the fourth is also the house of beginnings and endings). The Moon would move on to conjunct ingress Venus and Neptune, and trine ingress Mars the next day as the final details were being worked out.

ECONOMIC MELTDOWN

The Great Recession (some have called it a depression) began in early 2006, when housing prices peaked and began to decline. This led to the collapse of the sub-prime mortgage industry in early 2007, a year that saw the largest drops in home sales in the previous twenty-five years and the first price decline in many, maybe since the Great Depression of the 1930s.

As the next few years unfolded, the stock market lost nearly fifty percent of its value, countries around the world experienced serious financial problems, hundreds of banks failed, U.S. debt increased to trillions of dollars, and homes continued to decrease in value and go into foreclosure.

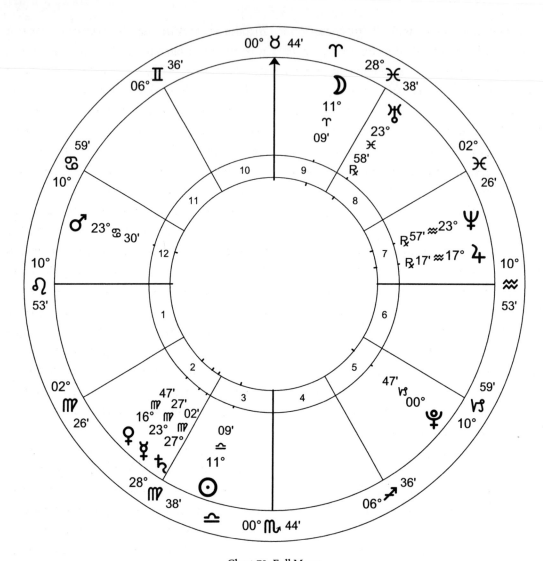

Chart 70: Full Moon
Event Chart / October 4, 2009 / 2:10:10 am EDT / Washington DC/ Placidus House

October 2009 was a particularly low point. The unemployment rate reached a recession peak of 10.1 percent as companies continued to lay off workers. Others, even those that were rich in cash, were not hiring. The American economy continued to spiral downward, aggravated by the reluctance of many to spend on all but necessities. Saving became a priority. All of this is reflected in the October 4, 2009, Full Moon chart (Chart 70) calculated for Washington, DC.

The most obvious indication of financial difficulties is the Venus-Mercury-Saturn stellium in the second house (the economy) opposition Uranus in the eighth house (country's debt). All four of these planets aspect Mars in the twelfth house by sextile or trine. The Sun and Moon in the solar third and ninth houses represent the worldwide nature of this crisis.

On its own, the Saturn-Uranus opposition in the second and eighth houses indicates a severe financial period. Saturn is the universal ruler of business and real estate, and Uranus represents change. Placed in the financial houses, this opposition would affect both. The Venus placement is another indication of the dire straights of housing/real estate as well as the overall economy. Note also that Mercury, the third planet in the stellium, rules the second house of the economy.

The sixth house represents the nation's workers. Although there are no planets in this house, it is ruled by Saturn in the second house. Its opposition to Uranus indicates a change in employment and in unemployment benefits.

The placement of Mars in the Full Moon chart suggests there was much activity behind the scenes of which the American people were unaware at the time. Confirmation of that can be seen in the Mars sextile to Venus, ruler of the tenth house of the president, and Mercury, ruler of the eleventh house of Congress. Mars sextile-trine the Saturn-Uranus opposition further suggests that the people involved were at odds (Saturn rules and Uranus co-rules the seventh house) over that month's hot topic: executive compensation and financial regulation.

However, despite the state of the economy and rising unemployment, the stock market continued to rise from its low point in March 2009. At first glance, Pluto in the fifth house doesn't look favorable for the market. But it was because Pluto is semisquare Jupiter, ruler of the fifth house, and Jupiter is approaching a conjunction with Neptune, ruler of the eighth house. So in the midst of all the dire indications, this financial sector was the exception, and a profitable one, for those who had the money to invest.

Such was not the case earlier in the year. The Dow-Jones Industrial Average hit a low of 6440 on Monday, March 9, 2009, and unemployment reached a new high of 8.9 percent the month before. This was in the midst of the U.S. Treasury Department's purchase of nearly $2 billion of preferred stock in U.S. banks and its restructuring of its previous assistance to American International Group (AIG), one of the companies heavily involved in the sub-prime mortgage crisis. AIG received $30 billion in TARP (Troubled Asset Relief Program) funds in exchange for $40 billion in stock. A $787 billion stimulus-spending bill was also signed into law.

These are only a few of the many events that occurred in the February-March 2009 time frame, with hundreds more throughout the

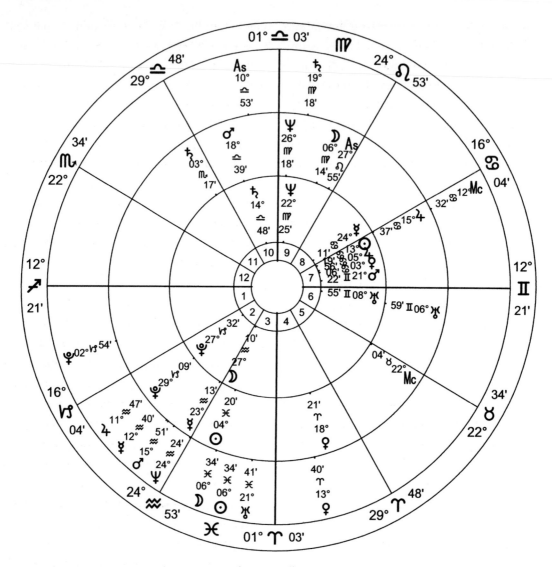

Chart 71: Full Moon
Inner chart: U.S. Birth Chart / July 4, 1776 / 5:10:10 pm LMT / Philadelphia, Pennsylvania
Middle chart: U.S. Chart Secondary Progressed SA / February 24, 2009 / 7:28:27 pm LMT / Philadelphia, Pennsylvania
Outer chart: New Moon / February 24, 2009 / 8:35 pm EST / Philadelphia, Pennsylvania
Placidus House

Great Recession and its aftermath. All of this is reflected in the U.S. chart.

Astrologers have debated the birth time (and even the date) of the United States for at least a couple of hundred years. The chart shown here (Chart 71 / Inner chart) is known as the Sibley chart because it was researched and promoted by Ebenezer Sibley, a well-known eighteenth century English astrologer and physician. Although the Sibley chart is the most widely used, there are many others that are used by various astrologers.

The United States progressed chart for February 24, 2009, is in the middle wheel, and the outer wheel has the planetary positions for the New Moon preceding the stock market low.

The most prominent influence is transiting Pluto in opposition to natal Venus, the universal planets of money. (This would be true of any United States chart for July 4.) Pluto returned to the same degree in December 2009, when several banks repaid the loans they had previously received from the U.S. Treasury Department. Note that Venus rules the sixth house of this United States chart, reflecting the high unemployment rate reached that year.

The February 24, 2009, New Moon in Pisces (Outer chart) was conjunct the progressed U.S. Sun and opposition the progressed Moon, forming a t-square with natal and progressed Uranus in the sixth house (a new high in unemployment). This New Moon-progressed planet configuration reinforced the realization that the struggling economy wasn't just a United States problem. It was a worldwide one that would continue to evolve through the summer months of 2010 as Saturn and Uranus formed their opposition in the third-ninth houses. During much of 2009 and into early 2010, the situation worsened as both these planets formed aspects to natal and progressed U.S. Neptune. And there was little the United States could do to lessen the impact of the global economy.

A more positive development associated with this New Moon was President Obama's announcement of a pull-out timeline for United States troops in Iraq. This war began in 2003, as transiting Pluto in Sagittarius opposed the U.S. natal Mars in Gemini. The progressed Moon was conjunct Mars at the time.

Mars rules the fifth house (stock market) of the U.S. birth chart, with Venus as co-ruler. At the time of the February New Moon, progressed Venus was opposition progressed Mars, and transiting Venus stationed retrograde conjunct-opposition these two planets the Friday before the market reached its low point. The New Moon also triggered the Venus-Mars opposition by semisquare and sesquisquare. Even though the market had been headed downward for some time, that trend was reversed under the influence of this New Moon as Neptune formed a conjunction to progressed Mercury for the final time.

You can learn much about mundane astrology and gain practical experience by observing how transits and progressions affect the chart of your city, state, country, or province. More knowledge and insights can also come from tracking the daily and monthly events indicated in monthly lunation charts, both at the time of the New and Full Moons and as the transiting planets aspect the planets and angles of the charts.

ASTROLOGICAL ORGANIZATIONS AND WEBSITES

ASTROLOGICAL ORGANIZATIONS

There are many local astrology groups in addition to the national and international ones listed here, some of which have chapters or affiliate groups in the United States and other countries.

American Federation of Astrologers (AFA)
6535 S. Rural Road, Tempe, AZ 85283
480-838-1751
www.astrologers.com
Offers certification testing and a correspondence course.

Association for Astrological Networking (AFAN)
www.afan.org

Faculty of Astrological Studies
www.astrology.org.uk
Offers classes and certification testing.

National Council for Geocosmic Research (NCGR)

www.geocosmic.org

Offers certification testing.

International Society for Astrological Research (ISAR)

www.isarastrology.com

Astrodienst

www.astro.com

Astrolabe

www.alabe.com

Matrix Software

www.thenewage.com

FREE ONLINE
CHART CALCULATION

You can get free charts at the following websites. For help obtaining an official U.S. birth certificate, visit this web page of the National Center for Health Statistics: www.cdc.gov/nchs/howto/w2w/w2welcom.htm.

AIR Software

www.alphee.com

RECOMMENDED READING

Thousands of astrology books have been written over the centuries, and new books are published every year. Included in this suggested reading list are books on nearly every astrological topic and for every level of astrological knowledge. Some are out of print, but you might find them at used bookstores and on the Internet.

ASPECTS

Antepara, Robin. *Aspects: Powerful Keys to Personal Transformation*. St. Paul, MN: Llewellyn Publications, 2006.

Avery, Jeanne. *Astrological Aspects*. Garden City, NY: Doubleday & Co., 1985; Tempe, AZ: AFA, 2005.

Carter, C.E.O. *The Astrological Aspects*. London: L. N. Fowler, 1930, Tempe, AZ: AFA, 2003.

Clement, Stephanie. *Aspect Patterns*. St. Paul, MN: Llewellyn Publications, 2007.

Hamaker-Zondag, Karen. *Aspects and Personality*. York Beach, ME: Red Wheel/Weiser, 1990.

Hamaker-Zondag, Karen. *The Yod Book*. York Beach, ME: Red Wheel/Weiser, 2000.

Kellogg, Joan. *The Yod: Its Esoteric Meaning*. Tempe, AZ: AFA, 1989, 2003.

Tompkins, Sue. *Aspects in Astrology*. Rochester, VT: Destiny, 2002.

ASTEROIDS

Donath, Emma Belle. *Asteroids in the Birth Chart*. Tempe, AZ: AFA, 1987.

_____. *Asteroids in Synastry*. Tempe, AZ: AFA, 1978, 2009.

George, Demetra. *Asteroid Goddesses*. Berwick, ME: Ibis Press, 2003.

Guttman, Ariel, and Kenneth Johnson. *Mythic Astrology*. St. Paul, MN: Llewellyn Publications, 1993.

———. *Mythic Astrology Applied*. St. Paul, MN: Llewellyn Publications, 2004.

BIOGRAPHY

Brahy, Gustave-Lambert. *Confidential Recollections Revealed*. Tempe, AZ: AFA, 2006. (Autobiography of Belgian astrologer Gustave-Lambert Brahy, 1930s and 1940s)

Christino, Karen. *Foreseeing the Future: Evangeline Adams and Astrology in America*. Amherst, MA: One Reed Publications, 2002.

CALENDARS AND ANNUALS

Llewellyn's Astrological Calendar. St. Paul, MN: Llewellyn Publications.

Llewellyn's Daily Planetary Guide. St. Paul, MN: Llewellyn Publications.

Llewellyn's Moon Sign Book. St. Paul, MN: Llewellyn Publications.

Llewellyn's Sun Sign Book. St. Paul, MN: Llewellyn Publications.

Maynard, Jim. *Jim Maynard's Astrologer's Datebook*. Ashland, OR: Quicksilver Productions.

CHIRON

Clow, Barbara Hand. *Chiron: Rainbow Bridge Between the Inner and Outer Planets*. St. Paul, MN: Llewellyn Publications, 2004.

Lass, Martin. *Chiron*. St. Paul, MN: Llewellyn Publications, 2005.

Reinhart, Melanie. *Chiron and the Healing Journey*. London: Starwalker Press, 2009.

COSMOBIOLOGY

Ebertin, Reinhold. *Applied Cosmobiology*. Tempe, AZ: AFA, 2006.

———. *Contact Cosmogram*. Tempe, AZ: AFA, 2011.

———. *Directions: Co-Determinants of Fate*. Tempe, AZ: AFA, 2011.

———. *Man and the Universe: An Introduction to Cosmobiology*. Tempe, AZ: AFA, 2011.

———. *The Annual Diagram: Forecasting Using 45-Degree Graphic Ephemeris*. Tempe, AZ: AFA, 2010.

———. *The Combination of Stellar Influences*. Aalen, Germany: Ebertin-Verlag, 1940; Tempe, AZ: AFA, 1994, 2004.

———. *Transits*. Aalen, Germany: Ebertin-Verlag, 1928; Tempe, AZ: AFA, 2001

Kimmel, Eleonora. *Altered and Unfinished Lives*. Tempe, AZ: AFA, 2006.

———. *Cosmobiology for the 21st Century*. Tempe, AZ: AFA, 1979.

———. *Fundamentals of Cosmobiology*. Tempe, AZ: AFA, 1979.

Simms, Maria Kay. *Dial Detective*. Kensington, NH: Cosmic Muse Publications, 2001.

DEGREES OF THE ZODIAC

Bovee, Blaine. *Sabian Symbols and Astrological Analysis*. St. Paul, MN: Llewellyn Publications, 2004.

Carelli, Adriano. *The 360 Degrees of the Zodiac*. Tempe, AZ: AFA, 1977, 2004.

Charubel. *The Degrees of the Zodiac Symbolized*. Bel Air, MD: Astrology Classics, 2004.

Henson, Donna. *Degrees of the Zodiac*. Tempe, AZ: AFA, 1981, 2004.

Jones, Marc Edmund. *Sabian Symbols in Astrology*. Santa Fe, NM: Aurora Press, 1993.

Kozminsky, Isidore. *Zodiacal Symbology*. Tempe, AZ: AFA, 1980.

ECLIPSES

Lineman, Rose. *Eclipses: Astrological Guideposts.* Tempe, AZ: AFA, 1984, 2004.

———. *Eclipse Interpretation Manual.* Tempe, AZ: AFA, 1986, 2004.

———. *Your Prenatal Eclipse.* Tempe, AZ: AFA, 1992, 2003.

Meridian, Bill. *The Predictive Power of Eclipse Paths.* New York, NY: Cycles Research Publications, 2010.

Teal, Celeste. *Eclipses.* St. Paul, MN: Llewellyn Publications, 2006.

ELECTIONAL ASTROLOGY

Hampar, Joann. *Electional Astrology.* St. Paul, MN: Llewellyn Publications, 2005.

Robson, Vivian. *Electional Astrology.* Bel Air, MD: Astrology Classics, 2005.

EPHEMERIDES

The American Heliocentric Ephemeris, 2001–2050. Exeter, NH: Starcrafts Publishing, 2007.

The American Sidereal Ephemeris, 2001–2050. Exeter, NH: Starcrafts Publishing, 2007.

The New American Midpoint Ephemeris, 2001–2020. Exeter, NH: Starcrafts Publishing, 2007.

The Uranian Transneptunian Ephemeris, 1900–2050. Exeter, NH: Starcrafts Publishing, 2007.

The Lilith Ephemeris, 2000-2050. Tempe, AZ: AFA, 2011.

Astro America's Daily Ephemeris, 2000–2010. Bel Air, MD: Astrology Classics, 2006.

Astro America's Daily Ephemeris, 2010–2020. Bel Air, MD: Astrology Classics, 2006.

Astro America's Daily Ephemeris, 2000–2020. Bel Air, MD: Astrology Classics, 2006.

Astrolabe World Ephemeris, 2001–2050. Atglen, PA: Whitford Press, 1998.

The New American Ephemeris, 2007–2020, with Longitude, Latitude and Declinations. Exeter, NH: Starcrafts Publishing, 2007.

The New American Ephemeris for the 20th Century, 1900–2000 at Noon. Exeter, NH: Starcrafts Publishing, 2009.

The New American Ephemeris for the 21st Century, 2000–2100 at Midnight. Exeter, NH: Starcrafts Publishing, 2006.

The New American Ephemeris for the 21st Century, 2000–2050 at Midnight. Exeter, NH: Starcrafts Publishing, 2010.

The New American Ephemeris for the 21st Century, 2000–2050 at Noon. Exeter, NH: Starcrafts Publishing, 2010.

The Asteroid Ephemeris, 1900–2050. Exeter, NH: Starcrafts Publishing, 2008.

Raphael's Ephemeris. (Single year.) Slough, England: W. Foulsham & Co.

Rosicrucian Ephemeris. (Single year, decade, century.) Oceanside, CA: Rosicrucian Fellowship.

Tables of Planetary Phenomena. Second edition. San Diego, CA: ACS, 1995.

FINANCIAL ASTROLOGY

Gillen, Jack. *The Key to Speculation on the New York Stock Exchange.* Tempe, AZ: AFA, 2009.

McWhirter, Louise. *The McWhirter Theory of Stock Market Forecasting.* Tempe, AZ: AFA, 2008.

Meridian, Bill. *Planetary Economic Forecasting.* New York: Cycles Research, 2002.

———. *Planetary Stock Trading III.* New York: Cycles Research, 2002.

Williams, David. *Financial Astrology.* Tempe, AZ: AFA, 1984, 2003.

FIXED STARS

Brady, Bernadette. *Brady's Book of Fixed Stars*. York Beach, ME: Red Wheel/Weiser, 1998.

_____. *Star and Planet Combinations*. Bournemouth, England: The Wessex Astrologer, 2008.

Ebertin, Reinhold. *Fixed Stars and Their Interpretation*. Aalen, Germany: Ebertin-Verlag, 1971; Tempe, AZ: AFA, 2001.

Noonan, George. *Fixed Stars and Judicial Astrology*. Tempe, AZ: AFA, 2009.

Robson, Vivian. *The Fixed Stars and Constellations in Astrology*. New York: Samuel Weiser, 1969; Bel Air, MD: Astrology Classics, 2004.

HISTORY OF ASTROLOGY

Holden, James Herschel. *History of Horoscopic Astrology*. Second edition. Tempe, AZ: AFA, 2006.

HORARY ASTROLOGY

Barclay, Olivia. *Horary Astrology Rediscovered*. Atglen, PA: Whitford Press, 1990.

Doane, Doris C. *Modern Horary Astrology*. Tempe, AZ: AFA, 1994, 2011.

Jones, Marc Edmund. *Horary Astrology*. Santa Fe, NM: Aurora Press, 1993.

Lavoie, Alphee. *Horary at Its Best*. West Hartford, CT: AIR, 2002.

Louis, Anthony. *Horary Astrology: Plain and Simple*. St. Paul, MN: Llewellyn Publications, 2005.

Simmonite, W.J. *Horary Astrology*. Tempe, AZ: AFA, 1950, 2009. (First published in 1896.)

HOUSES

Bryan, Gwyneth. *Houses*. St. Paul, MN: Llewellyn Publications, 2006.

Hamaker-Zondag. *The House Connection*. York Beach, ME: Red Wheel/Weiser, 1994.

Herbst, Bill. *Houses of the Horoscope*. San Diego, CA: Serendipity Press, 2005.

Mason, Sophia. *From One House to Another*. Tempe, AZ: AFA, 1993, 2008.

Oken, Alan. *Houses of the Horoscope*. Lake Worth, FL: Ibis Press, 1999.

Pelletier, Robert. *Planets in Houses*. Atglen, PA: Whitford Press, 1978.

Ruiz, Ana. *Interpreting Empty Houses*. Tempe, AZ: AFA, 2006.

Sasportas, Howard. *The Twelve Houses*. London: Flare Publications, 2007.

INTERCEPTIONS

Garrett, Helen. *Unlocking Interceptions*. Tempe, AZ: AFA, 2011.

McRae, I. I. Chris. *Understanding Interceptions*. Tempe, AZ: AFA, 2000.

Miller, Alice. *Intercepted Planets: Possibilities for a New Age*. Tempe, AZ: AFA, 2010.

_____. *Interceptions: Heralds of a New Age*. Tempe, AZ: AFA, 2009.

Wickenburg, Joanne. *Your Hidden Powers*. Tempe, AZ: AFA, 1992, 2001, 2011.

LILITH

Hunter, M. Kelley. *Black Moon Lilith*. Tempe, AZ: AFA, 2010.

Jay, Delphine. *Interpreting Lililth*. Tempe, AZ: AFA, 1981, 2010.

LOCATIONAL ASTROLOGY

Cozzi, Steve. *Planets in Locality*. St. Paul, MN: Llewellyn Publications, 1988; Tempe, AZ: AFA, 1997.

Davis, Martin. *Astrolocality Astrology*. Bournemouth, England: The Wessex Astrologer, 1999.

Penfield, Marc. *Bon Voyage*. Tempe, AZ: AFA, 1992.

Pottenger, Maritha, and Kris Brandt Riske, M.A. *Mapping Your Travels & Relocation*. St. Paul, MN: Llewellyn Publications, 2005.

MEDICAL ASTROLOGY

Blagrave, Joseph. *Astrological Practice of the Physick*. Bel Air, MD: Astrology Classics, 2010. (First published in 1671.)

Cramer, Diane. *Dictionary of Medical Astrology*. Tempe, AZ: AFA, 2003.

———. *How to Give an Astrological Health Reading*. Tempe, AZ: AFA, 1996, 2005.

———. *Managing Your Health & Wellness*. St. Paul, MN: Llewellyn Publications, 2006.

Cornell, H. L. *The Encyclopaedia of Medical Astrology*. Los Angeles, CA: Cornell Publishing Co., 1933; Bel Air, MD: Astrology Classics, 2004.

Culpepper, Nicholas. *Astrological Judgement of Disease/Decumbiture*. Bel Air, MD: Astrology Classics, 2003.

Darling, Harry F., M.D. *Essentials of Medical Astrology*. Tempe, AZ: AFA, 1981, 2004.

deMello, Joseph Silveira. *Decumbitures and Diurnals*. Tempe, AZ: AFA, 2002.

Faugno, Emily. *Your Fertile Hours*. Tempe, AZ: AFA, 1986.

Hill, Judith A. *Medical Astrology*. Portland, OR: Stellium Press, 2004.

Hofman, Oscar. *Classical Medical Astrology*. Bournemouth, England: The Wessex Astrologer, 2009.

Jansky, Robert C. *Astrology, Nutrition, and Health*. Atglen, PA: Whitford Press, 1977.

Ridder-Patrick, Jane. *A Handbook of Medical Astrology*. Edinburgh, Scotland: CrabApple Press, 1990.

Sellar, Wanda. *Introduction to Medical Astrology*. Bournemouth, England: The Wessex Astrologer, 2008.

Starck, Marcia. *Healing with Astrology*. Freedom, CA: The Freedom Press, 1977.

Starck, Marcia. *Medical Astrology: Healing for the 21st Century*. Santa Fe, NM: Earth Medicine Books, 2002.

MUNDANE ASTROLOGY

Campion, Nicholas. *The Book of World Horoscopes*. Revised edition. Bournemouth, England: Wessex Astrologer, Ltd., 2004.

Green, H. S., C.E.O. Carter, and Raphael. *Mundane Astrology*. Bel Air, MD: Astrology Classics, 2004.

Jones, Marc Edmund. *Mundane Perspectives in Astrology*. Stanwood, WA: Sabian Publishing Society, 1975.

Penfield, Marc. *Horoscopes of Africa*. Tempe, AZ: AFA, 2008.

———. *Horoscopes of Asia, Australia and the Pacific*. Tempe, AZ: AFA, 2006.

———. *Horoscopes of Europe*. Tempe, AZ: AFA, 2006.

———. *Horoscopes of Latin America*. Tempe, AZ: AFA, 2006.

———. *Horoscopes of the USA and Canada*. Second edition. Tempe, AZ: AFA, 2005.

———. *Stars Over England*. Tempe, AZ: AFA, 2005.

Riske, Kris Brandt. *Astrometeorology: Planetary Power in Weather Forecasting*. Tempe, AZ: AFA, 1997

Weber, Lind. *Astro-Geology of Earthquakes and Volcanoes*. Tempe, AZ: AFA, 1995.

NATAL ASTROLOGY

Adams, Helen J. *Understanding Retrogrades*. Tempe, AZ: AFA, 1982, 1996.

Arroyo, Stephen. *Astrology, Karma, and Transformation*. Sebastopol, CA: CRCS, 1992.

———. *Astrology, Psychology, and the Four Elements*. Sebastopol, CA: CRCS, 1975.

_____. Chart Interpretation Handbook. Sebastopol, CA: CRCS, 1989.

Avery, Jeanne. *The Rising Sign.* Garden City, NY: Doubleday, 1982.

Bloch, Douglas and Demetra George. *Astrology for Yourself.* Lake Worth, FL: Ibis Press, 2006.

Burk, Kevin. *The Complete Node Book.* St. Paul, MN: Llewellyn Publications, 2006.

Busteed, Marilyn, and Dorothy Wergin. *Phases of the Moon.* Tempe, AZ: AFA, 1982.

Carter, C.E.O. *An Encyclopaedia of Psychological Astrology.* London: W. Foulsham & Co., 1924; Bel Air, MD: Astrology Classics, 2003.

———. *Foundations of Astrology.* London: L. N. Fowler, 1947.

———. *Some Principles of Horoscopic Delineation.* London: L. N. Fowler, 1934.

———. *The Zodiac and the Soul.* London: Theosophical Publishing House, Ltd., 1928.

Christino, Karen. *What Evangeline Adams Knew: A Book of Astrological Charts and Techniques.* Brooklyn Heights, NY: Stella Mira Books, 2004.

Cunningham, Donna. *Astrology and Vibrational Healing.* San Rafael, CA: Cassandra Press, 1988.

_____. *Being a Lunar Type in a Solar World.* York Beach, ME: Samuel Weiser, 1990.

_____. *Healing Pluto Problems.* York Beach, ME: Red Wheel/Weiser, 1986.

_____. *Moon Signs.* New York: Ballantine Books, 1988.

Devlin, Mary. *Astrology and Past Lives.* West Chester, PA: Para Research, 1987.

Dobyns, Zipporah Pottenger. *The Node Book.* Tempe, AZ: AFA, 2010.

Falconer, Kim. *Astrology and Aptitude.* Tempe, AZ: AFA, 2005.

Forrest, Steven. *The Inner Sky.* San Diego, CA: ACS, 2001.

Garrett, Helen. *More About Retrogrades.* Tempe, AZ: AFA, 2011.

George, Llewellyn. *Llewellyn's New A to Z Horoscope Maker and Interpreter.* Fourteenth edition. St. Paul, MN: Llewellyn Publications, 2003.

Goldsmith, Martin. *Moon Phases: A Symbolic Key.* Atglen, PA: Whitford Press, 1988.

_____. *Zodiac by Degrees.* York Beach, ME: Red Wheel/Weiser, 2004.

Grebner, Bernice Prill. *Lunar Nodes.* Tempe, AZ: AFA, 1980, 2006.

Guttman, Ariel, and Kenneth Johnson. *Mythic Astrology.* St. Paul, MN: Llewellyn Publications, 1993.

———. *Mythic Astrology Applied.* St. Paul, MN: Llewellyn Publications, 2004.

Hand, Robert. *Horoscope Symbols.* Atglen, PA: Whitford Press, 1981.

———. *Planets in Youth.* Atglen, PA: Whitford Press, 1977.

Henson, Donna. *The Vertex: The Third Angle.* Tempe, AZ: AFA, 2003.

Hickey, Isabel M. *Astrology: A Cosmic Science.* Watertown, MA: Fellowship House Bookshop, 1974; Sebastopol, CA: CRCS, 1992.

Hill, Judith A. *Vocational Astrology.* Tempe, AZ: AFA, 2000.

Hone, Margaret. *The Modern Text-Book of Astrology.* Bel Air, MD: Astrology Classics, 2010.

Jones, Marc Edmund. *Guide to Horoscope Interpretation.* Stanwood, WA: Sabian Publishing Society, 1972.

Leo, Alan. *The Art of Synthesis.* London: L. N. Fowler, 1912, 1971.

———. *How to Judge a Nativity.* London: L. N. Fowler, 1909.

Lewi, Grant. *Astrology for the Millions.* St. Paul, MN: Llewellyn Publications, 1990.

———. *Heaven Knows What.* St. Paul, MN: Llewellyn Publications, 1995.

Lineman, Rose and Jan Popelka. *Compendium of Astrology.* Atglen, PA: Whitford Press, 1984.

Mason, Sophia. *You and Your Ascendant*. Tempe, AZ: AFA, 1998.

Oken, Alan. *Alan Oken's Complete Astrology*. New York: Bantam Books, 1988.

———. *Rulers of the Horoscope*. Freedom, CA: Crossing Press, 2000.

Parker, Julia and Derek. *Parker's Astrology*. London: DK Publishing, 2003.

Riske, Kris Brandt, M.A. *Llewellyn's Complete Book of Astrology: The Easy Way to Learn Astrology*. Woodbury, MN: Llewellyn Publications, 2007.

———. *Mapping Your Money*. St. Paul, MN: Llewellyn Publications, 2005.

Robson, Vivian. *Astrology and Sex*. Philadelphia: W. Foulsham Co., 1941; Bel Air, MD: Astrology Classics, 2004.

———. *A Beginner's Guide to Practical Astrology*. Bel Air, MD: Astrology Classics, 2010.

———. *A Student's Text-Book of Astrology*. Bel Air, MD: Astrology Classics, 2010.

Rodden, Lois. *Money: How to Find It with Astrology*. Yucaipa, CA: Data News, 1994; Tempe, AZ: AFA, 2006.

Rogers-Gallagher, Kim. *Astrology for the Light Side of the Brain*. San Diego, CA: ACS, 1995.

Silveira de Mello, Joseph. *Declinations*. Tempe, AZ: AFA, 2003.

Simms, Maria Kay. *Moon Tides, Soul Passages*. Kensington, NH: Starcrafts Publishing, 2004.

———. *Your Magical Child*. San Diego, CA: ACS, 1994.

Smith, Debbi Kempton. *Secrets from a Stargazer's Notebook*. New York: Topquark Press, 1999.

Spiller, Jan. *Astrology for the Soul*. New York: Bantam Books, 1997.

Tierney, Bil. *Alive and Well with Neptune*. St. Paul, MN: Llewellyn Publications, 1999.

———. *Alive and Well with Pluto*. St. Paul, MN: Llewellyn Publications, 1999.

———. *Alive and Well with Uranus*. St. Paul, MN: Llewellyn Publications, 1999.

———. *All Around the Zodiac*. St. Paul, MN: Llewellyn Publications, 2001.

———. *Dynamics of Aspects Analysis*. Sebastopol, CA: CRCS, 1983.

———. *The Twelve Faces of Saturn*. St. Paul, MN: Llewellyn Publications, 2002.

Tyl, Noel. *Synthesis & Counseling in Astrology*. St. Paul, MN: Llewellyn Publications, 1994.

Watters, Barbara. *Sex and the Outer Planets*. Washington DC: Valhalla, 1971; Tempe, AZ: AFA, 2010.

White, George. *The Moon's Nodes*. Tempe, AZ: AFA, 2004.

Wickenburg, Joanne. *In Search of a Fulfilling Career*. Tempe, AZ: AFA, 1992, 2003.

PREDICTIVE ASTROLOGY

Adler, Michelle. *Predictive Astrology*. Tampa, FL: Hidden Waters Publishing, 2006.

Brady, Bernadette. *The Eagle and the Lark*. York Beach, ME: Samuel Weiser, 1992.

Clement, Stephanie. *The Astrology of Development*. Tempe, AZ: AFA, 2010.

Cope, Lloyd. *Astrologer's Forecasting Workbook*. Tempe, AZ: AFA, 1995.

Forrest, Steven. *The Changing Sky*. Second edition. San Diego, CA: ACS, 2002.

George, Demetra. *Finding Our Way Through the Dark*. Tempe, AZ: AFA, 2008.

Hand, Robert. *Planets in Transit*. Revised edition. Atglen, PA: Whitford Press, 2001.

Leo, Alan. *The Progressed Horoscope*. London: L. N. Fowler, 1936; Bel Air, MD: Astrology Classics: 2007

Mason, Sophia. *Art of Forecasting Using Diurnal Charts*. Tempe, AZ: AFA, 1997.

Mason, Sophia. *Delineation of Progressions*. Tempe, AZ: AFA, 1998.

_____. *Forecasting with New, Full and Quarter Moons*. Tempe, AZ: AFA, 1994, 2001.

_____. *Lunations and Predictions*. Tempe, AZ: AFA, 1993, 2001.

Milburn, Leigh H. *The Progressed Horoscope Simplified*. Tempe, AZ: AFA, 1928, 1989, 2009.

Riske, Kris Brandt, M.A. *Mapping Your Future*. St. Paul, MN: Llewellyn Publications, 2004.

Rodden, Lois. *Modern Transits*. Tempe, AZ: AFA, 1978, 2010.

Rogers-Gallagher, Kim. *Astrology for the Light Side of the Future*. San Diego, CA: ACS Publications, 1998.

Ruperti, Alexander. *Cycles of Becoming*. Sebastopol, CA: CRCS, 1978; Santa Monica, CA: Earthwalk, 2005.

Rushman, Carol. *The Art of Predictive Astrology*. St. Paul, MN: Llewellyn Publications, 2002.

Sakoian, and Louis Acker. *The Transiting Planets*. Tempe, AZ: AFA, 2010.

Simms, Maria Kay. *Future Signs*. San Diego, CA: ACS Publications, 1996.

Teal, Celeste. *Identifying Planetary Triggers*. St. Paul, MN: Llewellyn Publications, 2000.

_____. *Predicting Events with Astrology*. St. Paul, MN: Llewellyn Publications, 2009.

Townley, John. *Astrological Cycles*. York Beach, ME: Red Wheel/Weiser, 1977.

Tyl, Noel. *Solar Arcs*. St. Paul, MN: Llewellyn Publications, 2001.

REFERENCE

Aldrich, Elizabeth. *Daily Use of the Ephemeris*. Tempe, AZ: AFA, 1971.

Bills, Rex. *The Rulership Book*. Tempe, AZ: AFA, 1971, 2007.

deVore, Nicholas. *Encyclopedia of Astrology*. New York: Philosophical Library, 1947; Bel Air, MD: Astrology Classics, 2005.

Doane, Doris C. *30 Years Research*. Los Angeles, CA: Church of Light, 1956; Tempe, AZ: AFA, 1985.

Donath, Emma Belle. *Houses: Which & When*. Tempe, AZ: AFA, 1989.

Koch, Beth. *Equal Houses*. Tempe, AZ: AFA, 1992.

Murphy, Peter, and Beth Rosato. *The Math of Astrology*. Tempe, AZ: AFA, 1998.

Rodden, Lois. *Astro Data II*. Revised edition. Tempe, AZ: AFA, 1997.

_____. *Astro Data III*. Tempe, AZ: AFA, 1986.

_____. *Astro Data IV*. Tempe, AZ: AFA, 1997.

_____. *Astro Data V: Profiles in Crime*. Yucaipa, CA: Data News, 1992.

_____. *Profiles of Women*. Yucaipa, CA: Data News, 1996.

Wilson, James. *Dictionary of Astrology*. Bel Air, MD: Astrology Classics, 2006. (Originally published in 1819.)

RELATIONSHIPS

Arroyo, Stephen. *Person-to-Person Astrology*. Berkeley, CA: Frog, Ltd., 2007.

Davison, Ronald C. *Synastry*. Santa Fe, NM: Aurora Press, 1983.

Devlin, Mary. *Astrology and Relationships*. Atglen, PA: Whitford Press, 1987.

Ebertin, Reinhold. *Cosmic Marriage*. Tempe, AZ: AFA, 1974, 2004.

Elgen, Rebeca. *The Shadow Dance and the Astrological Seventh House*. Houston, TX: Libra26Press, 2009.

Forrest, Jodie and Steven. *Skymates*. Revised edition. Chapel Hill, NC: Seven Paws Press, 2005.

Forrest, Steven and Jodie. *Skymates II: The Composite Chart*. Chapel Hill, NC: Seven Paws Press, 2005.

Geffner, Gayle. *Creative Step-Parenting*. Tempe, AZ: AFA, 2009.

Hand, Robert. *Planets in Composite*. Atglen, PA: Whitford Press, 1975.

Ruiz, Ana. *Prediction Techniques Regarding Romance.* Tempe, AZ: AFA, 2006.

Sargent, Lois. *How to Handle Your Human Relationships.* Tempe, AZ: AFA, 2006.

Suskin, Rod. *Synastry.* St. Paul, MN: Llewellyn Publications, 2008.

Townley, John. *Composite Charts.* St. Paul, MN: Llewellyn Publications, 2004.

———. *Planets in Love.* Atglen, PA: Whitford Press, 1978.

RETURN CHARTS

Louis, Anthony. *The Art of Forecasting Using Solar Returns.* Bournemouth, England: The Wessex Astrologer, 2008.

Penfield, Marc. *Solar Returns in Your Face.* Tempe, AZ: AFA, 1996.

Shea, Mary. *Planets in Solar Returns.* The Writers' Collective Associates, 1999.

Townley, John. *Lunar Returns.* St. Paul, MN: Llewellyn Publications, 2003.

TRADITIONAL ASTROLOGY

Al-Biruni. *The Book of Instruction in the Elements of the Art of Astrology.* Bel Air, MD: Astrology Classics, 2006.

Avelar, Helena and Luis Ribeiro. *On the Heavenly Spheres.* Tempe, AZ: AFA, 2010.

Bonatti, Guido. *Bonatti on 146 Considerations.* Minneapolis, MN: Cazimi Press, 2010.

———. *Bonatti on Basic Astrology.* Minneapolis, MN: Cazimi Press, 2010.

———. *Bonatti on Elections.* Minneapolis, MN: Cazimi Press, 2010.

———. *Bonatti on Horary.* Minneapolis, MN: Cazimi Press, 2010.

———. *Bonatti on Lots.* Minneapolis, MN: Cazimi Press, 2010.

———. *Bonatti on Mundane Astrology.* Minneapolis, MN: Cazimi Press, 2010.

———. *Bonatti on Nativities.* Minneapolis, MN: Cazimi Press, 2010

Brittain, Patti Tobin. *Planetary Powers: The Morin Method.* Tempe, AZ: AFA, 2011.

Holden, James H. *Five Medieval Astrologers.* Tempe, AZ: AFA, 2008.

Lilly, William. *The Astrologer's Guide.* Tempe, AZ: AFA, 2005. (Originally published in 1647.)

———. *Christian Astrology, Books 1 and 2.* Bel Air, MD: Astrology Classics, 2004. (Originally published in 1647.)

———. *Christian Astrology, Book 3.* Bel Air, MD: Astrology Classics, 2005. (Originally published in 1647.)

Masha'allah. *Six Astrological Treatises by Masha'allah.* Tempe, AZ: AFA, 2009.

Morin, Jean-Baptiste. *Astrologia Gallica, Book 13: The Proper Natures and Strengths of the Individual Planets and Fixed Stars,* translated by James H. Holden. Tempe, AZ: AFA, 2006.

———. *Astrologia Gallica, Book 14: The Primum Caelum and Its Division into Twelve Parts,* translated by James H. Holden. Tempe, AZ: AFA, 2006.

———. *Astrologia Gallica, Book 15: The Essential Dignities of the Planets,* translated by James H. Holden. Tempe, AZ: AFA, 2006.

———. *Astrologia Gallica, Book 16: The Rays and Aspects of the Planets,* translated by James H. Holden. Tempe, AZ: AFA, 2008.

———. *Astrologia Gallica, Book 17: The Astrological Houses,* translated by James H. Holden. Tempe, AZ: AFA, 2008.

———. *Astrologia Gallica, Book 18: Strengths of the Planets,* translated by Anthony Louis LaBruzza. Tempe, AZ: AFA, 2004.

———. *Astrologia Gallica, Book 19: The Elements of Astrology or the Principles of Judgements,* translated by James H. Holden. Tempe, AZ: AFA, 2006.

———. *Astrologia Gallica, Book 21: The Morinus System of Horoscope Interpretation,* translated by Richard S. Baldwin. Tempe, AZ: AFA, 2008.

———. *Astrologia Gallica, Book 22: Directions,* translated by James H. Holden. Tempe, AZ: AFA, 1994.

———. *Astrologia Gallica, Book 23: Revolutions,* translated by James H. Holden. Tempe, AZ: AFA, 2004.

———. *Astrologia Gallica, Book 24: Progressions and Transits,* translated by James H. Holden. Tempe, AZ: AFA, 2005.

———. *Astrologia Gallica, Book 25: The Universal Constitutions of the Caelum,* translated by James H. Holden. Tempe, AZ: AFA, 2008.

———. *Astrologia Gallica, Book 26: Astrological Interrogations and Elections,* translated by James H. Holden. Tempe, AZ: AFA, 2010.

Noonan, George. *Classical Scientific Astrology.* Tempe, AZ: AFA, 1984, 2005.

Pearce, A. J. *The Text-Book of Astrology.* Tempe, AZ: AFA, 2006. (Originally published in 1911.)

Porphyry. *Porphyry the Philosopher.* Tempe, AZ: AFA, 2009.

Ptolemy. *Tetrabiblos.* Bel Air, MD: Astrology Classics, 2002. (Written in the third century BC.)

Rhetorius. *Rhetorius the Egyptian.* Tempe, AZ: AFA, 2009.

Sahl ibn Bishr. *The Introduction to the Science of the Judgments of the Stars.* Tempe, AZ: AFA, 2008.

Zoller, Robert. *Arabic Parts: Lost Key to Prediction.* Rochester, VT: Inner Traditions, 1980, 1989.

GLOSSARY

angles: The Ascendant, Descendant, Midheaven, and IC.

angular house cusp: The cusps of the first, fourth, seventh, and tenth houses.

approaching aspect: A faster-moving planet that is approaching an exact aspect with a slower-moving planet.

Ascendant: The first-house cusp and one of the angles. It represents the individual and his or her outward expression of personality.

aspect: A geometric angle that connects the energy of two or more planets.

aspectarian: A grid that shows the aspects between the planets in a chart.

asteroids: The four major asteroids used in astrology are Juno, Vesta, Ceres, and Pallas Athena.

Chiron: A comet that is most commonly defined as the "wounded healer."

conjunction: A major aspect where two or more planets are within 0 to 8 degrees of each other. Its keyword is *intensity.* A conjunction can be an easy or hard aspect, depending on the planets involved.

contraparallel: An aspect that indicates two planets are at opposite degrees north and south of the celestial equator. The contraparallel functions like an opposition.

decanate: One-third of a sign. Each sign has three decanates—0° to 10°, 11° to 20°, and 21° to 30°—and each has its own ruling sign and planet.

declination: The degrees a planet is north or south of the celestial equator.

degree: The zodiac has 360°, and each sign has 30°. Degrees identify the position of a planet within a sign.

Descendant: The seventh-house cusp and one of the angles. It represents marriage and other close relationships.

detriment: A planet in the sign opposite its ruling sign, such as the Sun in Aquarius.

dignity: A planet in its ruling sign, such as Uranus in Aquarius.

easy aspect: The trine, sextile, and conjunction (depending on the planets in the conjunction) are easy aspects that represent a smooth flow of energy.

eclipse: Approximately four to six eclipses occur every year. A solar eclipse is also a New Moon, when the Sun and Moon are at the same degree and sign of the zodiac. A lunar eclipse is also a Full Moon, when the Sun and Moon are opposite each other.

element: Each of the twelve signs is classified according to one of the four elements—fire, earth, air, or water. The elements are also called quadruplicities.

ephemeris: A book or computer printout of the positions of the planets.

exaltation: A planet in the sign other than its ruling sign in which it functions well, such as Jupiter in Cancer.

fall: A planet in the sign opposite its sign of exaltation, such as Saturn in Aries.

fixed stars: The stars that make up the constellations.

Full Moon: A Full Moon occurs approximately every four weeks, two weeks after the New Moon. At the Full Moon, the Sun and Moon are opposite each other—180 degrees apart.

glyph: The symbol used for a planet, sign, or aspect.

grand square (grand cross): An aspect configuration formed by two oppositions at right angles to each other, forming a cross.

grand trine: An aspect configuration involving three (or more) planets, each 120 degrees apart and forming a triangle.

hard aspect: A square, opposition, semisquare, sesquisquare, or conjunction (depending on the planets in the conjunction) is a hard aspect that represents challenges and obstacles.

hemisphere: The four major sections of the horoscope—southern (top half of the chart), northern (bottom half of the chart), eastern (left side of the chart), and western (right side of the chart).

house: One of the twelve pie-shaped sections (houses) of the horoscope. Each house governs specific areas of life.

house cusp: The sign and degree of the zodiac at which a house begins.

IC (Imum Coeli): The fourth-house cusp and one of the angles. It represents home, family, and parents.

inconjunct: A minor aspect (also known as a *quincunx*) where two or more planets are 150 degrees apart. It indicates separation, strain, and uneasiness, because it is difficult to mix the energies of the planets involved.

intercepted sign: A zodiac sign that is contained wholly within a house and thus is not on a house cusp.

intermediate house cusp: The cusps of the second, third, fifth, sixth, eighth, ninth, eleventh, and twelfth houses.

latitude: The distance in degrees north or south of the equator, which is 0° latitude. Used along with longitude to define a geographic location.

longitude: The distance in degrees east or west of Greenwich, England, which is 0° longitude. Used along with latitude to define a geographic location.

luminaries: The Sun and Moon, which are also called the Lights.

Midheaven: The tenth-house cusp and one of the angles. It represents career and status.

mode: See *quality.*

Moon's nodes: The North and South nodes of the Moon are not actual bodies, but points. The North Node is similar to Jupiter, and the South Node is similar to Saturn.

mutual reception: Two planets in any aspect that are also in each other's ruling sign, such as the Moon in Aries and Mars in Cancer.

natural chart: A chart that shows the natural order of the zodiac from Aries through Pisces, beginning with Aries in the first house.

New Moon: A New Moon occurs approximately every four weeks, when the Sun and Moon are at the same degree and sign of the zodiac.

opposition: A major aspect where two or more planets are 180 degrees apart, or opposite each other, in the zodiac. Its keyword is *separation*.

orb: The allowable distance between two or more planets that puts them in aspect to one another. The closer the aspect, the stronger its influence.

out-of-sign aspect: An aspect between two planets that are in orb but not in the same mode or element.

parallel: An aspect that indicates two planets are at the same number of degrees north or south of the celestial equator. The parallel functions like a conjunction.

Part of Fortune: Also called the Lot of Fortune, this indicates luck, especially when in aspect to a planet or angle.

polarities: The opposite signs of the zodiac, such as Aries/Libra and Gemini/Sagittarius.

quadrants: The four sections of the horoscope that blend the influence of the four hemispheres—first quadrant (houses one, two, and three), second quadrant (houses four, five, and six), third quadrant (houses seven, eight, and nine), and fourth quadrant (houses ten, eleven, and twelve).

quality (mode): Each of the twelve signs is identified with one of the three qualities, or modes of expression—cardinal, fixed, or mutable.

retrograde: The period of time during which planets appear to move backward.

return chart: A chart calculated for the date and time that a planet returns to its natal place. The most common return charts are the solar return and lunar return.

rulership: Each planet has rulership over, or is associated with, one (or two) signs. A planet that rules the sign on a house cusp rules that house. The planets ruling other signs in a house are called *co-rulers*. Planets and signs also have natural rulership over specific areas of life, such as career, health, family, and money.

semisextile: A 30 degree angle between two planets. This aspect is mildly beneficial.

semisquare: A minor aspect where two or more planets are 45 degrees apart. It represents action and conflict.

separating aspect: This indicates that a planet is moving away from another planet after having formed an exact aspect with the second planet.

sesquisquare: A minor aspect where two or more planets are 135 degrees apart. It represents action and conflict.

sextile: A major aspect where two or more planets are 60 degrees apart. Its keyword is *opportunity*.

solar chart: A chart erected without a specific birth time, usually set for noon or sunrise, and with the Sun as the Ascendant.

square: A major aspect where two or more planets are 90 degrees apart. It represents action and conflict.

stationary planet: A planet that appears to stop before changing to direct or retrograde motion.

stellium: A group of three or more planets, all of which are conjunct.

synastry: A chart comparison method used to judge compatibility between two individuals.

t-square: An aspect configuration where two (or more) planets are in opposition and square a third planet.

trine: A major aspect where two or more planets are 120 degrees apart. It represents ease and luck.

trinities: The three houses associated with each of the elements—fire, trinity of life; earth; trinity of wealth; air, trinity of association; and water, trinity of endings.

Trinity of Life: The first, fifth, and ninth houses, which are associated with the fire element and represent initiative, dynamic energy, enthusiasm, faith, motivation, and confidence.

Trinity of Psychism: The fourth, eighth, and twelfth houses, which are associated with the water element and represent beginnings and endings, emotions, intuition, and karma.

Trinity of Relationships: The third, seventh, and eleventh houses, which are associated with the air element and represent partnership, friendship, social life, relatives, and associations.

Trinity of Wealth: The second, sixth, and tenth houses, which are associated with the earth element and represent money, possessions, reputation, achievements, career, work, and service.

unaspected planet: A planet that makes no aspects to other planets or angles.

Vertex: A calculated point that has a fateful connotation, indicating a person's destiny in life.

void-of-course Moon: The Moon's position from the time it makes its last major aspect in one sign until it enters the next sign.

yod: An aspect configuration in which a planet (the apex planet) is inconjunct two other planets that are sextile each other.